PROCEDURAL HISTORY OF THE 1940 CENSUS OF POPULATION AND HOUSING

ROBERT M. JENKINS

THE UNIVERSITY OF WISCONSIN PRESS

Published 1985

The University of Wisconsin Press
114 North Murray Street
Madison, Wisconsin 53715

The University of Wisconsin Press, Ltd.
1 Gower Street
London WC1E 6HA, England

Copyright ©1985
The Board of Regents of the University of Wisconsin System
All rights reserved

First printing

Printed in the United States of America

For LC CIP information see the colophon

ISBN O-299-10120-7

CONTENTS

PREFACE — vii

1 INTRODUCTION — 3

Evolution of the Bureau of the Census, 3
The Census Bureau in the 1930s, 4

2 PLANNING FOR THE 1940 CENSUS — 8

The Unemployment Census of 1937, 8
Data Processing Planning, 9
Geographical Planning, 9
Preparation of Schedules and Instructions, 11
The Inclusion of Employment and Income Questions, 12
Sampling Design, 13
The 1939 Special Census of St. Joseph and Marshall Counties, Indiana, 15
The Inclusion of a Census of Housing, 16

3 FIELD ENUMERATION — 17

The Structure of the Field Organization, 17
　Area Offices, 18
　District Offices, 18
General Preparations, 19
　Examination of Enumeration Districts, 19
　Receipt of Schedules and Supplies, 19
　Selection and Training of Enumerators and Squad Leaders, 20
　Public Relations, 21
The Enumeration Process, 21
　General Instructions, 21
　Filling Out the Population Schedules, 23
　The Housing Schedules, 26
　Enumeration Supervision, 27
　Progress Reporting, 28
Preliminary Population Counts: Announcements and Vouchers, 29
Return of Schedules and Final Reporting, 30
Special Situations, 30

4 PROCESSING AND TABULATION — 31

Initial Activities, 31
　Receipt and Examination of Population Schedules, 31
　Matching of Population and Housing Schedules, 32
　Population and Housing Hand Count, 35
　Transcription of the Preliminary Sample Data, 36
　Separation of Population and Housing Schedules and Other Materials, 39
　Control Room Operations, 40
Coding Operations, 41
　General Population Coding, 41
　Allocation of Unknown Ages, 45
　Verification of General Population Coding, 48
　Occupation, Industry, and Class of Worker Coding and Verification, 50
　Coding and Verification of the Housing Census, 52
Tabulation, 52
　Card Punching and the Sample Verification of Punch Cards, 52
　Machine Processing, 54
The Effect of World War II on the 1940 Census, 56

5 PUBLICATIONS FROM THE 1940 CENSUS — 57

Preliminary Releases, 59
Final Reports, 59
Territories and Possessions, 60

Contents

6 EVALUATION OF THE 1940 CENSUS   62

    Analysis of Employment Status Questions, 62
    Analysis of Class of Worker Questions, 63
    Analysis of Occupation and Industry Questions, 63
    Analysis of Income Questions, 64
    Analysis of Other Labor Force Questions, 65
    Analysis of General Population Questions, 65
    Underenumeration, 66

APPENDICES

Appendix I: 1940 Census Population and Housing Schedules, 71

Appendix II: Original Instructions and Addenda for General Population Coding (Operation 7), 77

Appendix III: Age Allocation Tables Used in 1940 Census, 109

Appendix IV: Instructions for Coding Occupation, Industry, and Class of Worker (Operation 9), 115

Appendix V: Description of Punch Cards (A–S) Used in 1940 Census of Population and Housing, 123

Appendix VI: Progress Report and Costs of the 1940 Census, 143

REFERENCES   147

INDEX   149

PREFACE

Robert M. Jenkins is the principal author of the *Procedural History of the 1940 Census*. Richard Cohn, Lori Hayward, Ann Kremers, and Barbara Weston of the Center for Demography and Ecology, University of Wisconsin–Madison, assisted in the preparation of the history. Frederick Bohme, Chief of the History Staff at the U.S. Bureau of the Census, provided important technical assistance in the collection of 1940 census documents and in the review of the manuscript. The history was greatly improved by the memories and scholarship of Margo Conk, A. Ross Eckler, Morris Hansen, Henry Shryock, and Conrad Taeuber, who served as reviewers.

The *Procedural History of the 1940 Census* was written as part of a project to create Public Use Sample files from the 1940 and 1950 Population Censuses. This material is based upon work supported by the National Science Foundation under Grant SES–7704135. Halliman Winsborough, Karl Taeuber, and Robert Hauser were the principal investigators in consultation with a board of scientific advisors and the U.S. Bureau of the Census, under a general plan approved by the National Science Foundation. Specific technical judgments as well as any opinions, findings, or conclusions expressed on the basis of those judgments are the sole responsibility of the principal investigators and not of the Bureau of the Census or the National Science Foundation.

**PROCEDURAL HISTORY OF THE 1940 CENSUS
OF POPULATION AND HOUSING**

1 INTRODUCTION

ARTICLE I, SECTION 2, of the United States Constitution directs that there be decennial censuses of the population for the purpose of determining the apportionment of representatives and direct taxes. The first census taken under this provision occurred in 1790, and subsequent censuses of the population have been taken every ten years.

The inquiries in the first census included little beyond the Constitutional provisions. The information provided by this enumeration included the names of the heads of families and the numbers of persons in five basic categories: free white males, 16 and over; free white males under 16; free white females; all other free persons; and slaves. With the evolution of the census both the nature and detail of the inquiries have expanded.

In 1800, the age classification was expanded and the location of family residence was obtained. The 1810 census saw the addition of inquiries on manufacturing. Information about foreigners and certain broad occupational groups was added in 1820. The 1840 census saw the addition of questions on school attendance and illiteracy, and a separate agriculture schedule. Throughout the remainder of the century the inquiries on the population schedule continued to expand and new schedules were introduced, until by 1880 and 1890 the volume had reached unmanageable proportions. The censuses from 1900 through 1930 were fairly modest, but with the advent of sampling in 1940 it was possible again to broaden the scope of inquiries and include a sizeable inventory of characteristics of the people and their homes.

The 1940 Census of Population, the Sixteenth Decennial Census, was taken under the legislative authority of the Census Act of June 18, 1929. This act removed the determination of specific inquiries from Congressional control, giving control instead to the Director of the Census subject to the approval of the Secretary of Commerce. The 1929 act also required persons enumerated to provide complete and accurate information under penalty of law. In addition, census employees were discouraged from making unauthorized disclosures of information through the provision of substantial penalties. The 1940 census was also covered by an act approved on August 11, 1939, that provided for a census of housing to collect information on dwelling units.[1]

Evolution of the Bureau of the Census

The organization responsible for taking the census changed considerably between 1790 and 1940. Federal marshals acted as enumerators for the 1790 census. The marshals had the authority to carry out the enumeration in their own way and they sent the returns directly to the President. Until 1900 the census was conducted by a temporary organization created to carry out the provisions of the corresponding census act. From 1800 through 1840 this temporary organization was under the direction of the Secretary of State. This responsibility was transferred from the Secretary of State to the Secretary of the newly created Department of Interior for the 1850 census. For the 1880 census, a temporary census office was created in the Department of Interior and, for the first time, a Superintendent of the Census (later renamed Director of the Census) was specifically appointed by the President. This office was disbanded after each census and forced to reassemble prior to the beginning of enumeration for the following census. It was not until the Permanent Census Act was adopted in March 1902 that a permanent census organization was created.

The permanent Bureau of the Census that had been

---

1. This information is based on U.S. Department of Commerce, Bureau of the Census "Manual of Census Bureau Activities." This document has no author or date, but was obtained from the library of the Census History Staff. See also, Eckler 1972, pp. 4–13, 42–48, 230–39.

created in 1902 was transferred from the Department of the Interior to the newly created Department of Commerce and Labor in 1903. The Secretary of this new department was given legislative authority to consolidate and reorganize government statistical work in the Department. The Director of the Census, Simon N. D. North, was a proponent of consolidation, presumably under the Bureau of the Census. However, pressures from the heads of bureaus involved in the collection of statistical information combined with jurisdictional disputes between the Department and the Bureau to prevent the consolidation of statistical work.

Although Director North failed in his attempt to get federal statistical programs consolidated into the Bureau, he did succeed in one endeavor which left a substantial mark on the Bureau. North considered the Bureau's annual rental contracts with the Tabulating Machine Company to be too expensive. Herman Hollerith, the inventor of the tabulating machine first used in the 1890 census, controlled this company. North first attempted to renegotiate the yearly contract with Tabulating Machine. When those negotiations proved fruitless, North received, from Congress, an appropriation for 1905–06 of $40,000 for experimental work in developing tabulating machinery. With this appropriation, the Census Machine Shop was established under the supervision of the Chief of the Bureau of Standards and employed former Hollerith employees. In 1907, the Census Machine Shop moved into quarters in the Census Building. The Bureau did later rent machines from Tabulating Machine, which became International Business Machines (IBM) in 1924. The Bureau, however, continued to use its in-house equipment produced by the Census Machine Shop (renamed the Mechanical Laboratory) until the advent of computers (Truesdell 1965, pp. 119–20, 139–42; and United States Department of Commerce [hereafter DOC], Office of Federal Statistical Policy and Standards [hereafter OFSPS] 1978, p. 118).

There were continued pressures to consolidate federal statistics within the Census Bureau. Consolidation was further hampered, however, by the division of the Department of Commerce and Labor into separate departments in 1913. Despite pressures for the creation of a central statistical agency from the American Statistical Association and the Federal Bureau of Efficiency's 1922 report, the collection of federal statistical information remained decentralized (Eckler 1972; DOC, OFSPS 1978, p. 11).

From 1921 to 1929, Herbert Hoover was Secretary of Commerce and, as such, was the Cabinet member responsible for the Bureau of the Census. A member of the American Statistical Association and the International Statistical Institute, Hoover viewed the Census Bureau as the central statistical agency of the federal government. He did not, however, press for the consolidation of federal statistical programs at the Bureau. Instead, Hoover was more interested in developing cooperative relations between the Department and the business community. He encouraged the systematization of business and economic statistics and their orientation toward use by business. Among other activities, Hoover directed the Census Bureau to compile the various series of business data and publish them as the monthly *Survey of Current Business* (DOC, OFSPS 1978, pp. 10–11; Scott 1968, pp. 40–41).

The Census Bureau in the 1930s

Hoover was elected President in 1928 and took office in March 1929. In the fall of that year, a business downturn began that evolved into the Great Depression. The resulting dislocations to the national economy and the federal government had an effect on the Census Bureau. Despite Hoover's view of the role of the Census Bureau as the statistical agency of the federal government, the Bureau was not exempt from the Economy Act of 1932. This act called for substantial reductions in staff in order to balance the federal budget. The Census Bureau was forced to reduce its staff drastically after completion of the 1930 census. Eckler (1972, p. 19) notes that "in 1933, the Bureau had only three Ph.D.'s and only one professional man under forty-five years of age" (DOC, OFSPS 1978, p. 25).

Franklin Roosevelt defeated Hoover in the 1932 election. Within months after taking office in March 1933 he had signed major legislation aimed at economic recovery and reform. This legislation established new programs in many fields, including industry, agriculture, welfare, securities and exchange, banking, and home mortgages. Corresponding to this expansion of government there developed a need for statistical information to aid in the administration of the recovery program.

Roosevelt's Secretary of Labor, Frances Perkins, requested that Stuart A. Rice, President of the American Statistical Association (ASA), appoint an Advisory Committee to the Secretary of Labor. With this Committee as a starting point, later talks between Rice and Meredith Givens, of the Social Science Research Council (SSRC), expanded to the Cabinet level, including the Secretaries of Agriculture and Interior and the Assistant Secretary of Commerce. These talks resulted in a decision, in June 1933, to establish the Committee on Government Statistics and Information Services (COGSIS), under the joint sponsorship of the ASA and the SSRC (DOC, OFSPS 1978, pp. 26–31).

COGSIS was created to assist in the improvement

and expansion of federal statistics. This mission was to be accomplished by providing statistical advisory services to the Secretaries of Agriculture, Commerce, Interior, and Labor. As a consulting committee, COGSIS handled only those cases brought before it by a particular agency. The Committee or its staff studied the problem at the agency involved and advised the responsible person at the agency of the recommended changes. Subsequently, the Committee specialist wrote a memorandum that was submitted to the agency and to COGSIS.[2]

One of the leading objectives of COGSIS was the "firm establishment of a central planning and coordinating statistical agency within the Federal Government" (Givens, 1934). COGSIS saw that the recovery program could be made the occasion of reorganization and coordination of federal statistical services. In a report of July 1933, COGSIS recommended the establishment of a central statistical board. Later in the same month, President Roosevelt created the Central Statistical Board (CSB) by Executive Order. COGSIS provided the initial staffing for the CSB. The legal authority for the CSB provided by the Executive Order limited its activities to the recovery program. Congress acted in 1935, however, to establish the CSB for a 5-year period. In 1939, the CSB was incorporated into the Bureau of the Budget.

Although the creation of CSB brought about central coordination of federal statistics for the first time, the recommendations of the final report of COGSIS urged that the diversity and decentralization of statistical programs and agencies within the federal government be maintained. The report emphasized that the existing organization of statistical programs had "advantages of a close relation to practical needs." Therefore, COGSIS sought to maintain a "delicate balance between central planning and decentralized responsibility." Within this perspective, COGSIS saw the central objective of the CSB as planning and coordination. The CSB was to remain an advisory board rather than being significantly involved in direct research (COGSIS 1937, pp. 3–13).

In addition to its concern with the CSB, COGSIS was actively involved in consultation on statistical questions. In January 1934, the Director of the Census requested that COGSIS survey the work of the Bureau in the fields of manufactures, agriculture, and population. COGSIS and staff members from the CSB cooperated in the study and the results of the inquiry were placed at the disposal of the CSB (COGSIS 1937, pp. 80–81).

One of the first tasks of COGSIS was the examination of the Bureau's tabulating facilities. Many of the new projects initiated by the Civil Works Administration and other agencies required mechanical tabulating, and the Committee sought to avoid duplication of facilities. As a result of the COGSIS study, arrangements were made for the Bureau's Division of Special Tabulations to provide the services needed by other agencies.

Since the next decennial census was still some time in the future, the study of the population census was aimed at broad issues of administration and policy rather than at the details of the decennial census operations. COGSIS began by sending letters to about thirty prominent users of the population data. COGSIS asked for candid and confidential criticisms of the population census and suggestions for improvements. On the basis of the replies, a memorandum making broad suggestions was prepared for appraisal by the Bureau and the CSB.

Recommendations with respect to the population schedule were both broad and specific. It was suggested that questions need not be asked (or tabulations made) simply because they had been asked (or made) in recent enumerations. Similarly, it was recommended that not every question had to be asked of the entire nation, and that tabulations of universally asked questions did not have to be made for the entire country. Specific questions, such as those on veterans, radio ownership, illiteracy, school attendance, citizenship, blindness, and deafness were recommended for discontinuation. Questions on mobility, place of employment, children ever born, length of separation of married couples, religious affiliations, and educational attainment were recommended for inclusion (COGSIS 1937, p. 82).

Several suggestions were made with regard to the tabulation program. These included extension of tabulations by census tracts in the larger cities and extensions of tabulations of occupations, families, and vacant dwellings. Recommendations for field operations included improving the training and examination of supervisors and enumerators, making more extensive use

---

2. Financed by a grant from the Rockefeller Foundation to the SSRC, COGSIS operated from June 1933 until December 1934, in space provided in the Department of Commerce building. COGSIS worked closely with the Advisory Committee to the Secretary of Labor. The combined staff of these committees numbered 57 people, more than 25 of whom later took positions within the agencies under review. The Census Bureau was one of the agencies which benefited from this infusion of new personnel. Rice, who was Acting Chair of COGSIS in the summer of 1933, served as Assistant Director of the Bureau from 1933 to 1935, and Calvert L. Dedrick, a former research fellow at SSRC and a COGSIS staff member, became the Bureau's Assistant Chief Statistician in 1937. See, Committee on Government Statistics and Information Services, 1937, pp. 129–31.

of squad leaders, conducting sample checkups in the field, giving more definite instructions to supervisors on checking the completeness of enumeration, and encouraging the development of local groups interested in accurate enumeration. The memorandum on the population census also suggested that the Population Division of the Bureau consider one of its major intercensal tasks to be the implementaion of sampling studies that would check outside sources to gauge the completeness of enumeration. It was also suggested that the census of population be taken every five years.

Another important memorandum was produced on the intercensal work of the Population Division. This memorandum recommended reducing the amount of time spent by the Division staff during the intercensal period on producing institutional reports and on miscellaneous routines. Suggestions were made as to what were considered to be essential functions to which the extra staff time could be devoted. These suggestions included the completion of a guide to unpublished census tabulations; the development of a sample-based, annual reporting system on population movements; analysis of census techniques and tests of validity of the decennial enumerations; and special tabulations for research in the population field.

In addition, the COGSIS report noted that detailed personnel requirements in the future depended upon the suggested tasks that were instituted. It did, however, make a point of noting that while there existed invaluable experience among the staff that was then employed, the fact that many on the staff were near retirement age provided "an inviting opportunity for building for the future by drawing in a number of capable young men with graduate training in social science and statistics, who can be systematically prepared for posts of leadership in the Division" (COGSIS 1937, p. 93).

With Stuart A. Rice as Assistant Director of the Bureau, the personnel recommendations of the COGSIS memorandum were implemented. He selected a nucleus of academically trained statisticians. Rice was responsible for Dedrick's appointment as Assistant Chief Statistician. In turn, Dedrick was responsible for starting Morris H. Hansen in sampling. While the formation of the nucleus of statisticians was not rapid, by 1938 the professional staff of the Bureau included 42 social scientists (Eckler 1972, p. 19; DOC, OFSPS 1978, p. 44).

At the time preparations for the 1940 census were beginning, the Bureau of the Census was a large organization consisting of many functional divisions: Agriculture; Business Census; Cotton and Oils; Current Business Statistics; Field; Geography; Machine Tabulation; Manufactures; Personnel; Population; Publications, General Information, Records, and Religious Statistics; Statistical Research; Statistics of States and Cities; Territorial, Insular, and Foreign Statistics; and Vital Statistics.

At the head of the Bureau organization were the offices of Director, Assistant Director, and Assistant to the Director. The Director of the Census was responsible to the Secretary of Commerce for the administration of the Bureau. William Lane Austin was the Director from 1933 to 1941. James C. Capt served as Director from 1941 to 1949. The Assistant Director served as administrative and technical advisor for those divisions involving economic statistics, as the Bureau's liaison for other governmental and private organizations, and as the person in charge in the absence of the Director. The Assistant to the Director was responsible for administrative and technical advice for those divisions that embraced the field of social statistics. In addition, there was an Office of the Chief Clerk, responsible for the Bureau's fiscal operations (accounting, payroll, purchasing); for equipment, space, and maintenance; for the mechanical laboratory; and for printing operations.

Of those Bureau divisions involved in planning and carrying out the 1940 census, the activities of the Personnel Division are probably the most obvious. In addition to handling appointments, promotions, and separations, Personnel was responsible for administering civil service and departmental regulations and public laws pertaining to the Bureau and its employees. Statistical Research, a Division established in August 1933, was formed by the restructuring of the Division of Revision and Results. The Statistical Research Division served as the Bureau's representative to the CSB, prepared or assisted in the development of official reports, memoranda, and letters for the Director's office, and prepared Census Bureau legislation—activities previously handled by the Chief Statistician and his staff. The Statistical Research Division was also involved in the preparation of reports, articles, and monographs that analyzed census statistics and data, census methods, and technical problems. This division was responsible for research and coordination in devising new schedules, instructions, and methods of editing, tabulating, and checking data.

The Division of Machine Tabulation was responsible for performing the tabulations of all census inquiries. It maintained an inventory of unpunched cards and had custody of all punched cards. Although functionally separate from the mechanical laboratory, which was under the administration of the Office of Chief Clerk, this division worked closely with the laboratory in the development of mechanical tabulating equipment. The Machine Tabulation Division also participated in design of schedules and punch cards and the development of tabulation programs. In addition to tabulating operations within the Bureau, this division performed tabulations for other bureaus of the Department of Commerce and for outside agencies and organizations.

The Division of Geography also played an important role in planning and carrying out the 1940 census. Its activities included establishing enumeration districts, preparing all civil and statistical area records for coordination and presentation of census statistics, compiling all graphic materials for Bureau publications and exhibits, and conducting research in geography, cartography, and graphics. These activities are described in greater detail in chapter 2.

The Field Division of the Bureau directed, coordinated, and supervised all censuses and special surveys conducted by the various divisions within the Bureau. The Field Division was created in December 1922, to help realize greater economies and more efficient procedures in the field phase of Bureau operations. Prior to that time each functional division had its own field operations. The Field Division participated in planning inquiries, cost estimates, and the field program. It was also responsible for the administration of canvasses—including responsibilities for the receiving and shipping of schedules and forms, travel authorizations, field personnel and payrolls, and equipment. These activities are described in greater detail in chapter three.

The Population Division was responsible for compiling the decennial population census and tabulating its returns; for collecting annual and decennial statistics on crime, delinquency, and prisoners; for making intercensal and postcensal population estimates; and for making special studies and reports. This large division was organized functionally into a number of sections. Some of these sections, such as correspondence, population estimates, crime statistics, and census of institutions were fairly permanent. Other sections, which were set up for the decennial census, were only partly active or were entirely inactive during intercensal periods. For the 1940 Census of Population, these latter subdivisions were quite extensive and included subdivisions for various types of census inquiries and for the various operations in the processing of returns. Greater detail on the role of the Population Division in the 1940 census is presented in chapter 2 and chapter 4.

2 PLANNING FOR THE 1940 CENSUS

Preparations for the Sixteenth Decennial Census began in 1936, with an analysis of legislative revisions necessary for the proper conduct of the census (DOC 1936, p. 17). The Bureau did not undertake extensive plans or large-scale preparatory work until it had received special appropriations and legislative authorization. It made its request for preliminary funds for the 1940 census during the next Congressional session.

To aid the Census Bureau in its work, the American Statistical Association (ASA) had appointed the members of a public Advisory Committee to the Bureau. This committee was charged with the coordination of the work of the special advisory committees that were established on specific topics. Members of the ASA committee during the preparations for the Sixteenth Decennial Census were Robert E. Chaddock, Columbia University, chairman; Murray R. Benedict, College of Agriculture, University of California-Berkeley; Paul T. Cherington, New York City; Frederick J. Dewhurst, 20th Century Fund, New York City; William F. Ogburn, University of Chicago; and Willard C. Thorp, Dun and Bradstreet, Inc., New York City (DOC 1939, p. 26).

The Unemployment Census of 1937

In 1937, Congress approved a national unemployment census. This census provided valuable experience which the Bureau was able to use in planning the decennial population census of 1940. Despite statisticians' advice to the contrary, Congress had sought the unemployment census as a voluntary registration of unemployed and partly employed persons in the United States (DOC, OFSPS 1978, pp. 44–45; DOC 1938, pp. 35–36). To direct the census of unemployment, President Roosevelt established a temporary agency, the Office of the Administrator of the Census of Partial Employment, Unemployment, and Occupations, under the direction of John D. Biggers. Biggers asked the Director of the Census, William Lane Austin, to provide staffing for the operation. Austin provided Calvert L. Dedrick, then the Chief of the Division of Statistical Research, and several other Bureau personnel to assist in management and machine tabulation for the project.

Dedrick had opposed the unemployment census before Congress, arguing that the manner of collecting the statistics would bias the results. Although he was unable to convince Congress, Dedrick did convince Biggers of the potential for substantial bias. At the urging of Dedrick, a check census was designed to represent the more than 80 percent of the U.S. population that was served by postal delivery routes. This sample was the first nationwide use of probability and area sampling to canvass a population for which lists were not available. This check census enabled more accurate estimates than the voluntary census and thus allowed estimates of the error in the voluntary figures.

The unemployment check census used a household enumeration form and sought to gather information on labor force activity in the week of November 14–20, 1937. Instructions were printed on the back of the form and Post Office Department employees conducted the field interviews. This check census was based upon a 2 percent sample of postal routes in the U.S., excluding a few business delivery routes in large cities.

The Bureau was involved in editing and tabulating the data and the preparation of final tables for publication. For this work, the Bureau received an appropriation of $850,000. In addition to providing the Bureau with an opportunity to test its procedures for examining, coding, and preparing punch cards, the work on the census of unemployment provided the first use of sampling techniques for the national probability sample. This latter experience was valuable in planning for the 1940 Census of Population.

Data Processing Planning

Throughout the thirties the Bureau was engaged in the modernization of existing and building of additional mechanical equipment used for tabulation of the census. Much of the equipment was designed and built in the Bureau's Mechanical Laboratory, which had been first permanently established as the Census Machine Shop in 1917.[1]

Four types of power-driven machines had been used in tabulating the 1930 census: (1) unit counters, which tabulated single-column characteristics; (2) adding tabulators, which summed quantities punched on successive cards; (3) sorters, which arranged cards in proper order; and (4) gang punches, which rapidly punched designations common to many cards in a series. During the mid-1930s, the unit counters were rebuilt in order to accommodate a change from 24-column cards used in 1930 to 45-column cards used in 1940. New gang punch heads were also built to accommodate the 45-column cards. In addition, the Mechanical Lab designed and built a new adding tabulator. These equipment changes were estimated to have saved the Bureau several thousand dollars in machine rentals (DOC 1936, pp. 29–30).

The introduction of commercially available equipment also played an important role in the 1940 Census (Truesdell 1965, p. 195). The IBM printer-tabulator was particularly important. This machine summarized data from consecutive cards, added items from different fields on the same card, and printed the results.

Geographical Planning

Another ongoing operation for the 1940 Census was the geographical preparation performed by the Bureau's Division of Geography. This division was a service branch with responsibility for preparing the maps used as guides for the enumerators and their supervisors, preparing the maps and charts used in Census Bureau publications, assisting in the establishment of special measurement units (such as metropolitan districts and census tracts), and allocating the schedules of persons not at their usual place of residence at the time of the population canvass. The Division of Geography had 75 people permanently employed as draftsmen, cartographers, and clerical help. During the preparations for the 1940 Census, the employment within the Division expanded to about 700 persons (von Struve 1940, pp. 275–80).

The largest preparatory task involving the Division was the preparing of the maps used by the census enumerators. The Division began this task by dividing the states of the United States into supervisors' districts. One or more counties were allotted to each supervisor's district. A "plan of division by enumeration district (E.D.)" was then prepared for each county. Enumeration districts were designed to be clearly defined areas—not including more than one incorporated place—that could easily be canvassed by a single enumerator in about two weeks in urban areas or a month in rural areas. The boundaries of E.D.'s were designed to follow either the boundaries of municipalities, wards, or minor civil divisions (civil township, election district, election precinct, school district, town, etc.); or roads, streets, railways, public survey lines, and other well-known lines. For purposes of the 1940 enumeration, the continental United States was divided into some 147,000 E.D.'s, an increase of 27,000 over 1930 (Proudfoot 1940b, pp. 301–3).

In order to define E.D.'s that could be canvassed in the desired time period, the Division of Geography had to take into consideration the number of inhabitants in incorporated places, the number of farms and inhabitants in each rural enumeration district, and the topography and access roads in rural areas. The Division also had to take into consideration the various statistical reporting areas such as states, counties, minor civil divisions, incorporated places, congressional districts, wards, and tracts for which the Bureau published data.

Rules formulated for the plan of division by enumeration district required that rural E.D.'s used in 1930 were to be used again in 1940 except in cases where the Field Division had recommended that the E.D. be divided, where changes had occurred in the minor civil divisions, or where the description of the E.D. was incorrect. The rules governing the establishment of new rural E.D.'s maintained that population should not exceed 1,500, and that there should not be more than 250 farms.

Urban enumeration districts used in 1930 were also to be used in 1940 except where changes had occurred in minor civil divisions, assembly districts, or ward areas that resulted in a fragmented E.D.; where there was an establishment or revision of census tracts; where the E.D. description was incorrect; where the E.D. had impractical boundaries; or where information on file indicated that the population was too large or too small. New urban E.D.'s established in 1940 were to meet definite population guidelines—1,000 persons on the

---

1. For a detailed account of the history of census processing in the late nineteenth and early twentieth centuries, including the development of tabulation equipment, see Truesdell 1965.

edge of a city and 1,400 persons within the built-up portion of the city.

Other rules governing the plan of division by enumeration district, regardless of whether urban or rural, included the requirement that each minor civil division or dependent incorporated place comprise one or more E.D.'s; that dependent incorporated places situated in two or more minor civil divisions or incorporated places situated in two or more counties be divided into at least one E.D. for each minor civil division or county, respectively; that incorporated places of at least 3,000 persons that were divided into wards were required to have at least one E.D. per ward. In addition, E.D. boundaries were required not to cross boundaries of census tracts, wards, assembly districts, congressional districts, supervisor's districts, incorporated places, minor civil divisions, or counties; and not to cut blocks unless it was to conform to the boundaries of the districts just named.

Separate enumeration districts were constructed for federal and state prisons, reformatories, mental institutions, and all other institutions having more than 100 inmates; for Roman Catholic institutions with 25 or more residents; for apartment buildings with 100 or more apartments in cities of 500,000 or more; and for national parks, lighthouses and lightships, Coast Guard stations, Civilian Conservation Corps camps, veteran's hospitals, and areas under military and naval jurisdiction. The Division of Geography was also instructed to provide instructions for showing separately on population schedules (but not making separate E.D.'s) non-Roman Catholic institutions having fewer than 100 inmates; Roman Catholic institutions having fewer than 25 residents; apartment houses having fewer than 100 but more than 49 apartments, in cities of 500,000 or more; unincorporated places having an estimated population of more than 100 persons; and islands and unoccupied military reservations.

The Division of Geography was responsible for making the original maps of these enumeration districts. Over 175,000 such maps were made for the 1940 Census. The division did not perform field mapping operations itself. Instead, the division compiled preexisting geographical information from a variety of sources: (1) a continually updated file containing several hundred thousand state, county, and city maps prepared by the civil governments and requested for use by the Bureau; (2) maps and map data collected by state highway departments and the Public Roads Administration and contributed to the Bureau; (3) aeronautical charts prepared by the Coast and Geodetic Survey of the Department of Commerce; (4) General Land Office maps showing accurate township range and section boundaries; and, (5) topographical survey maps prepared by the Geological Survey in the Department of the Interior.

In order to keep these map collections accurate and up-to-date, the Geography Division maintained a large correspondence with state, county, and municipal authorities on boundary changes and other data. For example, during the 1938 fiscal year, ending on June 30, 1938, some 1,850 letters were sent to city engineers concerning annexations and detachments and over 1,000 city and county maps were received. During the 1939 fiscal year, some 2,400 new county maps were obtained (DOC 1938, pp. 31; DOC 1939, p. 27). For the 1940 Census, base maps were prepared for 3,071 counties and 3,000 cities. In addition to the boundaries of these counties and cities, the boundaries of the approximately 52,000 minor civil divisions also had to be verified by local officials before final preparation of the maps.

The plans of division by enumeration district prepared by the Geography Division outlined and described each enumeration district and provided a map of it. The boundary description of each E.D. included the name or number of each minor civil division; the name of the incorporated place within which it was located or with which it was contiguous; and the township, range, and section numbers when the E.D. was so described. Boundary descriptions of incorporated places listed streets and highways, rivers, railroads, and other distinctive features forming the district boundaries. Boundary descriptions of rural E.D.'s included the roads, streams, railroads, and similar features used as boundaries. In cities with a 1930 population of 50,000 or more, all city blocks were numbered and used as enumeration units. E.D. descriptions in such cases included a numerical listing and description of each block.

The E.D. maps were colored by hand to mark the district boundaries. County maps were also made for use by district supervisors and area managers. These were multicolored maps that distinguished between minor civil divisions, enumeration districts, unincorporated places, wards, delimited unincorporated places, national parks, and other civil or political boundaries. Separate maps were also made for each incorporated place that had a 1930 population of 2,500 or more. Copies of the plans of division were made for the Geography Division, the enumerator, the district supervisor, the area supervisor, the Field Division, and the squad leader (in cities of 50,000 or more). Copies of maps were provided to the Geography Division, the enumerator, the district and area supervisors, and squad leaders.

In addition to this map making, the Geography Division prepared the charts and illustrative maps used in Bureau publications. The Division of Geography was also responsible for the allocation of nonresident and absent household schedules to their proper enumeration districts. The Division checked to make sure that the persons enumerated on these schedules were not also enumerated at their place of permanent residence. Such transient schedules numbered about 500,000 for the 1940 Census (von Struve 1940, p. 277).

The Division of Geography participated in the ongoing development of tabulation areas. During the period of planning for the 1940 Census, this work involved the establishment of metropolitan districts and guidance in the layout of census tracts of large cities.

In 1930, the Bureau had designated what were considered the principal metropolitan districts of the United States. These districts were required to have an aggregate population of 100,000 or more, with one or more central cities of 50,000 or more. In addition to the central city, the metropolitan district also included all contiguous civil divisions with a population density of at least 150 inhabitants per square mile.

The metropolitan districts designed by the Bureau were novel because they showed a city's geographic-economic, rather than political, boundaries. Business and industrial interests found these new tabulation areas to be useful and they sought an expansion in the scope and use of metropolitan districts as a basis for publications. The metropolitan district concept was also of interest to the cities, states, and the federal government in planning programs for the cities. In response, the Bureau appointed a committee to study a redefinition of these areas and the possible extension of their use as statistical reporting areas. This committee was composed of Paul T. Cherington, New York City, who represented marketing and advertising interests; T. W. Howard, the Chamber of Commerce of the United States, who represented manufacturers; and, Glenn E. McLaughlin, Bureau of Business Research, University of Pittsburg, who represented other statistical groups (DOC 1938, pp. 31–33; DOC 1939, p. 27).

Based upon the recommendations made by the committee, the Division of Geography established 140 metropolitan districts for the 1940 Census, according to the criteria outlined above. Metropolitan districts then served as a basis of tabulation and publication of statistics.

The Division of Geography was also involved in setting standards for the establishment of census tracts in the large cities. Unlike political units with boundaries subject to change, the census tracts were designed to be relatively permanent, nonpolitical boundaries within these cities that allowed chronologically consistent comparisons. The Geography Division established optimum requirements for tract delineation, but the actual tract boundaries were recommended by the localities in question. There were 71 cities that had established census tract grids as of the 1940 Census of Population (von Struve 1940, p. 278). The data for census tracts were not published but rather were only available for each city upon paying for the costs of tabulating the material desired for the tracts.

Preparation of Schedules and Instructions

The responsibility for development of specific census inquiries was first transferred from Congress to the Director of the Census Bureau, subject to approval by the Secretary of Commerce, by the Census Act of June 18, 1929. Prior to that time, the legislation authorizing each census had specified the questions to be included on the census schedules.

In early 1939, the Director of the Census asked the chief statisticians in charge of the divisions within the Bureau to develop a schedule that could be recommended for the 1940 census.[2] A tentative schedule was first presented for discussion at a general conference held March 3–4, 1939, and chaired by Dr. Louis I. Dublin of the Metropolitan Life Insurance Company. The proposed schedule was also discussed at a conference sponsored by the National Bureau of Economic Research on April 21–22, 1939. In addition to discussion of specific items, these conferences discussed the use of sampling techniques in order to incorporate questions that had been crowded off the main population schedule.

Groups representing the major departments and agencies of the federal government and business, labor, and other special interest groups were present at these meetings. The Bureau directly consulted more than a thousand persons in these preparations. In addition, the census Advisory Committee appointed a technical standing committee to serve in an advisory capacity for six meetings held between April and June 1939. Members of this technical advisory committee included Frederick F. Stephan, American Statistical Association, Chair; O. E. Baker, U.S. Department of Agriculture; Frank Lorimer, American University; P. K. Whelpton, Central Statistical Board; and Howard B. Myers, Works Progress Administration.

---

2. For the response of the Chief Statistician of the Population Division, see Bureau of the Census (hereafter BC) 1939 (National Archives, Record Group 29, NN364–101, Series C, Box 2).

Preliminary schedules, instructions, and other forms were tested in a special census in Indiana during August 1939. Based upon an analysis of the results from this trial, final copies of forms and instructions were drawn. The final schedule forms were approved by the Central Statistical Board, the ASA Advisory Committe, the Director of the Census, and ultimately, by the Secretary of Commerce (DOC 1937, p. 29; DOC 1940, pp. 38–39).

The Inclusion of Employment and Income Questions

One of the significant developments in the 16th Decennial Census of Population was the added emphasis on economic problems of the national labor force (Eckler 1941). New questions were added in recognition of the need for data bearing upon the problems of large-scale unemployment, underemployment, and irregular incomes.

The 1940 Census provided the first complete classification of work status for all persons fourteen years and over based on activity during a specific week. Work status was determined according to activity during the week of March 24–30, 1940. Persons were broadly classified as either in the labor force or not in the labor force and within each category further distinctions were made based on the activity of persons—working, actively seeking work, attending school, etc.—during this week.

This new concept of labor force status differed from the 1930 concept of "gainful workers." This earlier concept included all persons who reported a gainful occupation—one in which they earned money or a money equivalent, or in which they assisted in the production of marketable goods—as of the census date and, also, those who reported that they *usually* pursued gainful occupations. One class of considerable significance, new workers, i.e., those looking for work who have not been previously employed, was not included in the category of gainful workers. New workers were included in the labor force category in 1940. Seasonal workers, disabled and retired workers, and institutional inmates were not included in the labor force.

The age limits also affected the comparability of gainful workers in 1930 and the labor force in 1940. In 1940, all persons under 14 are classified as outside the labor force; in 1930, however, persons aged 10 to 13 were counted as gainful workers if they reported gainful occupations. This group had become so small by 1940 that the expense of the additional enumeration and tabulation was not justified (Hauser 1949).

The labor force statistics were designed largely to measure the volume of unemployment and the characteristics of the unemployed. In an attempt to determine the extent of underemployment or part-time employment, two new questions on hours worked and wage income were included in the 1940 Census. Furthermore, information on employment was provided by a question on the number of weeks worked in 1939.

The 1940 census also utilized a new classification scheme for occupations. This scheme, developed by Alba M. Edwards, had eleven occupational groups: professionals and semiprofessionals, farmers and farm managers, proprietors and other (nonfarm) managers, clerical workers, craftsmen, operatives, domestic service workers, protective service workers, (other) service workers, farm laborers and foremen, and laborers. Edwards had sought to develop a classification scheme based upon "social-economic status," which would separate "head workers" from "hand workers" and divide the latter according to skill level. At the same time, the Social Security Administration was seeking the separate classification of employers, "own account" (self-employed) workers, and employees. This need led to an increased importance for the class of worker question. In addition, the 1940 census used a new Census Industry Classification to classify workers by industry. This classification was based upon the Standard Industrial Classification prepared by the Central Statistical Board between 1937 and 1939 (Edwards 1941; Conk 1978).

At the time the 1940 Census was in the planning stages, economists were seeking data on income distributions in order to explain the long depression which the country was experiencing. In 1936, the Conference on Research in Income and Wealth sponsored by the National Bureau of Economic Research suggested that the census include income questions (Goldfield 1958, pp. 39–63). This suggestion was only one of many that the Census Bureau received for including income questions.

The inclusion of a wage-income question in the 1930 census had been discussed at a general conference in the summer of 1929. This conference also discussed a question on the value of owned homes and the monthly rental of rented homes. It recommended including this latter question in the 1930 census because it was felt that the "value or rental" question would be more readily answered, although sentiment favored the income question. Contrary to expectations, little objection to the income questions was encountered. The data gathered from this question came to be used as an index of purchasing power and economic status (BC 1940b).

During the 1930s, requests for income statistics continued to be presented to the Bureau from sources outside of government. In addition, requests for such data came from such governmental agencies as the Social Security Board, the Bureau of Labor Statistics, the Work

Sampling Design

Projects Administration, and the United States Housing Authority.

In response to these requests, Dr. Leon Truesdell, the Chief of the Population Division, included two questions on income in his recommendations for the 1940 population schedule. These two questions asked (1) the amount of money wages or salary received and (2) if the person made more than $50 from sources other than wages or salary. These questions were included on the preliminary schedules discussed at various conferences and were subsequently tested in the special census of St. Joseph and Marshall Counties, Indiana, in August 1939. The inclusion of these questions, somewhat modified, as questions 32 and 33 on the 1940 population schedule was approved by the Technical Advisory Committee on Population, the ASA Advisory Committee, the Director of the Census, and the Secretary of Commerce.

The Census Bureau had anticipated objections from the public and adopted certain methods to help obtain the income information. People were asked to report only the amount of money wages and salary which they had received during 1939. An exact amount was not asked if the person received over $5,000 of wage and salary income. For other types of income, the question asked was "Did this person receive income of $50 or more from sources other than money wages or salary?" In addition, the Bureau put the income questions at the end of the schedule so that other information would have already been obtained if the respondent protested reporting his or her income and refused to cooperate any further. A special procedure was also developed for persons who objected to giving the enumerators the answers to the income questions. This procedure involved the use of a confidential report form. The enumerator filled in identifying information on this form and gave it to the person being enumerated, who then provided the answers and mailed the form to Washington.

The inclusion of income questions on the population schedule sparked public criticism and adverse publicity, including newspaper editorials, cartoons, and articles. An important source of resistance was provided by United States Senator Charles W. Tobey of New Hampshire, who appeared on the floor of the Senate on January 3, 1940, to read a letter to the Secretary of Commerce. This letter denounced plans to ask income questions and requested that the Secretary eliminate the questions. When the Secretary refused, Tobey introduced a Senate Resolution that required deletion of the income questions from the population schedule. In February, Tobey made a nationwide radio address and hearings were held on his resolution. Despite the support that Tobey's resolution received, the Senate leadership failed to call the resolution out of committee for a vote by the full Senate. It was in response to this public concern, however, that the Census Bureau did develop the confidential reporting form for income (Eckler 1972, pp. 192–95; Scott 1968, pp. 45–46). Despite this publicity, the nonresponse rate for the wage and salary income question was 2 percent of the wage and salary workers, and only 200,000 confidential forms were used.

New questions on fertility, educational attainment, and migration were added to the 1940 census schedule.

The 1940 census gave more attention to the subject of human fertility than any previous census. A question asking the number of children ever born to ever-married women was added. This question and information on the number of children under the age of five in the household provided measures of fertility.

For the first time in census history, a question was asked to obtain information on the highest grade of school completed by each individual. The addition of this question was seen to provide new possibilities for the analysis of the relation of education to other important variables.

Another new question asked each individual age five or older for their place of residence five years ago. When crosstabulated with place of residence in 1940 this new question allowed the computation of direct statistics on population migration (Truesdell 1941; Shryock 1941; Proudfoot 1940a).

Sampling Design

Another new development in the 1940 Census was an innovation in census procedure: sampling was incorporated as an integral part of the complete enumeration. In addition to the information obtained in the complete count of persons, "supplementary" information was obtained from a sample of one in every twenty persons. The Bureau felt that the use of sampling in this manner both enlarged the scope of the census and facilitated tabulations (BC 1941; Hauser 1941b).

The incorporation of sampling techniques by the Bureau met with some resistance. Bureau Director Austin initially opposed the use of sampling because he felt that it did not have public acceptance. In addition, Leon E. Truesdell, one of the senior officials in the Bureau and Chief of the Population Division, opposed the use of sampling. Support for the use of sampling came from Dedrick and Vergil D. Reed, the Assistant Director. With the top officials at the Bureau divided over the incorporation of sampling techniques, the decision reverted to the Secretary of Commerce, Harry Hopkins, who held ultimate legal authority. Hopkins's Economic

Advisor, Willard L. Thorp, also favored the use of sampling. Hopkins decided in favor of the use of sampling in the 1940 Population Census (DOC, OFSPS 1978, pp. 45–46).

Philip M. Hauser, the Assistant Chief Statistician of the Population Division, and Dedrick planned the implementation of the sampling plan, using the consultative services of sampling expert Fredrick F. Stephan, then Secretary-Treasurer of the ASA, and Morris H. Hansen, of the Bureau's Statistical Research Division. To supervise the development of the sampling program, the Bureau sought out the services of Dr. W. Edwards Deming, a physicist and statistician in the Department of Agriculture (DOC, OFSPS 1978, p. 146).

The requests of both government and private groups for more information led the Bureau to consider additional questions in the decennial census. One of the benefits of using sampling in the census enumeration was the opportunity to include more questions on the schedule. This was made possible because the supplementary questions were only asked one-twentieth as often as the questions in the complete enumeration.

The Census Bureau considered another advantage of sampling to be that tabulations based upon a sample of persons could be finished months earlier than tabulations based upon the complete count. These earlier results proved to be beneficial in providing information needed for the emergency situation brought about by World War II. The greatly reduced cost of sample tabulations was considered an additional advantage, allowing more preparation and publication of such tabulations than would otherwise have been possible. In a similar light, the storage of the sample information on sample cards was considered more economical than the storage of cards from the complete count. Thus, subsequent tabulations could be produced as the need arose.

The Bureau acknowledged that in response to the changes brought by the Depression, there was an increased demand for an extensive body of statistical information regarding such concerns as unemployment, occupational shifts, migration, population growth, and other population changes. Since space on the schedule was necessarily limited, the adding of supplementary questions allowed the Bureau to expand its coverage to meet these needs. The use of sampling reduced the average time per interview that would have otherwise been necessary to obtain data, and substantially reduced the expanded costs of editing, coding, and tabulating the data.

In addition to being selected in a manner similar to the selection of the items for the full count on the main schedule, a consideration in the selection of the supplementary questions was the suitability of the questions for sampling. Since a sample is not a population inventory, the items chosen had to elicit information needed for generalizations, conclusions, and formation of policies for areas such as large cities, states, or geographic regions. The supplementary questions which appeared on the schedules included questions on parents' nativity, the language spoken in the respondent's home in earliest childhood (mother tongue), veteran status, social security information, usual occupation, usual industry and usual class of worker, nuptiality, and fertility. Most of these questions had appeared in earlier censuses in one form or another and their inclusion allowed comparison with these earlier censuses.

The sampling was designed to fit with existing census procedures. The sample was taken at the same time as the regular enumeration and the supplementary information was recorded in a separate section on the schedule.

The planners of the sampling at the Census Bureau felt that the sampling process should be kept as simple and automatic as possible. Since enumerators were employed for short periods of time, it was decided that it was impossible to provide enumerators with special training to conduct the sample. In order to avoid leaving anything to the discretion of the enumerator, the samples were designed to remind the enumerators when to ask the supplementary questions.

The 1940 population enumeration form was a "line schedule" with 40 lines each on the front and the back. A separate line was used for each person enumerated. The sample was selected by designating two of the 40 lines on each side of the schedule with the symbol, "Suppl. Ques." Enumerators asked the supplementary questions at the bottom of the population schedule for each person whose name fell on a line that was so marked. This line-sampling procedure yielded a sample of two out of 40, or five percent, of all the lines in each enumeration district, producing a sample that was stratified for geographic differences in population characteristics. The choice of a systematic pattern of lines within E.D.'s served, in effect, as the sampling unit.

The Bureau would have preferred a procedure of random sampling after the complete census listings had been made. This approach was impractical for administrative and financial reasons (Stephan, Deming, and Hansen 1940). It was decided that it was not possible to pursue random sampling of households or persons within each enumeration district simultaneously with taking the census without burdening enumerators and possibly introducing additional bias. The Bureau made the choice to sample at designated intervals and determined that sampling persons, i.e., schedule lines, was preferred over sampling households. This choice was based upon the possible controls for line bias that are described below. Thus, this procedure was found to be the simplest and most convenient of all procedures investigated from the standpoint of actual field experience. In addition, the inclusion of the supplementary questions at the bottom of the population schedule facilitated the matching of data on the main schedule with data on the supplementary schedule that occurred during the processing of returns.

The Census Bureau determined that it was necessary to overcome the bias inherent in the sample made up of designated schedule lines. Line bias occurs when designated lines persistently overstate or understate the frequency of certain characteristics and their proportions in the population. It was determined at the Bureau that such bias could arise from the nature of the systematic coverage provided by the census: enumerators in urban areas commenced enumeration at corner houses and worked around the block; in addition, within a household, the members were listed systematically from head through wife, children in order of age, other relatives, lodgers and their children, and servants and their children. The first few lines entered were thus biased in favor of corner houses and senior members of the household. Another source of bias could occur at the end and middle of the 80-line schedule where sheets were turned over or new sheets started. Here a disproportionate amount of blank lines would appear.

To reduce the possible effects of line bias, five different styles of the population schedule were used in enumeration. Each style was printed to show a different set of designated sample lines but was similar to other styles in every other respect. Four different styles ("W," "X," "Y," and "Z") were used to give direct representation to the 16 lines that presented the greatest variation (see table 2.1), while one style ("V") sampled the remaining 4 lines in an unbiased manner.

Table 2.1. Schedule Style, Sampling Line Numbers, and Their Proportions

Style	Proportion	Line Numbers
V	.80	14 29 55 68
W	.05	1 5 41 75
X	.05	2 6 42 77
Y	.05	3 39 44 79
Z	.05	4 40 46 80

The Bureau decided to provide each enumerator with only one style of schedule. Since each enumeration district was canvassed by a single enumerator, the 16:1:1:1:1 ratios were thus maintained by enumeration district. Differences in the size of enumeration districts were considered to be controlled by the shuffling of the population by style of schedule. The plan of distribution of styles was rotated on the following scheme: V V W V V V V X V V V V Y V V V V Z V V. This rotation pattern was made in the initial packaging and distribution of schedules but could not be fully implemented. The rotation pattern was repeated county after county, without breaking at county or state lines.

The 1939 Special Census of St. Joseph and Marshall Counties, Indiana

By the summer of 1939, the Bureau had developed the preliminary schedules, instructions, and other forms to be used in the enumeration of the 1940 census. These preliminary procedures were pretested in the special census of St. Joseph and Marshall Counties, Indiana, that began on August 14, 1939. Analysis of the results of this special census was used in the final decisions for preparations for the 1940 Population Census.

In addition to permitting tests of new forms and instructions, the trial census also provided an opportunity to test procedures for selecting enumerators through the use of objective examinations. Applicants for enumerator were given two tests. One test was based upon the abridged instructions to enumerators and covered the population schedule; the second test was based upon the instructions to enumerators and covered the supplementary schedule. The scores from these tests were then used in the selection of enumerators.

An innovation in the special census was the use of "field inspectors." The 170 enumerators hired for the special census were divided into groups of 10 to 20 enumerators. A field inspector was assigned to supervise each group of enumerators to act as the link between the enumerators and the supervisor. In the initial days of the enumeration, field inspectors were required to be available for enumerators' questions and to examine thoroughly completed population schedules and supplementary schedules for accuracy. Upon completion of an enumerator's assigned area, the field inspector was required to make a comparison of addresses on the population schedules with duplicate maps and descriptions of the enumeration district in an effort to ensure complete coverage.

The special census utilized two alternative forms of population schedules. One form, the white schedule, had 100 lines and followed the established practice of enumerating individuals sequentially by household. In addition, an experimental green schedule was also utilized. This was a household schedule with space for 12 persons. Only one household was enumerated on each green schedule. Each form was used in approximately half of the enumeration districts in the special census, with only one type of form used in each enumeration district. Enumerators were also required to fill out a supplementary schedule for each tenth household visited. This supplementary schedule provided a basis for a sample study of information not included on the regular schedules. Selection of households occurred systematically, with enumerators filling out the supplementary schedule for every household whose visitation number on the regular schedules ended in the digit "5."

Information appearing on the population schedules contained the address, structure visitation number, structure type, household visitation number, farm residence status, home tenure, home value or rent, and the number of rooms in the home.

Other information contained on the schedules included the name of each person enumerated, the relationship of persons to the head of household, sex, race, age at last birthday, marital status, school attendance, highest grade completed, place of birth, citizenship status, and residence five years previous. Employment status, occupation and industry, weeks worked, and income information also appeared on the population schedules.

The supplementary population schedules also included information on general identification, utilities and appliances in the home, mortgage indebtedness, female nuptiality and fertility, place of birth and mother tongue, usual occupation and industry, social security status, and veteran's status.

The information obtained from the special census was also used to train office employees. The preliminary editing and coding instructions, card forms, tabulations, and table forms for the final census reports of 1940 were all developed on the basis of the experience gained from processing the 1939 special census. Several statistical reports were also published.

The Inclusion of a Census of Housing

A Census of Housing was included in the Sixteenth Decennial Census by Congressional Act approved on August 11, 1939. This housing census was the first nationwide inventory of housing ever made. The act called for information on the number, characteristics, and geographical distribution of dwelling structures and units in the United States, Hawaii, Puerto Rico, the Virgin Islands, and Alaska. The act authorized $8,000,000 to cover the costs of such a census. The housing census was undertaken as part of the federal government's recognition of the importance of improving housing conditions and was designed to provide essential housing facts to guide government agencies interested in housing, as well as to aid local public and private concerns (Brunsman 1941).

The inclusion of the housing census required additional planning. Much of this work came from a special housing committee that included: Warren J. Vinton, U.S. Housing Authority, chairman; Shirley K. Hart, Federal Housing Administration; Corwin A. Fergus, Federal Home Loan Bank Board; Thomas J. Woofter, Farm Security Administration; Aryness Joy, Department of Labor; Samuel J. Dennis, Bureau of Foreign and Domestic Commerce; Calvert L. Dedrick, Bureau of the Census; and Leon E. Truesdell, Bureau of the Census (DOC 1940, p. 43).

3 FIELD ENUMERATION

THE ENUMERATION PROCESS for the 1940 Census of Population and Housing was the responsibility of the Census Bureau's Field Division. This responsibility included organization and training of the field staff, opening of field offices, execution of the enumeration, and preparation of preliminary population releases and pay vouchers. A description of these various activities is presented in this chapter. The population and housing schedules are also described.

THE STRUCTURE OF THE FIELD ORGANIZATION

The chief of the Field Division directed all field activities of the 1940 censuses. The United States and the territories and possessions were divided into three regions, each administered by an assistant to the chief of the Field Division. Each assistant was responsible for the progress and quality of work in his region. The chief and the assistants were headquartered in Washington.

The direct representatives of the Bureau in the field were 104 area managers appointed by the Director of the Census and located in cities designated by the chief of the Field Division. The territory under the supervision of the area manager was divided into districts, each headed by a district supervisor appointed by the Director.

Area managers were responsible for instructing the district supervisors and other field staff. They were also charged with providing assistance and supervision in all phases of district operations. The 529 district supervisors were responsible for directing collection of statistics from the start of the censuses of business and manufactures through the canvass of population and agriculture. Candidates for area manager and district supervisor were nominated either by members of Congress or by the Administration. Candidates for area manager were interviewed and trained by the permanent staff of the Bureau. These candidates received an eight-week training course during the fall of 1939. The course covered administrative and personnel procedures, schedules, forms, and instructions. Objective tests were administered and approved candidates received appointments. During December 1939, the area managers held one-week training courses for the district supervisors. Additional correspondence training was also provided for both area managers and district supervisors between January and March 1940 and nine regional training sessions were held during February and March (Eckler 1972, p. 162; DOC 1940, p. 40). Both the area managers and the district supervisors were provided with assistants and were authorized to employ stenographers and other clerical help as needed. The area managers were informed by the Field Division in Washington of the number of office employees allowed in their respective area and district offices.

In cities having populations of over 50,000, district supervisors were allowed to hire squad leaders to assist in directing the work of enumerators. Area managers were advised by Washington of the number of squad leaders allowed in the districts under their supervision. In those cities where squad leaders were allowed, they were hired to direct approximately 20 enumerators. Squad leaders and enumerators were appointed by district supervisors, under the direction of the area managers. The approximate number of enumerators for each district was predetermined by the amount of work to be completed in the allotted time. There were approximately 120,000 enumerators employed in 1940. All squad leaders and enumerators worked under the supervision of district supervisors. District supervisors were encouraged to find enumerators who could speak foreign languages for use in those enumeration districts in which a considerable number of people did not speak English. When such enumerators could not be found, the supervisors had to request authority from the chief of the Field Division to appoint interpreters to assist enumerators in those areas.

Area Offices

Area managers received training on the procedure and technical aspects of the canvass prior to the opening of their field offices. Once the training period was completed, area managers were responsible for arranging space, equipment, and telecommunications for their respective offices. The necessary forms and supplies for work in each office were shipped from the Field Division. When additional supplies were needed the area managers were instructed to requisition (Form F3-40) them from the chief of Field Division.

Before the beginning of the census of business and manufactures canvass, area managers brought together the district supervisors who had been conditionally assigned by Washington for training programs and subsequent examinations. Upon the completion of this program of training and evaluation, the examination papers and area managers' recommendations were forwarded to the chief of Field Division. Subsequently, the Director informed the area managers as to which supervisors would be appointed to each district.

Both area managers and district supervisors received "Plans of Division" (Form 16-3) showing the division of territory into enumeration districts, the piece-price rates to be paid enumerators therein, and the number of persons and farms reported from each district during the 1930 census. Area managers were instructed to require district supervisors to ascertain whether there had been any recent changes in the boundaries of minor civil divisions or in other political divisions. If such changes were found, the details of the changes, appropriate maps, and other evidence provided by county or local officials were sent to the chief of the Field Division. This procedure was required in sufficient time prior to the canvass in order that new descriptions and maps prepared by the Bureau would be available before the appointment of enumerators for the districts in question.

Area managers were encouraged to make regular visits to the headquarters of each district supervisor to make sure the canvass was being properly and satisfactorily conducted. They were instructed to make thorough checks of office records and to examine enumerator schedules to be sure proper entries were being made.

During the course of the canvass, area managers were authorized to subdivide established enumeration districts when necessary. The procedure to be followed allowed for the original enumeration district number to be retained and the parts to be marked "A," "B," etc. Complete descriptions of the proposed new districts were submitted to the chief of Field Division and accompanied by the reasons for the changes.

Area managers were responsible for the prompt completion of work in each supervisor's district. Upon an investigation showing that work in the district office had been satisfactorily completed, area managers were authorized to close the office and forward the office records to the chief of the Field Division. Thereafter, the area manager was responsible for any cleanup work necessary in the district.

District Offices

The territory under the jurisdiction of the area manager was divided into districts, each headed by a district supervisor. The district supervisor was directly responsible for the collection of statistics in the field. With the guidance and approval of the area managers, the district supervisors appointed and instructed all enumerators and other employees in the districts and directed their work throughout the canvasses.

The headquarters of each district supervisor was located in a city designated by the chief of the Field Division. In general, office space was utilized in federal or local government buildings. When such space was not available and space in a local chamber of commerce building was not available, the area manager was authorized to allow the rental of suitable quarters.

Although most communications in the field were conducted by mail, district supervisors were responsible for arranging telephone and telegraph service. They were also requested to make special arrangements with local postmasters for efficient mail delivery. All district correspondence with area managers and the Bureau was required to be in triplicate.

Schedules, forms, and other office supplies were shipped directly from Washington to the district supervisor's office. Additional supplies, when needed, were requisitioned from the area manager's office.

District supervisors were paid a sum of $2,000 to cover the entire period of both the business and manufactures census and the population, agriculture, and irrigation censuses. A part of this compensation was paid at regular intervals during this period, and a part was withheld until area managers furnished proof that work in the district had been satisfactorily completed. In addition, a bonus compensation was paid upon satisfactory completion of the district supervisor's work. This bonus was based upon the number of schedules completed within the district.

Both district and assistant district supervisors were

allowed traveling expenses and subsistence allowances, not to exceed $5 per day, during necessary absences from their headquarters. Such allowances were not paid when the employee traveled to the community in which he normally lived. At the time of appointment, district supervisors and their assistants were required to submit affidavits (Form F2–40) to the Director indicating their place of permanent residence. District supervisors were also authorized to incur necessary miscellaneous expenses not to exceed $25 during the period the office was in operation, for materials that could not be shipped from Washington, e.g., ink and glue.

The district supervisor was responsible for prompt preparation of all payrolls and expense vouchers in accordance with "Instructions for Accounting Procedure." Completed payrolls and vouchers were forwarded to the area manager for approval and transmission to the appropriate disbursing office.

GENERAL PREPARATIONS

Examination of Enumeration Districts

One of the first important duties of the district supervisor was to examine the list of enumeration districts outlined by the Bureau to make sure that they were clearly defined and that all incorporated places where included. Enumeration districts were to be small enough to allow an enumerator to finish his or her work in the time prescribed (about 2 weeks in urban areas and about 30 days in rural areas). In cases involving very small enumeration districts, district supervisors were allowed to assign an enumerator two or more districts once the first one had been completed. In such cases, separate returns were made for each enumeration district.

In examining the list of enumeration districts, district supervisors were to make sure that the descriptions and maps of the enumeration districts correctly represented the civil subdivisions of the counties in their districts. Similarly, the descriptions of enumeration districts in cities and other incorporated places were to be examined to ascertain that they represented actual boundaries as they existed. The district supervisors were to consult with county and city officials to verify the data that the Bureau had obtained.

The detection of mistakes in boundaries as shown on the enumeration district descriptions or the detection of unclear descriptions resulted in requests for the necessary changes, using the form "Request for Revision of Enumeration Districts" (Form 16–387). The original and two copies of this form went to the area manager. Included with this request were a map showing the boundary changes and a statement from a local official that could be made available to Washington. District supervisors were instructed not to enumerate these districts until they received a new set of descriptions from Washington. The geographer studied submitted changes; when the descriptions had been approved he notified the area manager and district supervisor. The geographer provided the district supervisor with new maps, descriptions, and enumeration district numbers for these new districts. If the changes were not approved, the district supervisors received an explanation and new instructions.

Other changes in enumeration districts occurred when it was necessary to split an enumeration district after enumeration had begun. This occurred only when it became clear that the enumeration district was too large to be completed in the allotted time. When such divisions were necessary, district supervisors were required to fill out "Split Enumeration District Report" (Form 16–5) in quintuplicate. The first four copies were mailed to the area manager, who returned a signed copy upon approval as the district supervisor's authority to make the changes and proceed with enumeration.

In dividing an enumeration district, each part of the district retained the original enumeration district number except that the letters "A" and "B" were added to identify the two parts. In the report filed by the district supervisor, the boundaries of each part were to be described accurately and in sufficient detail to prevent questions from arising. District supervisors were instructed to assume that their changes had been approved by the Division of Geography unless otherwise notified.

Receipt of Schedules and Supplies

Schedules, blank forms, and other supplies were sent to district supervisors in packages as needed. The population schedules and other supplies needed by enumerators were enclosed in portfolios. Each portfolio contained the materials necessary for one enumeration district. The boxes of portfolios and farm schedules were numbered consecutively in order of shipment. These boxes were to be retained and used in returning the completed schedules. Upon receipt of the final shipment of boxes, district supervisors were instructed to notify the chief of the Field Division as to the number of boxes received, the number of boxes damaged in transit, and the number of additional boxes needed.

As noted above, a separate portfolio was provided for each enumeration district. The portfolio contained copies of the various census schedules and other blank forms necessary to meet the enumeration requirements that were estimated for the particular district by the Census Bureau. The portfolio contained a printed label with the enumeration district number and space for entering the name of the enumerator and, where appropriate, the number of the squad leader's district. Pasted on the inside of the front cover of the portfolio were a description of the enumeration district and a map showing its outlines.

Portfolios were to be either mailed or delivered to the enumerators after they had been appointed, taken the oath of office, and received the necessary instructions. Enumerators were encouraged to promptly acknowledge receipt of the portfolios, in order to prevent delays in the work.

Selection and Training of Enumerators and Squad Leaders

All applicants for the position of enumerator were required to fill out application blanks. The district supervisor was encouraged to interview applicants whenever possible so that the applicants could speak freely about their qualifications. After examination of applications and interviews, the district supervisors were instructed to make a list of those applicants who could be reasonably expected to qualify as enumerators. This list became an eligibility list for the administration of a screening examination.

Persons not qualified for the job, as indicated by the screening process, were notified by the district supervisor that they did not have the necessary qualifications. The following criteria were used in eliminating applicants from the eligibility lists: their handwriting was not sufficiently legible, their applications indicated an inability to follow written directions, they were current or retired federal employees, they were under 18 or over 65, or they had been tax collectors or assessors since 1937.

District supervisors were instructed to give hiring preference to the following: war veterans and widows of war veterans (when equally qualified with others); crop reporters for the USDA (if not USDA employees); retired farmers; those who were attending or had attended agricultural colleges; school teachers; town clerks, recorders and other local officials (where state laws did not prohibit their employment); applicants who were at least high school graduates; and applicants whose appearance and manner indicated that they were suited for public contact.

Using this list of qualified applicants, district supervisors selected a number 50 to 100 percent larger than the number of enumerators required. The extra candidates thus produced provided a pool from which substitute enumerators could be drawn in case an enumerator was unable to continue his or her work. A number of training forms were then mailed to this group, with instructions to study these materials in preparation for testing. District supervisors made arrangements to administer the tests to the applicants and informed the applicants of these arrangements in the mailing of study materials.

Applicants were given the examinations in groups of 25 to 100. One hour was allowed for each test—I (population) and A–I (agriculture). The tests were then graded by the district supervisors. Applicants making the highest scores on Test I and Test A–I were selected to take the enumerators' training course.

Applicants who had been tentatively selected as enumerators were sent additional study materials prior to the beginning of this training course. The applicants were required to fill out sample training schedules and return them to the district supervisors for evaluation.

The training course began with the applicants reviewing the corrections made by the district supervisor on their sample training schedules. The training session then followed with a question and answer period centered on the schedules. Where time allowed, applicants were shown several training films. In addition, the supervisors scored the examinations and those persons receiving the highest passing scores were given appointments as enumerators. Persons making lower (but passing) scores were given further instructions before being allowed to begin as enumerators. District supervisors were instructed to encourage the enumerators to continue to study their instruction books after the formal training had ended.

Enumerator appointments were allowed without the prior approval of the Director. The enumerators received a letter of notification (Form 15–102) stating the rate of compensation and containing a blank oath of office (Form F8–40). Certificates of appointment were required for each enumeration district. Therefore, in cases in which an enumerator had more than one district, multiple certificates of appointment were required. The oath had to be signed, witnessed by a notary officer, and received by the district supervisor before the appointment certificate and any supplies were forwarded to the enumerator. District supervisors were required to forward to the area manager at the close of each day a list of names of enumerators from whom oaths had been received and to whom appointment certificates had been sent.

Upon taking the oath of office, enumerators were obliged to perform their work according to the procedures and subject to the penalties of the Census Act. Among the various penalties prescribed by the Census Act were up to a $500 fine on a misdemeanor for neglecting or refusing to perform duties; up to a $1,000 fine and/or two years imprisonment for publishing or communicating unauthorized information; and, up to a $2,000 fine and/or five years imprisonment for perjury or making false reports. Explicit warnings were made to avoid disclosing to any unauthorized person any information which they had secured. Additionally, enumerators were warned against failure to make an honest effort at securing full returns for their districts and against attempts to swell the size of their returns.

If a person declined to serve as an enumerator after taking the oath of office and receiving an appointment but before rendering any service, his or her certificate was cancelled. Clerical employees in the supervisor's office had to submit formal resignation notices (Form F7–40) addressed to the Director. Enumerators who resigned or terminated their employment were not required to submit resignations or notices of termination. According to the Census Act, enumerators could not retire from their appointment without "justifiable cause." District supervisors were instructed to make every attempt to convince enumerators to continue with their work and avoid the penalties prescribed by law. An additional instruction to district supervisors required that they make statements as to the efficiency of each employee working under their supervision. These statements were kept on file for use in future employment references.

In those districts where squad leaders were used, they were to be selected from the list of enumerator applicants on the basis of administrative experience and ability, as well as competence in understanding the schedules and instructions. District supervisors were encouraged to select squad leaders in advance of the training period for enumerators so they could assist in that training process. The training of squad leaders followed the procedures outlined above for enumerators. Once appointed, squad leaders were allowed to establish headquarters in public buildings apart from the district supervisor's office, so that they could maintain closer contact with enumerators.

Public Relations

Area managers and district supervisors were encouraged to make every effort to disseminate information regarding the needs of the census work. This effort was aimed primarily at local newspapers, radio stations, and any other available channels. The Bureau also encouraged area managers and district supervisors to establish contact with local organizations and officials in order to obtain their cooperation in promoting a complete and effective census. The Bureau's desire was to use organizational cooperation to create public interest in the census and to circulate information. While this cooperation was promoted, citizens and organizations were not allowed to be involved in any manner in the actual enumeration or to receive any census information except preliminary announcements.

The Division of Public Relations was responsible for the development and issuance of press releases throughout the entire nation during the canvass period. All area managers and district supervisors were instructed to contact civic organizations to secure their involvement in circulating this information to the press.

THE ENUMERATION PROCESS

According to law, the enumeration was to be made as of 12:01 A.M., April 1, 1940. The work of enumeration began on the following day, April 2. Enumeration was to be completed within 2 weeks in any incorporated place of 2,500 inhabitants or more in 1930, and within 30 days in all other districts. Additionally, persons in hotels, tourist camps, trailers, and flophouses were enumerated where they spent the night of April 8 (see below). It was the responsibility of district supervisors to arrange assistance needed for this canvass. The district supervisor was encouraged to have clerks in the office, as well as squad leaders, assist where necessary. The names of persons enumerated as of the night of April 8 were placed on separate sheets of the population schedule.

Squad leaders, used in the districts of 50,000 or more, assisted in the plans for the special enumerations on the nights of April 8 and 9, by obtaining from their enumerators a list of all places requiring special enumeration procedures and an estimate of the number of persons likely to be there on those nights.

General Instructions

Enumerators were instructed to begin their canvass by carefully checking for completeness and accuracy the map and description of the enumeration district which had been furnished to them.

Enumerators were told to visit every house, building, tent, cabin, hut, or other place in which a person might be living or staying. All women, men, and children (including infants) whose usual place of residence was in the enumeration district were to be enumerated. "Usual place of residence" was specified as meaning where people "*live*" or have their "*home*." This instruction to enumerate all persons including persons who were temporarily absent, persons who were in the district at the time of the enumeration but had no other place of usual residence at which they would be enumerated, and all persons who moved into the district after enumeration had begun but were not previously enumerated. Also to be enumerated were all inmates of prisons, homes for orphans, or similar institutions located in an enumeration district. All inmates of a jail, no matter how short their term of sentence, were to be enumerated as residents of the district. For convenience in enumeration, larger institutions were made separate enumeration districts and were enumerated, in most cases, by some employee of the institution. In addition, in cities which had a population of 500,000 or more in 1930, apartment houses with 100 or more apartments were made separate enumeration districts.

Enumerators were instructed to inquire of every household whether certain types of persons were members of the household: persons temporarily absent, either in foreign countries or elsewhere in the United States; persons attending schools or colleges; persons who lived in hospitals or sanitariums; persons who were servants or employees and lived in the same household or slept in the same dwelling; persons who were boarders or lodgers and slept in the house; and persons in the household who enrolled in the Civilian Conservation Corps. Such persons were to be enumerated as members of the households in the enumerator's district.

Similarly, enumerators were given instructions as to which persons they were not to enumerate, even though these persons might be present in the household at the time of enumeration. Such persons were considered to have usual places of residence other than the household, e.g., visitors, households temporarily in the enumeration district, transient boarders or lodgers, students living with the household whose home or usual place of residence was elsewhere, servants or other household employees who did not sleep in the same dwelling, and transient patients of hospitals and sanitariums (these persons were to be enumerated as residents of the household of which they were members).

Persons living in certain types of dwellings—hotels, tourist facilities, flophouses—were enumerated on particular evenings. On April 8, all persons living in tourist or trailer camps, missions, and cheap one-night lodging houses (flophouses) in an enumeration district were to be enumerated. Also on April 8, enumerators left a Hotel List (Form P–8) with the manager of each hotel. The manager was instructed to provide the names of all persons who spent the night of April 8 in his hotel including permanent residents who were not in the hotel that evening. Enumerators also left a supply of Individual Census Forms (Form P–7) to be filled out by each guest. Form P–7 requested all population schedule information including supplementary questions. On April 9, enumerators returned to collect these forms and interview persons on the Hotel List who failed to return an Individual Census Form. Enumerators were instructed to begin new sheets of the population schedule for the enumeration of these persons and to place these new sheets after the other schedules in the enumeration district, numbering them in sequence beginning with sheet 81. Additionally, enumerators were instructed to enter a "T" in column 3 of the schedule, rather than a visitation number, for the first person enumerated in each dwelling on those nights. Column 3 was to be left blank for subsequent persons in those places. Enumerators separated the Individual Census Forms into two groups. One group contained the forms of persons who indicated a usual place of residence other than the hotel. The information from all other forms (those of government guests, resident employees and transient guests not reporting another place of residence) was transferred to the sheets of the population schedule reserved for persons enumerated on the night of April 8.

Enumerators were provided with Enumerator's Record Books (Form P–6), in which they were required to enter five types of situations: (1) All households that had to be revisited; (2) households in which members were not expected to be present during the period of the canvass; (3) households temporarily in the enumerator's district but which claimed residence elsewhere; (4) households refusing to furnish required information; and, (5) vacant city blocks in an enumerator's district. In addition, enumerators were required to record necessary call-backs to obtain housing information. The enumerator's record book provided space for address, household visitation number, structure visitation number and unit number within structure (housing census), spaces reserved on the population or housing schedules, date of the first visit, a brief explanation of the reason for revisiting and any appointment information, and the date upon which the information was finally obtained. Upon completion of enumeration, the record book was turned in to the supervisor for inspection. The supervisor used the information to determine the adequacy of the canvass.

Enumerators received special instructions for those cases in which no member of the household was home at the time of a first visit. When a member of the household was expected to return during the period of the canvass, the enumerator was instructed to leave a copy of the Preliminary Population Schedule (Form P–11), assign a household visitation number, and record this information in the enumerator's record book. The entry in this case contained the address of the household to be revisited and the household visitation number. Where the enumerator was able to determine the number of persons in the household to be revisited, he or she was instructed to leave an appropriate number of lines on the population schedule. If the enumerator was unable to find out this information, the instructions were to proceed with the enumeration of the next household without leaving space on the schedule.

The preliminary schedule which was left at households to be revisited was designed to provide enumerators with required information, including supplementary questions, for each person in the household. Upon revisiting such households, the enumerators were instructed to check completed preliminary schedules for questionable entries and, if none were found, to transcribe the household data onto the population schedule. Responses to supplementary questions were transcribed only for persons whose names fell on the appropriately designated lines. If no preliminary schedule had been prepared, the household was to be enumerated in the usual manner. Households and persons for whom space was not reserved on the population schedule were enumerated on separate sheets beginning with sheet number 61. Also included on these separate sheets were individuals enumerated out of order but who were members of households enumerated in regular order. For such persons, the household visitation number of his or her household was entered in column 3 of the schedule, followed by *"cont'd."*

In cases in which a household was away from its place of residence for the entire period of the canvass, enumerators were instructed to attempt to obtain the name of the head of the household and the address at which he or she was residing. This information was to be entered in the Enumerator's Record Book and a "Report Card for Absent Household" (Form P–6) was to be turned in or mailed to the supervisor.

Enumerators were also given special instructions on how to enumerate those persons who claimed that their usual place of residence was outside the enumerator's district. Such persons were to be enumerated on the "Nonresident Schedule" (Form P–10), which differed from the population schedule in two ways. The nonresident schedule inquired about both the location of the usual place of residence and the place of residence at the time of enumeration. In addition, the nonresident schedule included supplementary questions to be asked of all persons in the household. Entries were made in the record book of each household enumerated on the nonresident schedule and completed nonresident schedules were mailed to the district supervisor at the end of each day's canvass for forwarding to the appropriate census office.

In those cases in which a household refused to give the information requested, enumerators were instructed to assign a household visitation number and record this number, the household address, and the structure information (if a housing census was being taken) in the record book. The enumerator was to report immediately such cases to the supervisor or squad leader. If the enumerator was able to obtain the names of the persons in the household, he or she was to leave an appropriate number of spaces on the population schedule. If the enumerator was unable to obtain such information, the squad leader or district supervisor was to do so. The use of tact and diplomacy in obtaining responses was recommended. Reference to the penalties provided for by the Census Act was allowed in extreme cases. The Census Act specified that any person over the age of 18 who refused to answer census inquiries was subject to misdemeanor prosecution and a penalty of up to $100 and/or 60 days imprisonment. In addition, such a person who willfully provided false answers was subject to a fine of up to $500 and/or imprisonment of one year. In those rare cases in which the district supervisor was unable to obtain information, a detailed report was sent to the area manager for action.

Enumerators were also given special instructions for recording any vacant housing units. In urban enumeration districts, the maps and descriptions of the enumeration districts showed the individual blocks making up each district. Each block had a block number. Enumerators were instructed to enter in their record book as a vacant block any one on which there were no residential structures of any kind. When enumerators encountered a vacant dwelling unit (either a house or an apartment) or a vacant room in a lodging house, they were required to leave a "Card for New Occupant." This card was to be mailed to the supervisor and provided notification of the need to return to enumerate the new occupant(s).

Filling Out the Population Schedules

Enumerators were given certain general instructions about filling out the population schedules.[1] Enumerators were instructed to use a separate numbered line for each individual enumerated and never to crowd individuals into spaces not numbered. Ditto marks were not allowed, although dashes were allowed in the sole case of repetition of a surname. Enumerators were requested to sign every form. They were also encouraged to seek information from a responsible adult member of the household.

The population schedule had three distinct parts: a

---

1. A facsimile of the population schedule is provided in Appendix I, Figure I.

heading, consisting of geographical and other identification information; "main lines," containing the items asked of all persons; and "supplementary lines," including additional items asked of five percent of those enumerated.

The heading on the population schedule was to be filled out completely before any persons were enumerated on the schedule (see Appendix I, Figure 2). The first entry for each enumeration district was to begin on a new sheet of the schedule. The sheets of the population schedules used to enumerate persons in regular order were numbered serially, beginning with sheet number 1. Sheets for persons enumerated out of regular order were numbered serially beginning with sheet number 61. Those sheets used to enumerate persons on the night of April 8th were numbered serially beginning with sheet number 81. Vacant lines were to appear only at the end of one of these three groups of schedules.

Once the heading information had been filled out, the enumerator began recording information in the columns of the population schedule (see Appendix I, Figure 3). The first two columns recorded the location of the household—the name of the street, road, etc., and the house number. Enumerators were asked to mark a heavy line across these two columns when they reached the end of any street.

General household data were recorded in columns 3 to 6. These entries were to be made only for the first line of any household, the one on which the head was listed. This information included a household visitation number—a sequential number for every household in the enumeration district. For census purposes, a household was defined as "a family or any other group of persons, whether or not related by blood or marriage, living together with common housekeeping arrangements in the same living quarters." In multiple-unit buildings (apartment houses, apartment-hotels, and tenements), there were as many households as there were separately occupied apartment or dwelling units. A hotel, boarding house, lodging house, or institution, however, constituted only one household. Servants, hired hands, boarders or lodgers who slept in the house and had no other actual place of residence were counted as members of the household. Also included in the general household data columns was information about whether the home or dwelling unit was owned by a member of the household or rented; the estimated market value of an owned home or the actual monthly rent paid; and, whether the household lived on a farm.

Column 7 of each schedule was reserved for the name of each person whose actual place of residence was with the household. These names were recorded surname first, followed by the given name and initial. In those cases in which the surname was the same as that of a member of the same household enumerated on the line above, a long dash was entered rather than the surname. If an entire household could not be entered on one side of the schedule, the enumerator was instructed to fill out all lines on the side and mark the box labeled "Household continued on next page" on the lower left margin of the schedule. In such cases, "cont'd." was to be written in columns 1 and 2 of the new page and columns 3 and 6 were to be left blank. An "X" with a circle around it was to be written after the name of the person in each household who furnished the information.

Column 8 of the schedule recorded the relationship of the person in column 7 to the head of the household. Lodgers, hired hands, chauffeurs, and servants were designated as such in column 8, and their relatives were designated as "lodger's son," "servant's daughter," etc. Institutional occupants were designated as officer, inmate, patient, pupil, etc., except for prisoners in penal institutions, whose prison numbers were entered in column 8.

Personal descriptions were entered in columns 9 to 12. This information included sex, race, age at last birthday, and marital status. Infants born between 12:01 A.M., December 1, 1939, and 12:01 A.M., April 1, 1940, had "Infant Cards" filled out in addition to the regular line entry on the population schedule.[2] Column 13 was used for response to the question of whether the person had attended school or college, except correspondence school, at any time since March 1, 1940. The last full grade of school or college completed by the person was entered in column 14.

Information on the person's place of birth was recorded in column 15. Column 16 was used to enter citizenship information for all foreign-born persons and persons born at sea. Four types of citizenship were recorded: (1) "NA"—naturalized citizens; (2) "PA"—declaration of intention to become naturalized—"first papers" taken out; (3) "AL"—alien; and (4) "AmCit"—American citizen at birth. In columns 17 to 20, the place of residence on April 1, 1935, of every person was entered. For persons under 5 years of age, a dash (—) was entered.

For persons 14 years old and over, questions in columns 21 to 33 requested labor force information. Questions 21 to 25 were designed to classify all persons 14 years old and over according to their work status during the week of March 24–30, 1940. These persons were

---

2. Infant cards were completed for a separate study of the coverage of newborn children in vital statistics programs, i.e., birth registration, and in the census itself.

The Enumeration Process

divided according to whether or not they were in the labor force. Persons who had a job, business, or profession in which they worked for pay or profit, or who were seeking work, were considered to be in the labor force. Persons in the labor force were categorized into four groups: (1) persons at work in private work or in nonemergency federal, state, or local government work; (2) persons at work on, or assigned to public emergency project work; (3) persons seeking work, not classified into one of the two categories above; and, (4) persons having jobs, businesses, or professional enterprises from which they were temporarily absent during the week of March 24–30. Special instructions were given to enumerators in communities in which there were only a few dominant industries. Here, enumerators were instructed to indicate as "seeking work" those individuals who may not have been actively seeking work only because the industries were shut down and there were no other possible jobs to be sought.

If persons did not fit into one of the above categories, they were classified as "not in the labor force," and further categorized as: (1) devoting most of their time to care of the home and housework; (2) in school; (3) physically unable to work; or, (4) in a residual category including retired persons and people choosing not to work.

For persons who were at work in either private or nonemergency government work, column 26 was used to record the number of hours worked during the week of March 24–30, 1940. Column 27 was used to enter the duration of unemployment, as of the week ending March 30, 1940, for all persons seeking work or assigned to public emergency work. For persons with previous work experience, this was the number of weeks since the last full-time private or nonemergency government job. For persons without previous work experience of one month or more, and for experienced persons who were seeking work after a period of absence from the labor force, the entry was the number of weeks since the person last began seeking work. Weeks of public emergency work, e.g., WPA, CCC, were counted as weeks of unemployment for the purpose of this question.

Columns 28 to 30 were used to enter occupation, industry, and class of worker information for those persons in the labor force. These columns were left blank for persons not in the labor force. The nature of the duties performed in the person's job was recorded in column 28 (occupation). For persons who were employed during this period in more than one occupation, the information recorded concerned the occupation at which the most time was spent. Persons who were seeking work and who had previous job experience were asked to give the occupational information from the last job on which they worked one month or more, including public emergency work. For those who were seeking work and had no previous job, the entry "new worker" was made in column 28, and columns 29 and 30 were left blank. Information on the kind of industry or establishment (factory, store, etc.) in which these duties were performed was entered in column 29 (industry).

Column 30 recorded the person's "class of worker": (1) "PW"—a wage or salary worker who was working for a private employer; (2) "GW"—all government workers, at all levels, including public emergency workers; (3) "E"—persons who were conducting their own business and employed one or more helpers other than unpaid family members or domestic servants; (4) "OA"—persons who conducted their own business or professional enterprise but did not employ helpers, i.e., persons working on their "own account"; and, (5) "NP"—an unpaid family worker who was working for a related family member and contributing to family income (housework and incidental chores not included).

For every person age 14 and over, except most institutional inmates, there was to be an entry in column 31 indicating the number of full-time weeks worked in 1939. This number included weeks on public emergency work or performing unpaid family employment. A "0" was recorded for persons who did not work for pay or profit during 1939. The total amount of money wages or salary paid in cash or check to each person for work done as an employee during 1939 was entered in column 32. This amount included commissions, tips, piece-rate payments, and bonuses; it also included work on public emergency projects. This amount did not include earnings by farmers or those engaged in business or the professions who did not work for wages or salaries but rather whose income was from business profits, sales of crops, or fees. Persons who did not receive any money wages or salary in payment for employment were given a "0" in this column. If a person made over $5,000 in money wages or salary, "5000+" was entered in column 32.

For each person aged 14 or over, either a "yes" or a "no" was entered in column 33 in response to the question: "Did this person receive income of $50 or more from sources other than money wages or salary?" Included in these other sources were the following: rents from roomers or boarders, business profits, fees, rents, interest or dividends, unemployment benefits, direct relief, and income in kind paid as wages. Not included as other sources were lump sum inheritances, lump sum compensation benefits, occasional gifts, reimbursements for travelling expenses, and receipts from the sale of land or securities. A "no" was recorded in this column for persons not receiving income amounting to $50 from one or more of the allowable sources.

Those persons who refused to provide the information for columns 32 and 33 were presented the option of answering the questions on a "Confidential Report on Wage or Salary Income, 1939" (Form P–16). Enumerators recorded at the bottom of this form the state, the enumeration district number, and the sheet and line number of the population schedule on which the person was enumerated. In the right margin of the schedule, they entered a "C"—for confidential report. While the person was entitled to fill out the form in private, enumerators were instructed to wait for the information to be placed in an envelope (Form C–131) addressed to the Director of the Census, sealed and returned to the enumerator for mailing. Enumerators were instructed to report any refusals to their supervisors, and to make the necessary entries in their record books.

Column 34 was used to record the number of the farm schedule filled out by any household member who operated a farm or other place requiring a farm schedule, e.g., a greenhouse.

The population schedule had 40 lines on each side. Two of these lines were designated to obtain certain supplementary information for the two persons whose names fell on the lines. At the bottom of the schedule there were two lines on which supplemental questions appeared and where responses to these questions were to be recorded (see Appendix I, Figure 4). This was the sample information described in the previous chapter. Supplemental questions were to be asked only of the member of the household whose name appeared on the designated line, regardless of the relationship to the household head. Column 35 was used to record the name of the person for whom the supplementary information was required.

The place of birth of the person's father was entered in column 36 and the place of birth of the person's mother was entered in column 37. The principal foreign language spoken in the person's home during earliest childhood was entered in column 38. "English" was entered in this column if no foreign language was spoken. In column 39 there was entered either a "yes" or "no" to the following question: "Is this person a veteran of the military forces of the United States—Army, Navy, or Marine Corps—or a wife, widow, or under-18-year-old child of a veteran?" Column 40 contained the response to this question: "If a child, is veteran-father dead?" Information on the wars in which the veteran or veteran-husband or veteran-father served was entered in column 41.

Social security information was entered in columns 42–44. This information included whether the person had a federal social security number (column 42), whether deductions for federal old-age insurance or railroad retirement were made from the person's wages or salary in 1939 (column 43), and, for those with the deductions named in the previous question, whether the deductions were made from (1) all, (2) one-half or more, or (3) part, but less than half, of wages or salary (column 44). In columns 45 to 47, information was entered about the person's usual occupation, industry, and class of work. This information was entered in accord with the instructions for entering information in columns 28–30. The information in columns 45–47, however, was not necessarily the same as that entered in the previous columns. If the person had never worked full time for a month or more, "none" was entered in column 45, and columns 46 and 47 were left blank.

For each woman on the supplemental line who had been married, widowed, or divorced (based on column 12), information was entered in columns 48–50. Column 48 contained the response to the question of whether the woman had been married more than once. The age of the woman at her first marriage was entered in column 49. Finally, the number of children ever born to this woman, excluding stillbirths, was entered in column 50.

The Housing Schedules

The inclusion of the housing census in the Sixteenth Decennial Census was designed to provide an inventory of housing facts. The housing census used two different schedules that were filled in by the enumerators conducting the population census. Both housing schedules incorporated precoded squares for some inquiries which, for the first time, allowed enumerators to record responses by checking the appropriate square.

The "Occupied-Dwelling Schedule" (Form 16–254) was used to enumerate all dwelling units that were occupied by a household enumerated on the "Population Schedule." The "Vacant-Dwelling Schedule" (Form 16–486) was used to obtain information on all dwelling units not occupied by enumerated households. Such dwelling units were primarily vacant and for sale or rent at the time of enumeration. Also, those units that were being held for the occupancy of absent households were listed on the vacant-dwelling schedule.

The entries on the occupied-dwelling schedules were arranged in several parts. Part I contained information on the location of the dwelling unit and household data. Specific items included the number of the structure in order of visitation and the dwelling unit number within the structure, the population line number of the head of the household, the block number (in cities of 50,000 or more), the race of the head, the number of persons in the household, farm residence, home tenure (owned or rented), and the value of the home or the amount of monthly rent paid. Part II contained data on the characteristics of the structure, such as number of dwelling units, the presence of a business within the structure, the year and purpose for which the structure was originally built, and the exterior material and need for major repairs. Information on the characteristics of the dwelling units, such as the number of rooms and the equipment present, was contained in part III. Part IV consisted of utility data, including any furniture that was included in the rent. Finally, financial data for each owner-occupied nonfarm unit was presented in part V of the occupied-dwelling schedule. This information consisted of the value of the property, the total mortgage debt, the first mortgage debt, the regular payments, the interest charged, and the holder of the first mortgage or land contract.

The vacant-dwelling schedules contained information in three parts. The location and general data in part I included the visitation and dwelling unit numbers, the block number, farm location, an occupancy status, and the monthly rental (or an estimate). Part II, the characteristics of the structure, and part III, the characteristics of the dwelling unit, were the same as on the occupied-dwelling schedule.

The housing census was designed to be taken along with the census of population. Enumerators filled in responses on the housing schedules as they completed the population canvass. The additional work of taking the housing census delayed the enumerators. Many enumeration districts that had been laid out for population and agriculture censuses were too large to be canvassed by one enumerator when the housing census was added. As a result, some enumeration districts were divided and in some E.D.'s the period for completion was extended (DOC 1940).

Enumeration Supervision

It was stressed to district supervisors that the instruction of enumerators and their supervision during the first two to three days of the canvass were essential in assuring that enumerators conducted their work promptly and efficiently. The concern of this early inspection lay principally with the form and completeness of entries and not with the thoroughness of the canvass. District supervisors were told to make sure that either they or their assistants checked to see that enumerators were carrying out instructions for filling out schedules and making proper entries in their record books. In those cities of 50,000 and over where squad leaders were used, each squad leader was responsible for inspecting those schedules filled out by enumerators. Squad leaders were instructed to meet with the enumerators at least every other day.

In urban supervisors' districts, enumerators were to submit the schedules completed in their first day's work at the close of the first day or early the second day. The district supervisor, assistant district supervisor, or squad leader then went over the completed work with them, commented on errors and omissions, and gave additional instructions, allowing the enumerators time to ask questions. All enumerators were to have their schedules examined and receive additional instructions within the first two days of the canvass.

The same plan was encouraged in rural supervisors' districts. Special provisions were designed for those cases where the necessary travel was difficult. In addition, rural enumeration districts were divided into four approximately equal subdistricts, which were canvassed as independent units. Enumerators were instructed to submit completed schedules for each subdistrict to the district supervisor for inspection and approval before beginning the canvass of another subdistrict. The completeness of enumeration was particularly stressed for rural districts.

The method of examining population schedules involved three steps. The first step required checking for complete heading information on every schedule that had been used. The second step consisted of a series of tests to assure the completeness of entries: entries were required in columns 2–6 for the head of every household, and only for heads of households; in columns 7–15 for every person; in column 16 for every person born abroad or at sea; in columns 17 and 20 for every person age 5 or over, except under certain conditions; only certain combinations of entries were excepted in columns 21–27 and only for those 14 years of age or over; entries were required in columns 21–33 for every person 14 years and older; in columns 35–50 for each person enumerated on a line marked "Suppl. Quest."; and an infant card was required for every infant reported as 0/12, 1/12, 2/12, or 3/12 years of age in column 11. Enumerators were to supply any missing information, if necessary, by revisiting the household.

The third step in the examination of schedules involved tests of accuracy: ditto marks were permitted only in column 7 to show the repetition of surnames; use of unauthorized symbols was not allowed; rents and values entered in column 5 were to be consistent with the entry in column 4 and with other values and rentals in the vicinity; names were to be entered in proper order; proper relationship to head of household entries were to be made; entries for sex, relationship to head, age, and marital status were to be consistent; the entry for highest grade completed was to be consistent with the age entry; occupation and industry entries in columns 28–29 were to be detailed; and entries for social security in columns 42–44 were to be consistent. Any needed corrections were made by the enumerator while the work was being inspected.

Squad leaders were assigned certain enumerators and charged with the responsibility of supervising the accuracy, completeness, and timing of the enumerators' work. Squad leaders were encouraged to keep records of all questions asked by enumerators that could not be answered. These questions were referred to the district supervisor. Upon completion of the enumeration, this record of questions was to be given to the district supervisor, who in turn was to mail it along with other office records to the chief of the Field Division in Washington.

After the initial inspection of enumerator entries had been made, it was no longer expected that all entries would be checked. Squad leaders were, however, encouraged to continue to inspect a "good portion" of the enumerators' entries during regularly scheduled meetings with the enumerators. Squad leaders were also instructed to inspect each record book to make sure that the enumerator had been using it according to instructions. Particular attention was given to making the necessary return visits to households where no respondent was at home at the time of the enumerator's first visit.

Squad leaders were provided with duplicate maps and descriptions of each enumeration district under their supervision in order to make sure that each enumerator had completely covered his or her assignment. In addition, squad leaders were instructed to verify approximately five percent of each enumerator's work by taking one completed schedule from each enumerator and making sure that each household had been contacted and that no occupied dwellings were omitted. Squad leaders were further encouraged to contact each household listed on the schedule to ensure the enumeration of the household was accurate.

The completeness of an enumerator's canvass was monitored through the district supervisor's knowledge of the territory, inspection of the enumerator's completed schedules and record book, examination of rural district maps, and comparison with city directories, voting lists, assessors' lists, telephone directories, and earlier censuses. When examination indicated that the returns for any district were incomplete or erroneous, enumerators were required to make the necessary corrections without delay. In those extreme cases in which the schedules of a district were too faulty to allow proper corrections, district supervisors were required to make a full report to the chief of the Field Division, who had authority to order a reenumeration of the whole district or any part that was needed to make the returns satisfactory.

Progress Reporting

The squad leaders were instructed to report each morning to the district supervisor's office. They were also required each day to fill out the "Squad Leader's Daily Report" (Form F–102). Although these instructions were developed for use in urban areas in which squad leaders were used, the instructions were also recommended for district supervisors who did not have squad leaders but who provided enumeration supervision themselves or through an assistant.

District supervisors were instructed that if during the course of the enumeration it became evident that work assigned to an enumerator was not likely to be completed within the allotted time period, supervisors should take measures to hasten the completion of the work. The measure recommended was to divide the enumerator's territory and assign a part to another enumerator. In the event that an enumerator resigned or was dismissed, district supervisors were also instructed to appoint new enumerators immediately. In such cases, the supervisor was instructed to send a complete statement of the facts of the case to the chief of the Field Division.

Included in enumerator portfolios was a set of "Daily Report Cards" (Form F–100). These cards were filled out each day and mailed to either the enumerator's squad leader, where they were used, or to the district supervisor. Before mailing these report cards, enumerators were instructed to post a record of them on the "Enumerator's Consolidated Production Record" (Form F–101). At the end of this production record was a "Certificate of Completion" of the enumeration district. When the enumerator had completed his or her district this certificate was to be signed and the consolidated production record mailed to the district supervisor.

From the enumerator's daily report cards, squad leaders made daily reports to the district supervisor informing him of each enumerator's progress. These reports were included in the squad leader's daily report. District supervisors posted these reports on a summary form. If there were no squad leaders in a supervisor's district, the summary sheet was completed directly from the enumerator's report cards. These postings served as records of progress in the enumeration of supervisors' districts and as a check for counting and verifying the population schedules. The cards were filed for each enumerator in order of their date and subsequently formed a basis for payment of enumerators and for the "District Supervisor's Daily Report to Area Manager" (Form F–104). This latter form reported the total number of enumerators at work and the status of the enumeration in the various enumeration districts under the district supervisor's authority. In those cases in which an enumerator failed to send a daily report card, the squad leader or district supervisor was instructed to send out a card indicating the "Failure to receive a daily report" (Form 15–122).

Area managers were required to mail weekly reports to the Washington office. These reports covered the week running from Thursday through the following Wednesday, and were due in Washington on or before Monday of the following week. Consolidated progress reports summarizing the activities of the entire Field Division for the previous week were then produced and distributed to the area managers.

Upon the completion of each county in a district, the district supervisor sent the chief of the field division a certificate of completion stating that all of the population and farms in the county had been enumerated and that the enumeration was complete.

Preliminary Population Counts: Announcements and Vouchers

District supervisors were instructed that upon the completion of the canvass of population and agriculture in their districts, an announcement was to be made of the population of each city of 10,000 persons or more and of each county in their districts, and the number of farms in each county. Announcement of population figures for smaller cities and minor civil divisions were left to the discretion of the district supervisors.

These announcements were sent to the chief of the Field Division, area managers, local officials, principal local newspapers, and other interested organizations, such as the chamber of commerce and boards of trade. The letter of transmittal that accompanied the announcement (Form P–116) invited these organizations to report the names of persons in their organization who might have been omitted from the census. The district supervisor was authorized to provide explanations to any queries, to make necessary investigations, and to have an enumerator correct or complete his or her enumeration. To reenumerate any district, however, the consent of the Director of the Census was necessary. Copies of all official correspondence concerning announcements, complaints, and criticisms were to be sent to the chief of the Field Division.

The information necessary for making these preliminary announcements was based upon a count made by the district supervisor for the preparation of the enumerators' pay vouchers. This count was a total of the number of persons on the population schedule, the number of farm schedules returned, and the number of infant cards. The population count made by the district supervisor from the examination of enumerator's finished population schedules was made on a "Population Count Slip" (Form P–113). For a given enumeration district, this count slip included the number of names and either blank lines or lines containing notations other than names for every sheet used in the enumeration of that district.

After examining and counting the schedules turned in by the enumerators and determining to their satisfaction that the returns were complete and the canvass thorough, district supervisors were to complete vouchers to pay enumerators. The rates of compensation for districts were established by the Census Bureau in Washington. The bases for compensation were the number of persons enumerated on the population and nonresident schedules, and the numbers of infant cards, farm schedules, and any other schedules (if any) returned. The counts used in the preparation of vouchers were those made in the district supervisor's office, not the counts in the enumerator's daily reports.

Enumerators were required to submit their consolidated production records, on which the certificate of completion statement appeared, and all daily report cards before the voucher was sent to them for their signature. District supervisors were required to check the signature on the signed voucher with the signature on the enumerator's oath of office for similarity. They were also instructed to hold the voucher for five days after the preliminary announcement of the population of the area of which the enumeration district was part in order to be sure there were no complaints. In the event of complaints, the vouchers were held until the enumerator's services were no longer needed. Once this period ended, the district supervisors attached the summary of the enumerator's daily work report, application, oath of office, and both copies of the certificate of appointment to the voucher and forwarded them to Washington for payment.

Enumerators were paid on a piece rate basis. These rates were shown on the certificate of appointment and were designed to produce an average salary of between $4 and $5 per day. Factors taken into consideration in determining rates of pay included population density, farm density, and transportation required. Any changes in the rates of pay established by the Bureau required the area manager's and the Director's approval.

Return of Schedules and Final Reporting

Once the preliminary announcement of the population and number of farms was made and enumerator's pay vouchers were certified, the district supervisor's office repacked the completed schedules in the boxes in which they had been originally shipped. The returns of each enumerator were to be kept together, except in those cases in which there were more than 15 farm schedules. In this latter event, the farm schedules were packed and mailed separately. Included in the box were the population schedules and the count slip, any agriculture schedules—plantation, irrigation, farm, ranch, abandoned or idle farm list—and the certificate of completion. Boxes were shipped to the Bureau of Census by registered mail as they were filled.

District supervisors were also required to notify the Bureau by invoice (Form F16–40) of the shipment of boxes of schedules. These invoices contained information including the box number, the enumeration district numbers to which the schedules pertained, and whether the box contained farm schedules. These invoices were made in quadruplicate for each day's shipment. The first copy was sent by mail to Washington, the second placed inside one of the boxes in the day's shipment, the third copy sent to the area manager, and the last copy retained by the district office.

District supervisors were required to make a full report of the work in their districts before completing their duties. This report was expected to include both a formal statement of beginning and completion dates of certain processes and the number of employees, and also a more general statement describing the conditions and difficulties encountered, and assessing the methods adopted. The report was to cover all phases of the enumeration process, including division of the territory into enumeration districts, selection and instruction of enumerators, supervision of enumerators' work, rates of compensation, cooperation, and publicity. District supervisors were also encouraged to make suggestions for the improvement of census methods.

Special Situations

In general, most persons residing on federal lands were enumerated by the federal agency or service with jurisdiction over the area. Military posts, naval stations, and Civilian Conservation Corps camps were made separate enumeration districts and enumerated by the service in question. Persons attached to posts or stations but living outside post limits were to be enumerated as members of the households which they usually kept rather than as members of the post. The War and Navy departments also provided census data for officers and enlisted men, and civilian employees on transports and naval vessels. Similarly, the Coast Guard provided enumeration of all officers and enlisted men and of all employees and their families living at their places of duty and working for the U.S. Lighthouse Service. Regular census enumeration was made of the families of those in the Coast Guard at their usual places of residence.

Most Indian reservations were enumerated by employees of the Bureau of Indian Affairs. Also, all persons having their usual places of abode within the boundaries of national parks were enumerated by the National Park Service. The necessary data for seamen and other employees on vessels who did not maintain homes on shore were obtained by the Bureau of Fisheries and the Coast and Geodetic Survey. The State Department enumerated all employees and their family members who were stationed abroad. Finally, special provision was made to enumerate the crews of vessels in foreign and intercoastal trade and on the Great Lakes. Even though these crew members had homes on shore they were not to be enumerated in the regular manner. Each vessel was enumerated on a separate 100–entry standard population schedule, sometimes by one of the ship's officers who was appointed as a census taker. The counts and characteristics were tabulated to special enumeration districts set up for this purpose, and the crew members were counted as part of the population of the port from which the vessel operated.

4 PROCESSING AND TABULATION

FOLLOWING THE COMPLETION of the enumeration process and field checks of the completed returns, the portfolios which contained the population and housing schedules were mailed to the Census Bureau in Washington, D.C. Once the schedules had been received at the Bureau they were processed and the information was transformed into tabular form. The system data processing was organized into a number of distinct operations that produced a flow of materials for the subsequent operations. This chapter traces this flow of processing operations from the initial receipt and checking of schedules through the tabulation of the data. The numbered operations are listed below.

Operations Procedures in the Processing of the 1940 Censuses

Operation 1	Receipt of Population and Housing Schedules by Field Division
Operation 2	Receipt and examination of schedules by Population Division
Operation 3	Matching of Population and Housing Schedules
Operation 4	Hand count of population and housing (and verification of matching)
Operation 5	Transcribing the preliminary sample data (and verification of hand count)
Operation 6	Separation of Population Schedules, Housing Schedules, and other materials
Operation 7	General population coding
Operation 8	Verification of general population coding
Operation 9	Coding Occupation, Industry, and Class of Worker
Operation 10	Verifying Occupation, Industry, and Class of Worker
Operation 11	General housing coding
Operation 12	Verification of general housing coding

INITIAL ACTIVITIES

Once the census schedules had been received and given a preliminary examination, they were passed through a series of steps that readied them for later coding and tabulation. An initial operation was the matching of the population and housing schedules. In this operation, all schedules and auxiliary forms were examined for data consistency and completeness. Following this match, hand counts were made of both the population and housing schedules, data from sample persons were transcribed on the preliminary sample sheet, and the schedules and auxiliary forms were separated for further operations or filing. This section on initial activities includes a discussion of the manner in which the Bureau maintained records on the flow of work.

Receipt and Examination of Population Schedules

Portfolios containing the completed schedules were received in Washington by the Field Division. In Operation 1, Field Division staff inspected each portfolio for the proper number of completed forms:

"Population Schedules" (Forms P–16–252),
"Infant Cards" (Form P–4),
"Occupied-Dwelling Schedules" (Form 16–254),
"Vacant-Dwelling Schedules" (Form 16–486),
"Enumerator's Record Book" (Form P–6),
"Population Count Slips" (Form P–113),
"Housing Count Slips" (Form HC–10).

The count of the number of population schedule sheets had to agree with the population count slip, the counts on the two dwelling schedule sheets had to agree with the housing count slip. In addition, the number of infant cards had to agree with the number recorded in the "Enumerator's Consolidated Production Record" (Form F–101). In the case of missing materials, the district supervisor was sent a list of missing materials and the portfolio was set aside until the materials were accounted for.

The staff in Operation 1 inspected the heading information on the first sheets of the population and dwelling schedules to see that it agree with the description and map of the enumeration district in the portfolio. Unexplained discrepancies were routed to the Geography Division for correction, as were any "Nonresident Schedules" (Form P–10) and "Absent Household Schedules" (Form P–110) needing assignment to the proper enumeration district. The contents of inspected and computed portfolios were listed on receipt forms and the portfolios containing the schedules were forwarded by the Field Division to the Population Division in county units.

In Operation 2, the population and housing schedules were received and examined by the Population Division. Receipt clerks compared the enumeration district (E.D.) number of each portfolio with the E.D. numbers listed on the delivery receipt for each county. When these numbers matched, the receipt clerk signed the receipt form and forwarded it to the control file record clerk. The receipt clerk then inspected the label on each portfolio, pasted a "Portfolio Memorandum" (Form P–302) on the outside of the portfolio, and delivered the portfolios to the section chief for assignment to examination clerks.

Examination clerks filled in identification information—E.D. number, state name, county name, the name of cities of 100,000 or more, or the name of the independent cities in Virginia—on the portfolio memorandum. Once this information had been recorded, the examination clerks removed from the portfolio all schedules and forms except for the population schedules and the dwelling schedules.

The examination clerks examined the schedules for consistency of E.D. numbers and compared heading information on the population schedule with the description of the E.D. pasted on the portfolio.

Each "Individual Census Form" (Form P–7) was examined to determine that the enumerator had transcribed onto the population schedule the information for persons residing in the E.D. These schedules were then divided into various groups to aid in the identification of problems. Forms which had not been completely transcribed onto population schedules were segregated for completion in Operation 3. Forms which had been transcribed onto schedules were examined at a rate of one in ten to determine that the information was complete, although consistency between the individual census form and the population schedule was not examined.

The "Preliminary Population Schedules" (Form P–11) were also removed from the portfolio. Every fifth schedule was checked to see that the information for the entire household had been transferred to the population schedule. Consistency between the two forms was not required. Clerks noted whether the information on the two forms appeared to be the same. If any of the preliminary population schedules thus checked had not been transferred onto the population schedule, the clerk was required to check all preliminary population schedules in the portfolio to see that all information had been transferred. Those preliminary population schedules which contained names not transferred were left in the portfolio, while any preliminary schedules on which all the names had been transferred were removed from the portfolio. A similar procedure was used to compare the preliminary housing schedules with the housing schedules.

Matching of Population and Housing Schedules

The matching of the population and housing schedules was carried out in Operation 3. This operation involved four main processes: (1) population and housing schedules were determined to be in the proper portfolio; (2) when necessary, information was transferred from auxiliary forms to the population and housing schedules; (3) infant cards were matched with entries for infants on the population schedule; and, (4) households on the population schedule were matched with dwelling units on the occupied-dwelling schedule.

The first step in the matching operation involved determining if the population and housing schedules were in the proper portfolio. Clerks were instructed to check both the "A" and "B" sides of each population schedule, occupied-dwelling schedule, and vacant-dwelling schedule to be sure that the E.D. number agreed with the E.D. number shown on the portfolio label. They also examined the heading information on each sheet of all the schedules for thoroughness and consistency of completion and supplied any missing entries which could be determined correctly. The geographer's map and description of the enumeration district were available on the inside cover of the portfolio for such use. In addi-

Initial Activities

tion, the clerks placed the schedules in numerical order according to type of schedule.

In the second step of Operation 3, information on supplemental forms was transferred to the population and housing schedules. The supplemental forms included individual census forms, preliminary population schedules, nonresident schedules, and absent-household schedules. Entries on these forms were compared with the entries on the population schedules to determine whether the persons enumerated on the supplemental forms had been enumerated on the schedules. If they had been enumerated, the forms were cancelled; if not, the information on the auxiliary forms was transferred to the population schedule.

The procedure for checking individual census forms began with noting whether a sheet and line number had been entered in the space provided on the form. If the information had been transferred, the form was set aside. If the space had been reserved but the information not transferred, the clerk transferred the information.

If the individual census forms did not contain these sheet and line numbers, the address at which the person should have been enumerated was to be listed on the form. In this case, the clerk found the sheets of the population schedule used for enumeration of persons on the same street. If a house number was reported, the entries for persons living at that address were examined to determine if the person on the individual census form was entered on the schedule. If the person was not listed at that address, the visitation number of the household at the address was compared with entries for household visitation numbers on the sheets used for persons enumerated out of order. When the entry could not be found on these sheets, the entry for the person was transferred from the individual census form to the sheets used for persons enumerated out of order, i.e., sheets numbered 61 and over.

In cases in which there was little or no address information present on the individual census form, the clerks were instructed to search among the names of persons in households enumerated on the same street or, if that information was not available, among the names of persons in the same E.D. in order to find the appropriate household. When the clerks had transferred all information which they determined possible, they marked the individual census forms to show either that the information had been transferred, including the sheet and line number of where the information was transferred, or that the information was not transferred.

The streets and house numbers on all preliminary population schedules were checked against the population schedule to determine if all persons in the household had been enumerated. If all members had been enumerated, the clerk initialed the preliminary population schedule and indicated on which sheet and line number of the population schedule the information could be found. In such cases, the two schedules were to be checked for consistency and any necessary corrections made.

If only some of the members of the household had information appearing for them on the population schedule, but space had been left for the rest of the household, the clerks were instructed to transfer the information for the rest of the household from the preliminary population schedule. If space was not reserved for these additional household members, the information for them was transferred to the first available line on the sheets used for persons enumerated out of order and the household visitation number on the population schedule was marked "cont." The sheet and line numbers to which the population was transferred were marked on the preliminary population schedule.

In those cases in which no space had been reserved on the population schedule for the household listed on the preliminary population schedule, the clerks transferred the information to the first available line on the sheets used for persons enumerated out of order. The assignment of a household visitation number was unnecessary in such instances. If the street and house number were not listed, the clerks compared the names on the preliminary population schedule with the names of persons for the entire E.D. in order to determine whether all or part of the household had been reported on the population schedules. When a household listed on the preliminary schedule could not be found on the population schedule, it was entered on the first available line on sheets reserved for persons enumerated out of order.

The procedures for transferring information from both the nonresident schedules and the absent-household schedules to the population schedule were the same. These procedures relied upon using the street and house numbers whenever possible. If these numbers were not available, the name was used to examine the population schedules in order to determine whether all or part of a household had been reported.

When the clerks found entries on the population schedule, they checked the information with that on the nonresident or absent household schedule for discrepancies. If only part of a household appeared on the population schedule, the information on the rest of the members was transferred to the reserved spaces, if any, or to space on the sheets reserved for persons enumerated out of order. Similarly, if none of the members of a household had been listed on the population schedule, their information was transferred to space reserved for the household, if any, or to space on the sheet for persons enumerated out of order.

Preliminary housing schedules were occasionally found in the portfolios; the clerks were required to compare the entries on them with the entries on the occupied-dwelling schedule. If the information for the dwelling unit was not already entered on the occupied-dwelling schedule, the clerks were to compare the address on the preliminary housing schedule with the same address on the population schedule. If a household was found at the same address on the population schedule and there was no housing information on either the occupied-dwelling or vacant-dwelling schedules, the information was transferred from the preliminary housing schedule to the occupied-dwelling schedule. When there was not a household listed on the population schedule, the clerks were instructed to find the dwelling unit on the vacant-dwelling schedule and to add the unit to that schedule if it appeared to constitute an additional dwelling. If the information necessary to make a determination was not present, the clerks marked the preliminary housing schedule "not transferred."

The third step in Operation 3 was the matching of infant cards with entries for infants on the population schedule. Infant cards were arranged in order by sheet and line number for each portfolio. The infant cards were then compared with the corresponding sheet and line numbers to see if the name of the child listed on the card was also listed on the population schedule. The information in the two entries was compared and corrected, if necessary, and a check mark was placed after the infant's name on the population schedule, to indicate that the infant card had been checked. The age of the infant was checked. If the age of the infant was over three months on the schedule and did not agree with the age on the infant card, the schedule was changed to agree with the card unless the date of birth on the infant card was prior to December 1, 1939. In this latter case, the infant card was cancelled by marking a large "X" through it.

If there was an infant card for an infant whose name did not appear on the population schedule but whose father and mother had been enumerated, the information was transferred to the population schedule. If a mother or father could not be found on the schedule, the infant card was marked "no such household."

After the infant cards had been compared to the entries on the population schedule and a check mark had been made on the schedule for each infant who had a card, the clerks then checked the schedule for all entries in column 11, the age entry.

Any entries of "3/12" or less should have had check marks beside them. If any such entries did not have check marks, infant cards were filled out for the infant based on the information appearing on the population schedule. Once all cards and entries on the schedules had been examined, the clerks returned the infant cards to the portfolio.

The fourth and final step in Operation 3 was the matching of population and housing schedules. The first sheet of the occupied-dwelling schedule was placed over the corresponding sheet of the population schedule. Line 1 on sheet 1 of the population schedule should have been filled out for the head of a household. For every person with an entry of "head" in column 8 there were to be entries in columns 3–6. The population schedule line number for the head was to appear in the space marked "Population Line No." on the occupied-dwelling schedule. If the two numbers corresponded, the clerks placed a check mark on the occupied-dwelling schedule. The clerks repeated the process for each line on the population schedule for which entries appeared for a "head," until every head of household enumerated had been checked. Certain types of households were excepted from entries on the occupied-dwelling schedule. These exceptions were institutional households, hotel households, and households for which all entries on the population schedule had been made by the clerk in the second step of Operation 3.

There were households enumerated on the population schedule for which no dwelling unit had been enumerated on the occupied-dwelling schedule. If such instances occurred more frequently than once per sheet, they were referred to the section chief. Certain rules were developed for handling less frequent occurrences. If there were entries in columns 3–6 of the population schedule but the person in column 8 was not designated head, the clerk cancelled the entries in columns 3–6 only. When there were no entries in columns 3–6 but the entry in column 8 was "head," the clerks were instructed to cancel the "head" entry. Finally, if there were entries in columns 3–6 and an entry of "head" in column 8, the clerks compared the entry for number of persons on the occupied-dwelling schedule for the previous dwelling unit with the number of persons listed in the previous household on the population schedule. When the entry for number of persons in the previous dwelling unit included the persons in both the previous household and the household in question and the street address of the two households was the same, the entries in columns 3–6 and column 8 for the "head" of this household were cancelled. If either of the addresses of

Initial Activities

the two households were different or the entry of the number of persons in the previous dwelling unit on the occupied-dwelling schedule did not include persons in the questioned household, the clerk was instructed to assume that the dwelling unit had not been enumerated on the occupied-dwelling schedule. The clerks then made entries on this schedule based upon information present on the population schedule. The clerks also cancelled the entry for the dwelling unit if it appeared on the vacant-dwelling schedule.

The clerks were also instructed how to treat dwelling units for which no head of household had been enumerated on the population schedule. The clerks first compared the names and addresses on the occupied-dwelling schedule with the names and addresses on the population schedule. If the name and address appeared on the population schedule but was not designated "head" in column 8, the clerks cancelled the entry in that column and replaced it with the entry "head" for a person who was 18 years old or over and not the wife of the head.

If columns 3–6 were blank for these persons, the information was transferred from the occupied-dwelling schedule to the population schedule. Clerks were instructed to check the number of persons in the previous and succeeding dwelling units and compare these numbers with those entered on the population schedule in order to be sure that any new household created had not already been included in another household. If the clerks could not find the name on the occupied-dwelling schedule or the population schedule, or if they found the name but the person was under 18 or wife of a household head, they cancelled the entry on the occupied-dwelling schedule and transferred the information to the vacant-dwelling schedule. Such transfers were not made until matching of all households and dwelling units was completed.

With the completion of the matching of every dwelling unit on the occupied-dwelling schedule with a houschold on the population schedule, the clerk was instructed to check the block number entries on the occupied-dwelling schedule with the number on the population schedule. Block numbers appeared on both schedules for all cities of population 50,000 or greater. If the block numbers did not agree, the clerks checked the street names and house numbers with the map of the enumeration district and corrected the wrong entries.

The clerks also had to check for completeness the entries on the occupied-dwelling schedules for which the information could be obtained from the population schedule. If any information was missing on the dwelling schedule it was transferred from the population schedule. Similarly, the clerks checked the entries in columns 3–6 of the population schedule for each person designated "head" in column 8. If any information was missing in these entries it was transferred from the occupied-dwelling schedule to the population schedule.

An occupied-dwelling schedule sheet was required for every sheet of the population schedule. The sheet numbers of the occupied-dwelling schedules were to correspond to the sheet number of the population schedule containing the line on which the head of the household was enumerated. In cases where there was more than one sheet of the occupied-dwelling schedule for one sheet of the population schedule, the extra dwelling schedule sheets were lettered. Any renumbering done by the clerks required the changing of the count slip in the portfolio.

Population and Housing Hand Count

Operation 4 of processing the schedule data involved the verification of the matching of population and housing schedules and the hand count of population and housing. This operation consisted of three successive steps beginning with verification and two hand counts.

In the verification procedure, the clerks were required to keep a tally of the number of lines on the population schedule and the number of sections on occupied-dwelling and vacant-dwelling schedules upon which corrections were necessary. With the completion of the verification step of the matching operation, the clerks filled out a "Verifier's Report of Errors Found" (Form P–305) based upon the tally of required corrections.

The clerks checked the heading information to ensure that it agreed with the geographer's description and to see that the instructions for Operation 3 had been followed. The auxiliary forms and any entries made on the schedules in Operation 3 were then inspected. This inspection was designed to ensure that information had been transferred when necessary and that there were no duplicate entries. The clerks examined the population schedules to be sure that an infant card had been filled out for every line with an entry of "0/12 to 3/12" in column 11. Clerks were instructed to supply missing infant cards. If an infant card was determined to have been inappropriately cancelled in the previous operation, the clerks "reinstated" the card; and if an infant card could not be found for an entry for which it was required, the clerk created a new infant card based upon the information on the population schedule. The clerks were instructed to pay particular attention to the date of birth listed on the population schedule.

The clerks examined the entries for head of household on the population schedule to see that they corresponded with similar entries on the occupied-dwelling schedule. This procedure was performed for both sides of all population and occupied-dwelling schedules in the portfolio. Missing information or discrepancies between the two schedules were corrected. The clerks also checked the sheet numbers of both schedules.

The second step in Operation 4 was the hand count of population. The clerks first began this step by filling out "Population Count Slips" (Form P–113a), using the heading information on sheet 1 of the population schedule. One slip was used for each enumeration district. The clerks then placed the population schedules in numerical order and examined each schedule to be sure that only one name appeared on each line.

Once the schedules had been ordered, the clerks began to inspect names on the "supplementary lines," those lines at the bottom of the schedule that were used to record information in columns 35–50.[1] If the name appearing in column 35 did not match the name on the corresponding main line, the portfolio was referred to the section chief along with a "Problem Referral Slip" (Form P–365) indicating the location and nature of the problem. If the enumerator had omitted a name and the supplementary information, the clerk entered the name in column 35 and left columns 35–50 blank. If it appeared, however, that the enumerator had omitted all or nearly all of the supplementary lines, the portfolio was also referred to the section chief with an attached problem referral slip. Clerks were instructed not to make a point of inspecting the supplementary lines for consistency, but if they did notice inconsistencies they were to refer them to the section chief.

After inspecting the supplementary lines, the clerks were required to examine the main lines on both sides of the schedule, line by line, and to cancel line numbers on the left side of the schedule on any line not used to enumerate a person. Thus, any blank lines and lines used by the enumerator for information or explanation were cancelled. When a main line number marked "Suppl. Quest." was cancelled, the corresponding supplementary line number was also cancelled. In addition, supplementary line numbers on blank sides of the schedules were cancelled though the main lines on such sides were not. Supplementary lines were only cancelled under these two circumstances.

If the enumerator had cancelled a name or otherwise indicated that a person should not have been enumerated, the clerks cancelled the corresponding line number. Main lines on which the person was listed as "Ab." in column 8 *and* as "Inst." in column 21 were also cancelled. If, in such cases, the person cancelled was listed as the "Head," the information in columns 3–6 was transferred to the next person in the household, who then was marked as "Head." In this circumstance, the entry on the occupied-dwelling schedule for population line number of the "Head" was also changed. Any other questions about cancellation were referred to the section chief.

The clerks next recorded on the population count slip the number of uncancelled main lines and the number of cancelled main lines on each sheet. All blank main lines of a schedule were counted as cancelled lines. The correct sum of both entries for each sheet was always 80. After the count of main lines was complete, the clerk counted persons enumerated on supplementary lines. These counts were also entered on the population count slip. There was only one entry, however, each for the uncancelled supplementary lines and for the cancelled supplementary lines. The total of these two was equal to twice the number of sheets of population schedules in the portfolio.

The final step of Operation 4 was the hand count of housing. In a manner similar to the procedures for the hand count of population, the clerks first inspected the occupied-dwelling and vacant-dwelling schedules and cancelled each section not used by the enumerator. Some of these sections had been cancelled in Operation 3. Once all appropriate sections had been cancelled, the clerks began to record on the "Housing Count Slip" (Form HC–11) the number of occupied units and the number of blanks listed on each sheet of the occupied-dwelling schedule. Next, the clerks entered the number of uncancelled vacant units and the number of blanks from the vacant-dwelling schedule on the housing count slip. Any problems were referred to the section chief for handling. With this step, the work in Operation 4 was completed. The clerks were instructed to place the materials into the portfolio in the same order in which they had been received and to attach both count slips to the outside of the portfolio, enter the required information on the portfolio memorandum, and return the portfolio to the section chief.

Transcription of the Preliminary Sample Data

Operation 5 consisted of both the verification of the hand count done in Operation 4 and the transcription of preliminary sample data. Two different types of clerks were used in Operation 5. First, comparison clerks com-

---

1. These supplementary lines corresponded to two of the "main lines" on the top part of the schedule which were used to record information for columns 1–34. These two main lines were marked "Suppl. Ques.," and comprised a 5 percent sample of the population.

Initial Activities

pared the hand counts made in Operation 4 with the hand counts made in the field, corrected any discrepancies between the field and office counts, totalled the results of the office hand count, and then transcribed the preliminary sample employment data. Following these steps, verification clerks verified certain hand count totals and the transcription of the preliminary sample employment data.

Comparison clerks were furnished with portfolios containing population count slips from the field (Form P–113) and office (Form P–113a) and housing count slips from the field (Form HC–10) and office (Form HC–11). The comparison clerks first had to verify the heading information which the clerks in Operation 4 had filled in on the office population count slip. They then verified the accuracy of the counts on these slips and totalled the results. The office population count slip contained counts of the number of entries on main lines (i.e., the number of persons enumerated), the number of blank and cancelled main lines, and the number of persons for whom the supplementary information was or should have been obtained. These counts were for an entire enumeration district.

In verifying the accuracy of these counts, the comparison clerks were required to inspect each sheet of the population schedule to see that the clerks in Operation 4 had made cancellations only where required. If the comparison clerks found that an Operation 4 clerk had failed to make necessary cancellations of main lines, they were to make the cancellations. Similarly, if the comparison clerks found main lines cancelled incorrectly, they were to circle the line number. The office population count slip was corrected in accordance with any changes made by the comparison clerks.

The comparison clerks then added the number of entries and the number of blanks on the office count slip. Each line which did not total 80 was marked with an "X." Then, for each sheet of the population schedule, the number of entries recorded on the office count slip was compared with the number of entries on the field count slip. Whenever these two totals did not agree, the comparison clerks placed an "X" in the sheet column of the office count slip. The comparison clerks recounted the number of entries and the number of blanks on sheets for which they had marked an "X" and corrected either the field or office count slip. The number of entries on the office count slip was totaled and posted on the slip and the number of blanks on the office count slip was totaled and posted. The sum of these totals was required to equal 80 times the number of sheets of population schedule used. If it did not, the comparison clerks were required to repeat the procedure. In addition, the totals on the field count slip were required to equal the totals on the office count slip. When the two sums agreed, the figure was posted at the bottom of the office population count slip and on the portfolio memorandum.

Verification of the count of supplementary lines involved examining the name in column 35 to see that it was identical with the name in column 7 for the corresponding main line marked "Suppl. Quest." If there was no correspondence, the portfolio was referred to the section chief with a problem referral slip attached. In addition, supplementary lines were checked to see that they were cancelled when the corresponding main line was cancelled. If such lines had not been cancelled, the comparison clerks cancelled them. The clerks also checked to be sure that the only supplementary lines cancelled were those for which the corresponding main line had been cancelled. If a supplementary line had been inappropriately cancelled, the comparison clerks circled it to restore it. Next, the comparison clerks counted the number of uncancelled supplementary lines to see if they agreed with the total on the office count slip.

The comparison clerks were required to verify the accuracy of the hand count of housing and total the results. The clerks inspected each line of the office housing count slip to ensure that the sum of occupied units and blanks or the sum of vacant units and blanks totaled 30. The clerks then compared each sheet of the office count slip with the corresponding sheet of the field count slip to see that the number of occupied units on each agreed. Whenever the two numbers did not agree, the clerks recounted the number of occupied units and the number of blank or cancelled sections on the office count slip.

The clerks also verified the number of vacant units for sale or rent or not reported, the number of units held for absent households or occupied by nonresidents, and the number of blanks on each of the vacant-dwelling schedules, and made necessary corrections on either count slip. The numbers on the office count slip were added and posted on the office slip. The comparison clerks then totaled the number of occupied units on the office count slip and posted the number on the slip. Similarly, the number of blanks appearing on the occupied-dwelling schedule was totaled and posted on the office count slip. Any changes made on the field count slips were checked to see that they corresponded to the office count slips and when they did not agree, the clerks made the necessary corrections. When the sums agreed, the clerks initialed the count slips and returned them to the portfolio. The comparison clerks also filled out the verifier's report of errors found, entering the total population and the number of errors which the clerk had corrected on both the office count slips—housing and population.

Once the comparison clerks had completed the verification of the hand count they began the transcription of the preliminary sample employment data. This step involved transcribing certain information for each person enumerated from a population schedule main line marked "Suppl. Ques." onto a "Preliminary Sample Transcription Sheet" (Form P-316). This transcription sheet contained 32 lines, with each line containing four questions—one section for each person enumerated on a line marked "Suppl. Ques." on each sheet of the population schedule.

After making sure that the population schedules in the portfolio were in numerical order, the clerks entered the state, county, E.D. number, and, when applicable, the name of the incorporated place on the transcription sheet. The clerks entered in the first column of the transcription sheet the sheet number of the population schedule. In column A of the transcription sheet, a "1" was entered if the person for whom the information was being transcribed lived on a farm, and a "0" if that person did not live in a farm. If the main line marked "Suppl. Ques." had been cancelled, an "X" was entered in column A and the remaining columns in the section were left blank. When all the main lines so marked were left blank it was unnecessary to fill a line on the preliminary sample transcription sheet for that schedule.

The entry in column B of the transcription sheet was "1" if the entry for sex in column 9 on the schedule was "M," and "2" if the entry was "F." When column 9 was blank, the comparison clerk made a determination of the sex of the person based upon the name in column 7 and the relationship in column 8, and then entered the proper code.

Column C of the transcription sheet was coded for the race of the person. A "1" was entered when column 10 of the schedule had an entry of "W" and a "2" was entered when column 10 was other than "W." If column 10 was blank, the comparison clerk determined the race of the person by reference to the entry in column 10 for other persons in the household. When this information was not available, the entry for column C was made on the basis of the race of the head of the preceding household on the schedule.

The comparison clerks transcribed the age entry in column 11 of the schedule to column D of the transcription sheet, except when it was over 100 or a fraction. For any age over 99, an entry of "99" was made in column D. A fractional age in column 11 on the schedule was transcribed as "00." When an "Un" (for Unknown) appeared in column 11, the entry transcribed was "VV."

Entries in column E of the transcription sheet were for work status and were based upon the entries in schedule columns 21-25, and upon schedule column 28 when a "yes" had been entered in column 23. The clerks first inspected the initial sheets of the population schedules to determine whether there were errors that might affect codes assigned on the transcription sheet. Such errors included (1) a "yes" in columns 21-24 for persons who were housewives working in their own homes (identified by an entry of "H" in column 25 or "Housework, own home," etc. in columns 28-30). In those cases the "yes" entries in columns 21-24 were cancelled; (2) entries of "no" or "blank" in all columns 21-24 for a person with an entry in columns 26 or 27, 28, 29, and 30; (3) entries of "yes" in more than one of columns 21-24 or of "yes" in one of these columns along with an entry of "Ot." in column 25; (4) an entry of "yes" in columns 21 or 24 along with WPA or NYA in columns 28, 29, or 30; (5) entries other than "Inst." for inmates of an institution; and (6) blanks or entries of "Inst." for persons in institutions other than certain types. If the comparison clerks found errors of types (2) or (6), they referred the portfolio to their section chief.

Table 4.1 Summary of the Coding Scheme for Column E

Schedule Entries	Column E Code
If there was a "Yes" in columns 21-24:	
If "Yes" in column 21	1
If "Yes" in column 22	2
If "Yes" in columns 21 and 22	2
If "Yes" in column 23 and not new worker in column 28	3
If "Yes" in column 23 and new worker in column 28	0
If "Yes" in column 24	4
If "Inst." in column 21	9
If there was no "Yes" in columns 21-24 and no "Inst." in column 21:	
If "H" in column 25	5
If "S" in column 25	6
If "U" in column 25	7
If "Ot" in column 25	8
If no "H," "S," "U," or "Ot," in column 25 and:	
If "1" or more in column 26	1
If "1" or more in column 27	3
If "1" or more in both columns 26 and 27	blank
If blank in both columns 26 and 27	blank

When there were entries in columns 21-25 for persons whose age had been recorded as 13 years or less, the clerks were instructed to leave column E blank.

Initial Activities

When the comparison clerks had completed preparation of the preliminary transcription sheet they returned all materials to the portfolio, entered the required information on the portfolio memorandum, clipped the count slips and transcription sheets to the inside of the portfolio, and returned the portfolio to the section chief.

In the final step of Operation 5, verification clerks examined the work done by the comparison clerks. The verification clerks first compared the figures entered for total population on the office population count slip with those entered on the field population count slip. The verification clerks also had to verify the total listed on the office housing count slip and make any necessary corrections. Corrections were also made on the field housing count slip when it did not agree with the verified count.

The verification clerks verified the entries on the preliminary sample transcription sheet, and changed any incorrect entries on the transcription sheets. When the clerks found errors, they reported them on a line on the verifier's report of errors found. Following this, they replaced the materials in the portfolio, entered the information required on the portfolio memorandum, and returned the portfolio to the section chief.

Separation of Population and Housing Schedules and Other Materials

Operation 6 was performed by separation clerks and numbering clerks. The separation clerks were responsible for removing the housing schedules from the population portfolios and preparing housing portfolios; removing the infant cards from the population portfolios and preparing them for transmission to the Divison of Vital Statistics; removing auxiliary and blank schedules from the population portfolios and preparing them for filing, and removal and routing of count slips and transcription sheets; inserting the "Confidential Reports on Wage or Salary Income, 1939" (Form P–16) in the population portfolios; and inserting on certain population portfolio memoranda notations identifying the E.D. as either in need of examination for location of industrial homeworkers or as "urban–1930." The numbering clerks were responsible for entering the portfolio number on the housing portfolios and verifying the separation clerks' entries on the housing portfolio memoranda and "Separation Sheets" (Form HC–13).

The population portfolios were arranged in order by E.D. number. The clerks checked to see that the portfolios were all from the same county or city. The occupied-dwelling and vacant-dwelling schedules for four consecutive E.D.'s were removed and placed in a housing portfolio. On a blank separation sheet the separation clerks entered the state and E.D. number of the first E.D. in the group. The clerks transcribed information from the office housing count slip onto the separation sheet regarding the total cards to be punched (the sum of the number of occupied units, vacant units for sale or rent, and vacant units held for absent households or occupied by nonresidents). This information was entered in a column designated "Total number of dwelling units." The occupied-dwelling and vacant-dwelling schedules were then removed from the population portfolio and placed with the separation sheet.

The envelope containing the infant cards was then removed from the population portfolio and was set aside for transmittal to the Division of Vital Statistics.

All count slips were removed from the portfolio and placed in a manila envelope. Count slips for E.D.'s in the county or city were also placed in the envelope. The state name and the county symbol were entered on the outside of this envelope.

The separation clerks then removed the preliminary sample transcription sheet. The name of the state and county, or city, was entered on the "Jacket for Preliminary Sample Transcription Sheets" (Form P–317). All preliminary sample transcription sheets for a county or city were placed in one jacket, except when the county or city had more than 50 E.D.'s. In such cases, more than one jacket was used and each jacket was marked with the E.D. numbers it contained.

Also removed from the population portfolio were individual census forms, preliminary population schedules, nonresident schedules, absent household schedules, preliminary housing schedules, and any blank population and dwelling schedules. The forms were fastened together and set aside for transmittal to the files.

The housing portfolios prepared by the separation clerks, the population portfolios, the central control card, the count slips for a county or city of 100,000 or more, and the filled jacket for preliminary sample transcription sheets were then assigned to a numbering clerk.

The numbering clerks then compared for each E.D. the figures entered for total number of dwelling units on the portfolio memorandum with the "Total cards to be punched" indicated on the office housing count slip. The clerks then totaled the "total units" of each E.D. and posted this sum on the portfolio memorandum. The entries on the jacket for preliminary sample transcription sheets were also verified. They also inspected each population portfolio memorandum to be certain that notations of "Industrial Homeworkers" were made or omitted according to the entry on the control car. They then returned the housing and population portfolios, the count slips, the filled jacket for preliminary sample transcription sheets, and the central control card to the control desk.

Control Room Operations

An important part of the Bureau's processing operations was the maintenance of the production records. This function was performed in Operation A. As clerks in the processing operations completed work on a portfolio assigned to them, they entered the following information onto the portfolio memorandum: their section number and name, the hours worked on that portfolio, and the date on which the work on that portfolio was completed. This information was then posted by the section chief to other production records.

The section chiefs in each process kept records of the work in their sections on the "Section Chief's Daily Production Record" (Form P–304). The form contained information indicating the state and process on which work was underway, the section number, and the date. The section chief entered the name of each clerk employed in the section on that date and the E.D. numbers of all E.D.'s assigned to each clerk. When a clerk completed work on an E.D. and returned it to the section chief, the section chief noted on the daily production record form the completion of the E.D., the population of the E.D., and the hours worked in processing the E.D. At the end of each day, the section chief prepared a new daily production record for the next day, entering the names of the clerks and listing the E.D.'s assigned to each clerk. The original copy of each day's form was signed and delivered to the production records chief. A duplicate copy of each day's form was retained by the section chief, and provided the information for the posting of "Individual Production Records" (Form P–308).

The section chief or assistant section chief maintained the individual production records for all clerks employed in a given section. When clerks were transferred from one section to another, their production records were also transferred. The information shown on the section chief's daily production report was transferred to the individual production record. The information transferred included the date, operation, state, E.D. number, E.D. population, and the hours worked. In addition, data were entered from the "Verifier's Report of Errors Found" (Form P–305). These data included the verified population and the numbers of errors reported.

The central production record section maintained for each operations section a "Section Production Summary" (Form P–309) as a continuous record of the work of the section during the entire period for which the section was engaged on a specific operation. Each day, the clerks in the central record section entered on one line of this record the total work completed in a section on that day. These totals were transcribed from the section chief's daily production records at the close of each day.

The production record section also prepared the "Daily Production Summary by Operation" (Form P–311). From the section production summary, the clerks added to the daily summary, posted by operation the number of E.D.'s and the population processed that day. This summary included calculations of the clerk days worked each day and cumulatively for each operation.

Finally, the central record section maintained for each state a "State Production Summary" (Form P–310). The clerks in the central record section daily sorted the section chief's production records by state and operation and then summarized this sort to obtain state totals for each operation. These totals were posted to the state production summary. At weekly intervals, totals for the previous week were added to the cumulative totals. These totals were then used in the preparation of the "Weekly Production Report by State and Operation" (Form P–312).

In addition to the maintenance of production records on employees and sections, records were also maintained in the Central Control Room in order to permit the location of any portfolio and provide a record of the progress of work. This record maintenance operation was designated Operation B. The unit for recording purposes was the population portfolio (which included housing schedules through Operation 6; after Operation 6, similar controls were established for the housing portfolios). The basic control record was the "Central Control Card" (Form P–301). Before the portfolios were received from the field, a series of cards had been prepared for each county, and for each city of 100,000 or more. As the portfolios were received the date of receipt was posted on the card for the county, and as portfolios were routed to an operation the date and section number were posted on the card under the name of the operation.

The chief of the control room used a central peg board as the principal guide in directing the flow of work through the various operations. This board contained a series of individual pegs, each representing an operation for a given state. Discs were hung on the pegs to show the number of portfolios being processed in each operation for each state at a given time. These discs were moved to correspond with the actual movement of the portfolios.

Once the population and housing schedules had been received and examined in Operation 2, the portfo-

Coding Operations

lios were forwarded to the control room before going to Operation 3. Transfers of each group of portfolios from one operation to another were recorded on a "Routing Slip" (Form P–303) indicating the state, county (or city of 100,000 or more), date, a listing of the E.D. numbers of the portfolios transferred, the section and process from and to which the portfolios were transferred, and the signatures of those accountable for each transfer.

The portfolios to be transferred from the control room to a section in Operation 3 were designated by the chief of the control room and routing slips were prepared by the routing clerk. The routing clerk entered the state, county (or city of 100,000 or more), and the date on the routing slip and listed the contents of the portfolio in numerical order. A control room messenger then took the portfolios to the control clerk in the wing where the matching process (Operation 3) was being carried out. After Operation 3, whenever portfolios were ready for transfer to the next process, the assistant section chief filled out the routing slips as the routing clerk had originally done. The rest of the delivery process was the same as that described above and was maintained throughout the remaining processing operations.

The portfolio movement indicated by the routing slips was recorded on the peg board by moving the discs corresponding to the portfolios to the peg representing the operation to which the portfolios had been delivered. The E.D.'s listed on the routing slips were also recorded as transferred on the central control card for the county by indicating the date and section number on the control card under the column heading of the process to which the portfolios were sent. Once this entry had been made on the control card, the routing slip was stamped and sent to the permanent file of routing slips, maintained by state and date.

CODING OPERATIONS

In the second phase of the processing and tabulation operations, clerks coded and verified the coding of both the population and housing schedules. The coding operations were essential steps in which nonnumerical entries were translated into numerical codes that could be tabulated by mechanical equipment. In addition, certain items were edited for consistency during the coding operations. Once the coding of schedules was completed, the codes which had been entered were subjected to verification in order to ensure accuracy.

There were four basic coding and verification procedures. First, the population schedules were coded. Second, these schedules were verified in a separate operation. Third, occupation, industry, and class of worker codes were determined and verified in the same operation. Finally, the housing schedules were coded and verified in the same operation. Also, included in this section is a discussion of the allocation of values for unknown ages, an operation which occurred after the general population coding.

General Population Coding

The general coding of the population schedules was performed by clerks in Operation 7. These clerks were provided with specific instructions on how to make cancellations and corrections on the population schedules (see Appendix II). Complete cancellation of an item on the schedules was indicated by drawing a horizontal line through the entire column in which the entry appeared. Corrections were also made by drawing a horizontal line; however, the line was only through the entry. The correct entry was then made to the side or above the original entry in the same column space. The original entries had been made in black and the corrections were made in red.

Special lettered columns were provided on the population schedule for most of the alphabetic codes which had to be translated into numeric codes. There were occasional columns for which a numeric code had to be entered in the same column as the enumerator's entry. For example, an entry of "M" in column 12 for marital status was occasionally coded "7." Such coding was handled as a correction: a horizontal line was drawn through the original entry and the correct code was written in the same column space.

The coding in Operation 7 did not include coding of columns 1–5, 7, 28–30, 34–35, or 45–50. In addition, no entries were made in columns F, J, or U. Occasionally, problem referral slips were attached to the portfolio. These contained additional instructions about which columns were not to be coded.

Before the actual editing and coding, the clerks checked to see that the sheet numbers on each schedule were arranged in consecutive order. In addition, the confidential wage or salary income forms were arranged in sheet and line number order. The information on these forms was then transferred to the appropriate person's line on the population schedule. Column 32 contained information about the "amount of wages or salary received in 1939," and column 33 reported whether the person received "income of $50 or more from sources other than money wages or salary."

The first entry that required coding was the question on farm residence in column 6. When a "yes" to the question of farm residence had been entered for the head of a household, the coders entered a "1" for all other members of the household. When the response was "no," blanks were left for all other household members. The coding clerks were instructed to make sure that they checked the person entries on sheets 61 and over—the sheets for persons enumerated out of order—to see that column 6 had an appropriate code.

Column 8 contained the relation of the person to the head of the household. An entry in this column was required for every person. If the column was blank, the coders were required to determine the probable entry based upon the name appearing in column 7, the sex in column 9, the age in column 11, and the marital status in column 12. The codes assigned for the alphabetic entries are shown in Appendix II (Operation 7: Instructions for General Population Coding), paragraph 19 and its amendments. The numeric codes for the relation question were recorded in column A on the population schedule.

When the person enumerated as the head of a household was female and a husband was also listed, the clerks assigned the head code in column A to the husband, and coded the female as wife of head. In such cases, the enumerator's entries in column 8 were not changed. They change was made only in column A.

Special relation-to-head codes were given for institutions and hotels. The person most likely to have been the head of the household (manager, superintendent, principal, etc.) was given a code of "V" and all other persons in the institution or hotel were coded "9." The exception to this rule was when an enumerator had listed officers or other employees and their families who lived in separate quarters as separate households. In these cases, the clerks coded the household in the same manner as households not living on institutional grounds.

The coding scheme also distinguished between employees who performed personal services for the household and those employees whose labors contributed to the family's income. The entries in column 8 were checked for consistency with the employment entries in columns 21–25 and 28–29. Relatives of the employees were given a separate code.

Column 9 recorded the sex of the person enumerated. If this column was blank the clerk made determination of the sex of the person based upon the name and relation entries. Obvious errors were also corrected. Column 10 contained the entry for the race of the person enumerated. When this column was blank, the coding clerk entered the race of the other persons in the household. When the race entries for entire household were blank, the clerk entered the race of the head of the preceding household. No coding was required for entries of "W" and "Neg." Other entries were coded according to the list given in Appendix II, paragraph 32, as amended.

An entry for the age of the person enumerated appeared in column 11 of the schedule. When column 11 was left blank or illegible, or contained an entry of "Un," the clerks were required to complete form P–306, "Persons of Unknown Age." This form was then secured to the outside of the portfolio at the time the portfolio was returned to the control desk. The codes for these ages were assigned in another operation (see the description below). The clerks were also instructed to pay close attention to the enumerator's entries in column 11 for children under one year of age. These numbers were listed as fractions and the clerks were instructed to make sure that the entire fraction appeared within the column space. When the fraction extended beyond the column space, the clerks cancelled the enumerator entry and entered the codes shown in Appendix II, paragraph 34.

Column 12 contained the entry for marital status. An entry was required for every person. If no entry existed, the clerks provided an entry based upon other information on the schedule—in particular, the relation to head and age entries. When it was impossible to determine a marital status, a code of "S" or "Single" was entered unless information on the schedule indicated that the person was a parent. When such a relation was indicated, a "Wd," for widowed, was entered if the person was age 55 or over and a code of "7," indicating "married, spouse not present," was entered if the person was under age 55. The coding clerks were also instructed to cancel the "M" in column 12 for any person whose husband or wife was not enumerated as a member of the household. The cancelled entries were replaced with an entry of "7."

Education information appeared in columns 13 and 14. The entry in column 13 was either a "yes" or "no" to the question of current school attendance. Enumerator entries were accepted without change. If column 13 was blank, the coding clerk was instructed to first check the entry in column 25 for an "S," indicating student. If an "S" occurred in column 25, an entry of "yes" was made in column 13 when the person was within the compulsory school ages of the state in which he or she resided. The compulsory school ages used are shown on the last page of Appendix II. The highest grade of school completed was shown in column 14. These entries were translated into numeric codes and entered in column B on the population schedule. The numeric entries for column B are shown in Appendix II, paragraph 38, as amended.

The place of birth entered in column 15 of the popula-

Coding Operations

tion schedule was coded in column C of the schedule according to the code schemes for states and countries listed at the end of Appendix II. A code symbol in column C was required for every person. If an entry for place of birth had been omitted, the clerk attempted to determine it from the entries for other members of the household. In such cases, the clerk did not write the name of the place in column 15, but simply entered the code in column C. If column 15 was blank and a code could not be determined from the entries of the other household members, the clerk entered a code for unknown. The codes used for persons whose place of birth could not be determined are shown in Appendix II, paragraphs 40–43, as amended.

Column 16 of the population schedule contained entries on the citizenship status of foreign-born persons. Appropriate codes included "NA," "PA," and "AL."[2] Any entries of "Am. Cit." were cancelled by the clerks, as were entries for persons born in the United States and its territories and possessions. The clerks were instructed to attempt to supply missing entries for column 16 based upon the rules described in Appendix II, paragraph 45.

Information on place of residence on April 1, 1935, was recorded in columns 17–20 of the schedule. Column 17 contained the city, town, or village, if this place had more than 2,000 inhabitants. If the population was under 2,000, an "R" was entered. If the person was living in the same house in 1935 as at the time of enumeration, an entry of "same house" was made in column 17. For persons living in the same city or town but in a different house, an entry of "same place" was made in column 17. In both these instances, columns 18–20 were left blank. Column 18 contained the entry for the county of residence in 1935. Similarly, column 19 contained the entry for the state, territory, or foreign country of residence in 1935. Column 20 indicated whether or not the place of residence was on a farm.

The coding clerks received detailed instructions for determining four-digit migration codes based upon the information in columns 17–20. These instructions are shown in Appendix II, paragraphs 47–73, as amended. The migration codes indicated those persons who were living in the same house or same place, as described above. For those persons who were not living in the same house or place, the codes indicated the state, subregion of the state, and the type of place: rural nonfarm, rural farm, rural—farm residence unknown, urban place of 2,500 to 10,000, urban place of 10,000 to 25,000, urban place 25,000 to 100,000, and city of 100,000 or more. The four-digit migration codes were entered in column D on the population schedule. Codes were entered for all persons except children under five.

Problems with enumerator entries for the 1935 residence question led the Bureau to use special migration editors on both the day and night shifts. The problems occurred when enumerators did not adequately distinguish between the entries for "same place," "same house," and "same farm." In the course of editing and coding enumerator entries, regular coding clerks were instructed to refer problem portfolios to the special migration editors. Portfolios from 12,341 enumeration districts received such special editing (Shryock 1957).

The entries in columns 21–25 pertaining to the person's work status during the week of March 24–30, 1940, were coded in column E of the population schedule. The coding scheme for column E was the same as that used to code column E of the preliminary sample transcription sheet. This scheme is detailed in the earlier description of Operation 5.

The coding clerks also inspected entries in column 26, the number of hours worked during the week of March 24–30. When "Inst." had been entered in column 21, the clerks cancelled any entries in columns 26 and 27 and entered a code in column 26 to indicate the type of institution. The institution codes are presented in Appendix II, paragraph 77. The information on the type of institution was to have been recorded by the enumerator on the schedule heading. Except in cases where institution codes had been entered, entries were cancelled in column 26 for any persons other than those who had received a code in column E of "1." When column 26 was blank the coders left it blank, and when the entry was 100 or over, it was cancelled and "99" (the highest number tabulated) was entered in column 26.

The coding clerks were also instructed to cancel entries in column 27 except for persons who had been coded as "2" or "3" in column E. The clerks also cancelled entries of "100" or more and replaced them with the codes described in Appendix II, paragraph 79. Columns 28–30 and F were not coded in this operation (see the description of Operation 9, below). In column 31, weeks worked in 1939, all entries of more than 52 were cancelled and replaced with "52."

When column 32, money wages or salary received in 1939, contained a blank, the coding clerks were instructed to leave the column blank, except for those cases for which the entry in column 31 was "0." In such cases, the clerks entered a "0" in column 32. The clerks were also instructed to cancel any entry of 6,000 or over in column 32 and write in "5,000+." Any amounts en-

2. The meaning of these codes is discussed in chapter 3, p. 24.

tered in column 33 for other income were cancelled and replaced with a "1" for "yes," when the amount was $50 or more, or a "no," when the amount was under $50. Blanks in column 33 were left as such. No coding was done in column 34.

All uncancelled supplementary lines were coded, even when columns 35–50 were completely blank. When columns 35–50 were completely blank or cancelled, a code of "8" was entered in column I on the supplementary line of the schedule. No coding was done, however, in columns 35, 45–47, J, 48–50, U, and Z, in this operation.

The places of birth of the person's father and mother appearing in columns 36 and 37 were coded in column G on the schedule. Column G was left blank when the entries in columns 36 and 37 indicated that both persons were born in the U.S., its territories, possessions, at sea, or in a place that could not be determined. When the person's father was born in a foreign country, the code for the country in column 36 was entered in column G, and the mother's place of birth was disregarded. When the father was born in the U.S., its territories, possessions, at sea, or in a place that could not be determined, but the person's mother was born in a foreign country, the code for the country given in column 37 was entered in column G. The codes used to code the foreign countries are given at the end of Appendix II. The entry in column 38 for mother tongue was coded in column H according to the codes given at the end of Appendix II. When the language appearing in column 38 was "English," column H was left blank.

The entries in columns 39–41 pertaining to veterans' information were coded in column I. The codes used in column I are given in Appendix II, paragraphs 89–90. Similarly, the codes for the social security information appearing on the schedule in columns 42–44 are given in Appendix II, paragraph 91, as amended.

A code was entered in column K on the supplementary line for every person enumerated on that line. This code was based upon the entry appearing in column 4 for the head of the household in which the person was a member. When an "O" appeared in column 4 for the head of the household, it meant that the home was owned and the code entered in column K was "0." When an "R," for rented, appeared in column 4, a code of "1" was entered in column K. Finally, when the person enumerated on the supplementary line was a lodger, servant, hired hand, etc., or a member of an institutional household, the code entered in column K was a "2."

An entry was made in column L for each person enumerated on a supplementary line for whom an "0" or "1" had been entered in column K. This code indicated the value of an owned home or the monthly rental of a rented home. The value should have appeared in column 5 on the line for the head of the household. The coding clerks were instructed, however, to use the value which appeared in column 5 for any related number of the households. The codes used in column L are given in Appendix II, paragraph 95.

The coding clerks entered in column M a code corresponding to a crossclassification of the entries in column 6, farm residence, and column 9, sex. Blanks in column 6 were treated as "non-farm." Column M was coded for all persons and the codes are summarized in Appendix II, paragraphs 97–98.

The code entered in Column N on the schedule was a race and nativity code constructed on the basis of a combination of entries for the person in columns 10, C, 36, and 37. These codes are listed in Appendix II, paragraph 99, and essentially distinguished among Whites by place of birth of the person and his or her parents, and distinguished Negroes and other races.

The age or age code entered in column 11 was transcribed by the clerk in column O. When the entry in column 11 was blank or "Un," the clerk left column O blank. Similarly, column P was coded according to the marital status of the person entered in column 12 of the schedule. The codes for column O are given in paragraph 101 in Appendix II. The code appearing in column B for the person was transcribed in column Q. When column B was blank, column Q was left blank. The citizenship status of the person entered in column 16 was coded in column R on the schedule. These codes are shown in Appendix II, paragraph 103.

The code appearing in column E was transcribed to column S. When column E contained a blank space, column S was left blank. When the entry in column S was 1, 2, or 3, column T was coded on the basis of the appropriate entry or code from column 26 or 27. These codes for hours worked or duration of unemployment are given in Appendix II, paragraph 105. A code was entered in column V for weeks worked based upon the entry in column 31 of the schedule. These codes are shown in Appendix II, paragraph 107.

The clerks coded column W based upon the entry for wage and salary income that appeared in column 32. When column 32 was blank, column W was left blank. When the entry in column 32 was 1,000 or more, the first two digits of the entry were transcribed in column W. When the entry in column 32 was between 100 and 999, the first digit, preceded by a zero, was transcribed in column W. If the entry in column 32 was between 1 and 99, the clerks entered a code of "0V" in column W; and when a "0" appeared in column 32, a code of "00" was entered in column W. In column X, the entry in column

Coding Operations

33 for other income was coded. These codes are shown in Appendix II, paragraph 110. Finally, the clerks transcribed the relationship code in column A to column Y.

Once the coding had been completed for all schedules in a portfolio, the clerks made the proper notations on the portfolio memorandum indicating that the process had been completed and returned the portfolio to the control desk.

Allocation of Unknown Ages

For the 1940 Census of Population, the Bureau developed and implemented a method for eliminating unknown ages during the processing of returns (BC 1942). Although in the four censuses from 1910 to 1940 the percentage of unknown ages had only ranged from a low of 0.08 percent (1930) to a high of 0.18 percent (1910), the Bureau felt that both the use of age distributions in demographic research and the expense of the space required to print and tabulate unknown ages justified the development of an age allocation routine. This routine was developed under the direction of W. Edwards Deming, the Bureau's mathematical adviser, and Leon Geoffrey, who was responsible for the details and execution of the method.

Prior to its use in the processing of schedules in 1940, the method was tested in two experimental trials. The first test was made during the initial development of the allocation method and was tried on 2,000 randomly selected entries from the 1939 Special Census (pretest) of St. Joseph and Marshall Counties, Indiana. The second test was carried out using 2,000 comparisons from the 1940 schedules. In both tests, the recorded age was covered and the age estimator was used to assign an age based upon the available information on the schedule. In the first test, 43.6 percent of the 2,000 ages were estimated correctly or within one year, while in the second test 46.2 percent were estimated correctly or within one year. Some 20.5 percent of the estimated ages in the first test were in error by more than five years, while the corresponding figure for the second test was 17.8 percent.

The Bureau felt that results of these tests indicated that the methodology was satisfactory, although it was cautious about the extent to which the results could be generalized, since the circumstances which lead to blank or partial entries for age could also lead to incomplete or absent information needed to estimate age in the census. In addition, the tests were likely to have contained proportionately more children and family members, for whom age allocation was easier, and proportionately few lodgers, for whom age allocation was more difficult.

Operation 7, the general coding process, had involved both the translation of certain non-numeric entries into numeric codes and the editing of specified items for consistency. The age entry occurred in column 11 on the population schedule, and a whole number or fraction was required in this column for every person enumerated. In those cases in which column 11 was blank or illegible or contained an entry of "Un," for unknown, the coders in Operation 7 were instructed to make an entry on the "Persons of Unknown Age" form. This form was fastened to the outside of the portfolio when the portfolio was returned to the control desk at the end of this operation. Before the portfolios of coded schedules went to Operation 8 for verification, those portfolios with unknown ages were segregated and sent to the age allocation operation. The general coding operation was at its peak between September and December 1940. In December there were 848 coders working in two shifts, coding approximately 1,342,000 persons per day. There were seven age-assigners at work, three per shift with one assigner overlapping and instructing. The maximum number of ages estimated by a single assigner in a 7-hour shift was 450; however, the average number of ages assigned daily ranged from 245 in the weeks following training to 380 near the end of the operation (BC 1942).

The age-assigners received a month of training before they were allowed to work alone. Persons selected to be age-assigners all had college degrees, with some statistical or sociological training. Several held masters' degrees and one had a doctorate. The age-assigners were paid at the rate of assistant section chiefs, $1,620 per annum.

The general population coders worked in sections of 20 each and the age-assigners worked with this population. The age-assigners worked on a table near each section chief where the portfolios containing unknown ages from that group were placed. Attached to each portfolio was the "Persons of Unknown Age" form which identified the portfolio by state and E.D., and indicated the sheet and line number of any schedule requiring attention. Estimated ages were entered on the schedule in green ink, to distinguish these entries from the black enumerator entries and the red edited entries. The estimated ages were also recorded on the referral form.

The various paraphernalia for age-assigning—the master indicator, ages of compulsory school attendance of each state, ages of husbands and wives, age from school grade, the various card decks, and index of occupations (for descriptions of these, see below)—were placed on a hand truck which constituted a portable desk for the age-assigners. They traveled from section to section, where there were usually about one to six portfolios for attention.

There were six types of problems that occurred in the process of general coding which led to referral to age assignment: (1) a complete blank; (2) a partial entry; (3) an illegible entry; (4) an inconsistency with other information on the schedule; (5) an ambiguous entry, such as "over 21," "21+," "legal," etc.; and (6) entries of "0" or "under 1." In all, there were 207,211 ages assigned for the entire census. The most common problem was blank entries. The second problem, that of partial entries, could have occurred when an enumerator was interrupted or when the informant did not know the exact age but could place it within a decade. The enumerator was only able to record the age within a decade, thus making an entry which left the unit digit blank. Occasionally, entries which were present in the age column appeared inconsistent with other data on the schedule. There were about 2,000 inconsistencies that were referred to age assignment, but only 831 were treated as unknown ages. The remainder were allowed to stand, e.g., when a child was shown as older than the father or there were two or more children a few months apart. In such unusual situations, if the entries were not impossible they were left as enumerated. Estimation of infant ages arising from a "0" or "under 1" entry was made with an infant deck.

Two general principles were utilized in the assignment of ages. Assignment was to be guided by whatever age-indicative information appeared on the schedule, and the estimated age could not be inconsistent with any information on the schedule which was considered to be reliable.

The relationship between the age of children in school and the highest grade completed was considered to be very close and was given precedence over other information. This basis for age estimation was applicable, however, only for a person designated in column 13 as "in school," and for whom there was an entry in column 14 for highest grade of school completed. This information was then used to assign the average age for the highest grade completed during the previous academic year (see Appendix III, Figure 1).

Employment information was also utilized in this step of the assignment process. For those who had completed either seventh or eighth grade, an age of "13" was assigned if there was no employment information (columns 21–33), and an age of "14" was assigned if such information was present.

When information on the relation between school attendance and highest grade completed was absent, the next highest priority was given to the age relation between husband and wife. If this information was also absent, the unknown ages were distributed according to certain types of controls. In this regard, a "Master Indicator" (see Appendix III, Figure 3) was used in the age allocation scheme to assist the age-assigners in using the data in the schedule. The assigner started at the top of the master indicator and worked down along the appropriate path until he or she arrived at an estimated age which was satisfactory. The general rule operating in this process was that the assigner should choose a path which led to the quickest and most definite allocation of age. Once a temporary age had been assigned, the assigner was required to check the estimate for consistency with the other information on the schedule.

In using this allocation method, the assigner was instructed to go first to column 12 on the population schedule. This column contained the marital status of the person in question. Since this information had been coded prior to the age assignment operation, there were no unknown data in this column. If column 12 indicated that the person was married and the age of the spouse was given on the schedule, the assigner looked up the appropriate age in a table that provided the relationship between the ages of husbands and wives (see Appendix III, figure 2).

The table of the age relationship of husbands and wives was based on Mortimer Spiegelman's work on the frequency distribution of the ages of husbands and wives among the native white population of Pennsylvania in 1930. The Census Bureau operated under the assumption that the same age distribution would hold for the 1940 population of any other state, and for any race. This table look-up was only applicable if the age of one of the spouses was present on the schedule.

If the spouse was not listed or his or her age was unknown, the age-assigner was instructed to observe the relationship to the head listed in column 8. If the person with the unknown age was a parent, the procedure was the same for those married (age of the spouse unknown), widowed, or divorced. The procedure for parents involved determining the sex of the person from column 9. Then, for female parents, the age-assigner was instructed to look up the "Mother Deck." This deck consisted of 250 cards, each stamped with a number representing an age and occurring in proportion to the number of mothers having that age at the birth of their first child. When the age of the oldest child listed on the schedule was thought to be that of the oldest child, this deck was used by adding the age shown on the top card of the deck to age of the oldest child shown. The sum of these two figures was the estimated age of the mother. Once an age had been assigned to the mother, the table providing the age relation between husbands and wives was used to estimate the husband's age.

The cards of the Mother Deck, along with those of the other decks used in age estimation, were used in a similar manner. The cards were first stamped with an age. After being shuffled, the cards were numbered serially from 1 to 250 on their reverse side to provide an order. When a deck was consulted, the top card was drawn but only used if the age given on it was consistent with information available on the schedule. If the age given on the card was inconsistent, the next card was tried. Cards from which assigned ages were taken were placed at the bottom of the deck and when the deck was used once through the cards were again placed in serial order. The Census Bureau felt that the advantage of this procedure was that it ensured the frequency distribution of assigned ages among the class of persons for whom the deck was constructed. The procedure also had the advantage of placing each assigned age as close as possible to the correct cell in any table in which age was cross-classified with some other results.

In those cases where the spouse was not listed or the spouse's age was unknown and the entry in column 8 indicated that the person was not a parent, a different procedure was used. The first control used was the person's occupation entry. It was assumed by the Bureau that within the 13 broad occupational groups of 1940 (see Appendix III, Figure 4), the age distribution of each sex was homogenous. In fact, the Bureau found that some of the age distributions of the broad groups were similar and could be combined. Three decks of 250 cards were assembled, with each deck representing a number of occupations with the same age distribution (Appendix III, Figure 4). The number of cards belonging to any age class was in proportion to the frequency with which that age class occurred for the broad occupational group and sex group in the 1930 Census of Population. The procedure for using the occupation cards was the same as that for using the Mother Deck.

For those cases in which the person with the missing age was listed on the schedule as married, divorced, or widowed, but the other information on the schedule was too limited to provide for the use of the other lookups thus far described, the assigner was instructed to use Part C of the "General Deck." The General Deck contained 250 cards that showed ages in proportion to the combined male-female age distribution of the country as a whole in 1930, except that children aged 5 to 20 attending school were excluded. This deck was divided into three parts based upon the age range represented by certain questions on the schedule. Part A contained cards in which the age ranged from zero, i.e., less than one year, through 4, and corresponded to no entries for the questions on residence 5 years earlier in columns 17–20. Part B contained cards for the age range from 5 through 13 and was obtained from the entry in column 13 for current school attendance. The Bureau had no cards in this deck for ages 9 to 13 because it felt school attendance was sufficiently close to universal and therefore any assignment other than in relation to highest grade completed would have over-represented such children. Finally, Part C contained cards for ages 14 and over, based upon entries for employment and occupation in columns 21 through 30. The procedure for using the General Deck was the same as for the other decks.

A somewhat different procedure was used for those persons with missing ages whose marital status in column 12 was single. This procedure involved determining from the entry in relation-to-head, column 8, whether the person was a child, grandchild, niece, or nephew of the head. If it could be determined that the person did have such a relation to the head, the assigner sought to determine if the person was 5 or over, based on the information on previous residence in column 17. An additional check included determining if there was information on employment in columns 21 through 34, indicating that the person was at least 14 years of age.

Those persons determined to be children, grandchildren, nieces, or nephews of the head were directed into one of three allocation paths depending upon the entries noted above. The first path included those who had no entry on the previous residence item, column 17, or the employment items, columns 21–34. If there was no entry for highest grade completed, or if the entry was "0," the assigner was instructed to use general deck A to assign an age. If the entry in column 14 was "1" to "H-4," the assigner was instructed to use the table estimating age from highest grade of school completed. Finally, if the entry in column 14 was above "H-4," assigners were to use General Deck C with the table of age and highest grade completed as minima.

The second path for this type of unknown age involved those persons for whom there were entries for the employment questions, columns 21–34, whether or not there was an entry for the previous residence question, column 17. This procedure involved checking the school attendance question in column 13. If this entry was either "No" or blank, the assigner made an estimate based on either the Occupation Deck or on General Deck C. If there was an entry in column 13, the assigner next examined the entry in column 14 for highest grade completed. If there was no entry in column 14, the age estimate was made from the Occupation Deck or from General Deck C. If the entry in column 14 was from "7" to "C-4," the assigner was instructed to use the table estimate for the age related to highest grade completed. Finally, if there was any other entry in column 14, the estimate was made from the Occupation Deck or General Deck C.

The final path for this type of single person was for

those persons with an entry in column 17, previous residence, but no entries for the employment information, columns 21–34. The procedure involved determining the entry for current school attendance, column 13. If the person was then attending school, the assigner was instructed to check the entry in column 14 for highest grade completed. If there was no entry, the age estimate was made from General Deck B. If the entry in column 14 was from "0" to "H–4," the estimate was made from the table indicating the average age for highest grade completed.

If the entry in column 13 indicated that this person was not currently attending school, the assigner also next checked the entry in column 14, highest grade completed. If there was no entry in column 14, the assigner was instructed to use General Deck B for the age estimate. If the entry in this column was above "H–4," the estimate was made from General Deck C, with the table for highest grade completed used as a minimum. If the entry in column 14 was "H–1" to "H–4," only the table for highest grade completed was used. In those cases in which there was an entry of "0" to "8" in this column, special methods were used. If it appeared that the enumerator had failed to report school attendance but it could be assumed that the child was in school, then the table for highest grade completed was used. If the highest grade completed was reported as "0" and the entry for previous residence was considered valid, the ages of "5" and "6" were assigned alternately. When the highest grade completed was listed as "0" but the entry for previous residence was questionable, the assignment was made as "5" one-third of the time, as "6" one-third of the time, and from General Deck A one-third of the time. This latter procedure was required by the fact that there were a large number of portfolios presented to the age-allocation operation on which the enumerator had experienced difficulty with the question on residence 5 years ago—about one-third of the children under 5 were listed with residence 5 years ago.

For those single persons whose relation to head did not show them to be child, grandchild, niece, or nephew, the next step involved determining whether there were entries in columns 21–34 for employment information. If this information was present, the assigner made the age estimate based upon the Occupation Deck or General Deck C. If there was no employment information, the next step involved determining the entry for previous residence. If there was no entry for column 17, the estimate was made from the General Deck A. If there was an entry in column 17, the estimate was made from General Deck B.

General Deck A provided for age allocation in the range of 0 through 4 years of age. Whenever this deck turned up the age 0, the assigner was required to use the Infant Deck. This deck consisted of eight cards, used in rotation, ranging from 4 months through 11 months. Only rarely were the cards for 0 months through 3 months used. This special deck was designed to avoid having to fill out an "infant card" during processing. In 1940, the infant card was an innovation which enumerators were asked to fill out for every infant of three months or less. These cards were turned over to the Division of Vital Statistics to allow it to cross reference the completeness of birth registrations. Thus, these cards were only used when there was some definite indication that the age of the infant was under 4 months. As with the other decks used in age assignment, the procedure for using the Infant Deck was the same as that described above for the Mother Deck.

Once the detailed method for age assignment had been used to arrive at an estimated age for those persons with unknown ages, the age-assigner was then required to check the estimate to see if it was consistent with other reliable information on the schedule. In addition, certain rules were adopted for checking consistency: (1) the gap between the age of a child and younger parent could not be less than 14 years; (2) the gap between the age of a child and a grandparent could not be less than "30" years; (3) nieces and nephews could not be older than their aunts or uncles; (4) the head of a household could not be under "18;" (5) an apprentice or new worker could not be over "25;" and (6) the age assigned to a person at work on a WPA, CCC, or NYA project had to be within the regulation age limits of those agencies. If these consistency checks were failed, the age had to be reassigned taking into consideration the information with which the estimate had been inconsistent. If the consistency checks were passed, the assigned age was written on the schedule in green ink to distinguish it from the enumerator's entries which were written in black ink and from the red editorial markings.

Verification of General Population Coding

In order to ensure accuracy, the work of the coders and the card punchers was verified. In the preparation of data which were not required by the legal purposes on the census, it was possible to introduce sample inspection into the processing. The object of sample inspection was accuracy in the production of statistical tables, while at the same time maintaining a minimum cost for the inspection. It was estimated that the total savings from the use of sample verification in the processing of returns in 1940 amounted to $263,000. The fol-

Coding Operations

lowing is a breakdown of the savings from the use of sample verification:[3]

Process in which sample verification was used	Savings
Preliminary employment transcription	$ 3,000
General population coding	82,000
Occupation coding	68,000
General housing coding	15,000
Individual population card punching	73,000
Housing dwelling card punching	22,000
Total savings	$263,000

It was considered necessary that coders and punchers have a history of consistently accurate work before sample verification took the place of 100 percent verification. Once performance records showed the work of coders and punchers to be accurate within control limits, small but frequent samples of their work sufficed for maintaining control of the processing. It was necessary to keep a record of the production and errors of each individual and to monitor this record daily and weekly. This record was kept on the verifier's report of errors found. The principles behind the sample verification of the coding operations were the same as the principles which were applied to the sample verification of card punching.

In Operation 8, verification of the general population coding was performed to correct errors made by the Operation 7 clerks, to discover those cases where the systematic coding errors indicated misunderstanding or misinterpretation of the instructions by the coding clerk, and to determine whether the age estimator made the correct entries in columns 13, B, and D.

Before starting the verification process, the clerks were required to become familiar with the "Instructions to Enumerators" (Form PA–1), the "Instructions for General Population Coding" (Form P–327a), and the "Instructions for Punching Population Individual Cards A and B" (Form P–345), the last of which indicated how the puncher used the various code numbers and corrections. As in other editing operations, the clerks in the general coding verification made all corrections with red pencils. Entries made by enumerators were not erased, merely cancelled and corrected. Entries made by the coding clerks, however, were allowed to be erased when necessary.

The clerks in Operation 8 were required to fill out a verifier's report of errors found for each day's work and for each section verified when more than one section number of Operation 7 was examined. A separate line was filled out on this form for every person whose work was being verified. The information recorded on the form included the name of the coder, the state, the E.D. number, and the population. A tally of the number of entries or codes changed was kept and entered in the column "Number of Errors Found." Also recorded on the verifier's report of errors found was an entry indicating the types of errors that appeared frequently in the coding.

The amount of a coding clerk's work which was verified depended upon the clerk's experience. In the initial stages of coding, all work of each clerk was verified. As the clerks gained experience, however, the section chiefs were allowed to provide specific instructions to the verifiers that adjusted the amount of work verified for particular clerks, depending on the number of errors made by the coding clerk. The criteria used in determining which coding clerks were eligible for this sample verification were the same as those described below in the section on sample verification of card punching.

The verification process began with the verification of the transcription of the confidential report of wage or salary income forms. Once any necessary corrections were made, the clerks clipped the forms together, attached a slip of paper identifying the forms by state, E.D., and the notation "transcribed," and held them for return to the control clerk when the coding of the entire portfolio had been verified.

The verifiers were instructed to follow a procedure of verifying column by column rather than line by line, except in cases where other entries on a line or on other lines for other members of the household had to be examined to determine the accuracy of a code. During the later stages of verification, however, when coders had become experienced and sampling had been introduced into the verification process, the verification was done line by line. Schedules were verified one side at a time and the verifiers were instructed to keep the general coding instructions in mind as they checked the schedules.

When the verification of the coding was completed, the verifiers made the proper notations on the portfolio memorandum and returned the portfolio and confidential report forms to the control desk. At the end of each day's work, the verifiers turned in to their section chiefs the verifier's report of errors found. This form was filled out in duplicate. One copy was kept by the verifier's section chief and the other copy went to the section chief where the coding had been performed.

---

3. For this and the description and results of sample verification of card punching below, see Deming and Geoffrey (1941).

Occupation, Industry, and Class of Worker Coding and Verification

Operation 9 consisted of the coding of occupation, industry, and class of worker entries on the population schedule, columns 28–30, F, 45–47, J, and U. The Operation 9 instructions are reproduced in Appendix IV. In the preparations for this coding an occupation index was prepared in two volumes: a Classified Index with more than 25,000 occupational designations arranged according to occupation or occupation group, and an Alphabetic Index of the occupational designations indicating to which of the 451 occupations and occupation groups the classification belonged (BC 1940a). The Alphabetic Index also included approximately 9,500 industry designations and symbols indicating to which of 132 titles of the industry classification the designations belonged. This index was prepared by Dr. Alba M. Edwards, with assistance from Ernest J. McCormick, and was based upon the "Standard Industrial Classification" developed under the auspices of the Central Statistical Board between 1937 and 1939.

Each occupation coding clerk was provided with a copy of the Alphabetic Index of Occupations and Industries and a large card, "List of Principal Occupations and Industries with their Symbols," on which several of the principal occupations and industries in the index were printed. These coding aids were used to look up each entry of an occupation (column 28) and of an industry (column 29). The symbols given in the index for each were entered in the first two sections of column F of the schedule. In addition, columns 45 and 46 of the "Supplementary Questions" section of the schedule were coded according to the instructions for coding columns 28 and 29. Only those persons who were considered to be in the labor force were given occupation, industry, and class of worker codes. Such persons were determined by the codes appearing in column E (for a description, see table 4.1). Only persons with column E codes of "1," "2," "3," or "4" were considered to be in the labor force.

An "occupational designation" consisted of a complete return of an occupation of the person and the industry, business, or place in which the person worked. Each occupational designation was represented in the Alphabetic Index by a five-digit code symbol. The first three digits of the code indicated the occupation and the last two digits represented the industry. In cases in which an occupation occurred in many industries, the code for the industry in the occupational designation was "Ind.," indicating that the code for the particular industry listed in the Industry Index was to be used.

The entry in column 30 of the schedule was for class of worker. These entries were coded in the third space in column F, according to the following scheme:

Schedule Entry	Code	Meaning
PW	1	Wage or salary worker in private work
GS	2	Wage or salary worker in government work
E	3	Employer
OA	4	Working on own account
NP	5	Unpaid family worker
New worker	6	Person without previous work experience

Coders were instructed to consider as unpaid workers all children under 18 years of age and women of any age who were enumerated with their family on a farm and returned as farm laborer, garden laborer, or other agricultural laborer, with no entry for column 30, unless there was information indicating otherwise. All other persons returned as farm laborer, garden laborer, or other agricultural laborer, with no class of worker entry were coded as wage or salary worker in "private work." Coders were also instructed to check the occupation entries of "farmer" and "farm laborer" to see that they were consistent with the entry in column 34 for farm schedule number. In almost all cases, anyone filling out a farm schedule was coded as farmer, whereas farm laborer was coded if a farm schedule had not been filled out. Persons living on farms who were returned as "Laborer—odd jobs," "Odd jobs," or "Working out," were given the code for farm laborer.

The index was designed to cover most occupational designations, but it was not exhaustive. When an occupational return was not found in the Alphabetic Index, or was not covered by it, the case was referred to the coding supervisor. In addition, the coders were instructed that when they encountered children under 18 years of age in certain occupations, they were to provide codes for alternative occupations, usually apprenticeships. Examples included the following: blacksmith, boilermaker, brickmason, cabinetmaker, carpenter, cooper, coppersmith, designer, draftsman, dressmaker (not in factory), electrician, machinist, mechanic, milliner, plumber, printer, stonemason, tailor, and tinner were coded blacksmith's apprentice, boilermaker's apprentice, etc.; cook and housekeeper were coded servant; dairy farmer and farmer were coded (dairy) farm laborer; and nurse was coded child's nurse. There were also occupations for which children were not deemed to possess the necessary physical or mental

Coding Operations

requirements—proprietary, official, supervisory, or professional pursuits. When children under 18 were returned in such occupations, the cases were referred to the section chief. In some cases, the occupational codes that were provided differed from the schedule entries.[4]

There was also a list of "peculiar occupations for women." When a woman was returned as following such an occupation, the schedule was examined to determine whether an error had been made either in the occupation or in the sex of the person. This list included the following occupations:

Auctioneer	Hostler
Baggageman	Inspector, mine/quarry
Blacksmith	Ladler or pourer, metal
Boatman	
Boilermaker	Laborer, coalyard
Boiler washer	Laborer, lumberyard
Bootblack	Laborer, pipeline
Brakeman	Laborer, road or street
Butcher	
Butler	Locomotive engineer
Cabinetmaker	
Captain	Loom fixer
Conductor	Lumberman
Cooper	Machinist
Craneman	Manager, mine or quarry
Deck hand	
Ditcher	Marine
Electrician	Marshal
Engineer (any)	Master
Engine hostler	Mate
Express messenger	Mechanic
Fireman (any)	Millwright
Flagman, railroad	Miner
Foreman, lumber camp	Molder (any metal)
Foreman, mine/quarry	Motorman
	Pilot
Foreman (any construction industry)	Plasterer
	Plumber
	Pressman, printing
Forester	Puddler
Freight Agent	Railroad official
Furnace Man	Railway mail clerk
Garbage man or scavenger	Roofer
	Sailor
Gas or steam fitter	Sawyer
Heater	Slater
Smelter man	Switchman, railroad
Stevedore	
Stonecutter	Teamster
Stonemason	Tinsmith
Street cleaner	Tool maker
Structural iron worker	Woodchopper

Persons on or assigned to public emergency work, i.e., Works Progress Administration, National Youth Administration, Civilian Conservation Corps, or local relief work, were coded the same as other workers for their occupation entries. For their industry entries, such persons were also coded the same as workers in private employment when an industry was reported. When the return merely indicated the program, such as "WPA," the industry code was given as government. When a person reported two jobs, the first return was coded.

When the coders received portfolios for coding, they first checked the portfolio memorandum to see if the portfolio was to be examined for industrial home workers. An industrial home worker was defined as one who worked in his or her home for a *commercial* employer who furnished the materials or products on which the person worked. A proper return for an industrial home worker included the words "at home" following the occupational entry in column 28. The kind of business or factory by which the person was employed was entered in column 29. The coders were instructed to distinguish carefully between industrial home workers, who were working for commercial employers, and persons who worked in their own homes for themselves. Each person identified as an industrial home worker was recorded on a line on the "Industrial Home Worker Transcription Sheet" (Form P-358).

When the coding of a portfolio was complete, the coders made the proper entries on the portfolio memorandum and noted that the data for industrial home workers, if any, had been transcribed. The portfolios were returned to the control desk.

Verification of the occupation, industry, and class of worker coding was done by clerks in Operation 10. Not all of the coding was verified. Instead, sample verification was used. The proportion verified was determined by the percentage of error in their previously verified work.

When portfolios were given to the verifiers, they went over several sheets and verified the accuracy of the occupation, industry, and class of worker symbols assigned by the coders. When an incorrect symbol was found, the verifiers changed it to the correct symbol and made an entry on a "Verification Slip" (Form P-355). This slip entry included the sheet and line of the E.D. on

---

4. For a discussion of this issue and, in particular, the issue of coding women in "unusual" occupations that is discussed below, see Conk (1981).

which the error was found and the occupation, industry, and, if involved, class of worker entries on the schedule, the symbol the coder assigned, and the corrected symbol. The clerks also verified any symbols entered in column J of the "Supplementary Questions" section of the schedule and checked to see that the transcription of symbols from column F to column U had been properly made.

Coding and Verification of the Housing Census

The coding of housing schedules was performed in Operation 11. This operation involved three main processes: completion of entries for added dwelling units, examination of specified items for completeness and consistency, and provision of code symbols for entries not precoded.

The housing schedules were contained in separate portfolios after Operation 6. The examination of the housing schedules was made section by section. Corrections were made by cancelling the original entry and writing the correct entry above or beside the old entry, or by checking the correct box.

Entries on the occupied-dwelling schedules were arranged in several parts. Part I contained information on the location of the dwelling units and household data. Specific items included the number of the structure in order of visitation and the dwelling unit number within the structure, the population line number of the head of the household, the block number (in cities of 50,000 or more), the race of the head, the number of persons in the household, farm residence, home tenure (owned or rented), the value of the home or the amount of monthly rent paid. Part II contained data on the characteristics of the structure, such as number of dwelling units, the presence of a business within the structure, the year and purpose for which the structure was originally built, and the exterior material and need for major repairs. Information on the characteristics of the dwelling units, such as the number of rooms and the equipment present, was contained in part III. Part IV consisted of utility data, including any furniture that was included in the rent. Finally, financial data for each owner-occupied nonfarm unit was present in part V of the occupied-dwelling schedule. This information consisted of the value of the property, the total mortgage debt, the first mortgage debt, the regular payments, the interest charged, and the holder of the first mortgage or land contract.

The vacant-dwelling schedules contained information in three parts. The location and general data in part I included the visitation and dwelling unit numbers, the block number, farm location, occupancy status, and the monthly rental (or an estimate). Part II, the characteristics of the structure, and part III, the characteristics of the dwelling unit, were the same as on the occupied-dwelling schedule. The details of the coding process for the housing census are provided in the "Coding Instructions for Housing Census" (Form HC–15).

Verification of the housing census was performed in Operation 12 according to the same basic procedures used to verify the general population coding. This procedure included an initial verification of all work by each coder. As the coders became experienced and met established error rates, the verification of a coder's work was done on a sampling basis. Throughout the verification operation, clerks were required to fill out the verifier's report of errors found for each coder whose work was checked, for each day of verification. When verification was finished, the portfolio memorandum was marked and the portfolio was returned to the control desk.

TABULATION

The first tabulation of the census data was the count made in the field by the district supervisor. This count was made by totaling the number of persons on the population schedule and served as the basis for both the enumerators' pay vouchers and the preliminary population announcements. A similar process was performed by the clerks in Operation 4. In this operation, the clerks produced a hand count of the population by counting the number of persons and dwelling units enumerated on population schedules. This hand count served as the official population count used in the apportionment process and was the basis for the first series of state bulletins on population and the first volume of the final population report (Truesdell 1935).

While these counts were tabulations they were not classifications of the data according to detailed characteristics of the population. To present the data obtained from the census schedules in detailed form, the data were transformed into a format permitting machine processing. The conversion of the data on punch cards into tabular form represented the final step in the processing of census returns.

Card Punching and the Sample Verification of Punch Cards

The use of punch cards in the processing of census returns began in the 1890 Census of Population. Punch cards used in processing this census were blank and required reading boards in order to show the proper positions for making punches. Throughout the next 40 years, substantial developments occurred in the technology of card punching (Truesdell 1965). By 1930, commercial key punches had replaced the reading boards. A standardized punch card of 24 columns had been developed for use on the commercial key punches. Between 1930 and 1940, the Bureau adopted a 45-column punch card and altered its machines to handle these new cards. This change was significant because it allowed extra fields on which to punch information from the census schedules.

In the processing of census returns in 1940, card punching was done by operators working in groups of 20. Each section of punch operators was supervised by a section chief and an assistant section chief. The operators transferred information appearing on the schedules to the cards by punching designated keys on hand-operated punch machines. Detailed instructions explained the translation of schedule entries into codes to be punched in designated columns, or fields, on the punch cards. Codes and editorial changes had been made on the schedules in previous operations. There were eight different types of cards punched. A complete description of these cards is given in Appendix V. An additional card (Card W) containing 1910 Census fertility information was produced as a Works Progress Administration project and used by the Bureau for comparative fertility analysis.

As noted above, one of the innovations in the 1940 processing of census returns was the use of sample inspection in the verification of different operations. The sample verification of card punching was central to the card punching operation.

Initially, a verification clerk examined all of a card puncher's work. Error rates of the card punchers were recorded on the verifier's report of errors found on a daily basis and plotted on a weekly basis. When the work of a puncher met predetermined criteria, the work of the puncher became subject to sample verification. To qualify for sample inspection, the punchers had to show for a 4-week period an average error rate of not more than one wrong card per 100 cards punched and no week of an average of 2 wrong cards per 100 punched. Additionally, only one of those four weeks could include a portfolio for which there were more than 3 wrong cards per 100 cards punched. A puncher was disqualified from sample verification when the average error rate for any week, determined on a sample basis, exceeded 3 wrong cards per 100 cards punched, or if it exceeded 2 wrong cards per 100 cards punched for two weeks out of a 4-week period.

The sample verification lasted 7 months. During this period, 51,000,000 (29 percent) of the 175,600,000 cards punched were subjected to sample verification. During the peak of activity, records were being kept on 1,265 punchers and 498 verifiers. The maximum number of punchers who qualified for sample verification at any one time was 473 (39 percent). Only 13 of the punchers who qualified for sample verification were later disqualified. Additional staff included seven people in record maintenance, three in training and supervision of verifiers, two doing studies of the error records and special problems, and one supervisor under the direction of the mathematical advisor, Dr. Deming (Deming and Geoffrey 1941).

The sample verification operation involved the selection of 5 percent of the cards in each portfolio punched by a "qualified" puncher. This averaged about one card per 8 minutes of work by the punchers. The selection of cards for sample verification was done through systematic sampling of the cards. A random starting point was used and changed daily for each verifier. Any errors found by the verifier in the sample were corrected. In addition, the verifier was instructed to verify all cards in a portfolio whenever the error rate of the sample exceeded 3 wrong cards per 100. About 2 percent of the work of qualified punchers was reverified in this manner. Visual verification of certain columns was also performed by holding together cards for which holes were to be punched in the same place on each card. An additional 7 percent of the work of qualified punchers was verified in this manner. The sorting and tabulating machinery was also set to reject cards with certain inconsistent punches. These cards were then corrected.

Five 5,000-card samples of incorrectly punched A cards were studied to learn about the nature of the errors made in card punching (Deming, Tepping, and Geoffrey 1942). The study showed that when sample verification was used, the net effects of incorrect punches were often negligible. In many fields, errors tended to compensate for each other. It was also found that the units column of a field was more often incorrectly punched than earlier columns in the field; thus, errors in numerical fields were mostly of small magnitude. As an example, age was incorrectly punched on 3,210 cards of the sampled 25,000 cards. Still, 41.8 percent of these 3,210 cards were punched within the correct 5-year age group and 40 percent of the remaining cards were punched in adjoining 5-year age groups. The study found that the pattern of incorrect punches in other fields analyzed—wage income, farm residence, race, citizenship, and marital status—was essentially the same for all. Errors tended to compensate for one another, i.e., the distribution of the errors was not greatly different from the distribution without the errors.

The study also determined factors associated with

the occurrence of incorrect punches. The clustering of incorrect punches on cards having more than one incorrect punch was examined. It was found that 86 percent of the incorrect cards had only one error, while 9 percent had two errors and only 5 percent had three or more errors. An investigation of the 3,535 cards with two or more errors showed that the multiple incorrect punches were related, as when a column was skipped, thereby making the punches for subsequent columns incorrect.

The distribution of incorrectly punched cards according to the schedule line number was also examined. It was found that there was a gradual decrease in the number of incorrect cards for successive lines of the population schedule. This was expected since earlier lines were filled out more often than later lines. In addition, the number of incorrect cards for certain lines was considerably greater than for others. The four lines designated for supplementary questions and the first line of the schedule showed a prominence over the other lines. The study concluded that the source of the errors on the lines designated for supplementary questions was in the column on the card which indicated that the schedule line was designated as a supplementary line. Lines not so designated had substantially fewer errors in this column. The greater error rate on the first line of a schedule was attributed to breaks in the puncher's rhythm caused by the removing of a completed schedule and insertion of a new in the schedule holder behind the card punch machine. In particular, it was found that the longer interval before the first line of the first sheet of a portfolio was associated with the greater number of incorrect punches.

The frequency of certain codes in relation to incorrect punches was also analyzed. It was found that for certain fields of the A card, there occurred punches which were far more frequent than any other punch in the field. For instance, the punch of "Native" in the citizenship field was far more frequent than any other of the possible punches in the field.

Machine Processing

Central to the processing of census data has been the incorporation of changes in machine technology. These changes were designed to increase both the efficiency and the accuracy with which the data from individual returns could be tabulated. By 1940, the Census Bureau was using census-built sorting machines, unit counters with 60-column recording sheets, and reproducers—used to transfer punched items on one to any position on another card (Truesdell 1965, pp. 195–97).

The sorting machine was used to sort punch cards according to the values punched in a column on the cards. The sorter could only sort on one column at a time. A multicolumn sorter was not developed in the Bureau until 1947. Thus, any complicated sort required several passes through the sorter.

After preliminary sorting, punch cards were passed through a unit counter. The unit counter kept counts of the number of individuals with specific characteristics. This machine was capable of counting up to 7 separate fields, or columns, from each card. Through a system of relays these columns could be combined, thus eliminating some preliminary card sorting. The number of separate characteristics that could be counted was limited when the codes for characteristics occupied more than one field on a card. The results of a run through the unit counter were printed on 60-column recording sheet or result slip.

Runs through the unit counter were made for relatively small areas. In order to obtain county or state totals, the figures for these small areas had to be consolidated. To do this, consolidation data from the unit counter result slips were first transferred to summary cards through the use of manually operated key punches. These summary cards were 45-column cards onto which were punched the small-area totals. Then printer-tabulator machines developed by IBM accumulated information from consecutive summary cards. These machines could also add items punched in different fields of the same card to provide needed totals and subtotals. The results were then printed approximately as they were needed for publication. This machine replaced an earlier process of copying the unit-counter result slips onto consolidation sheets, from which totals and subtotals were obtained by using manually operated adding machines.

An initial count was made from the tabulation of the "Preliminary Sample Cards" (S cards). These cards had been punched from information on the preliminary sample transcription sheet. The information on these sheets had been obtained in Operation 5 for those persons whose line entry on the population schedule had fallen in the 5-percent sample, i.e., on a line marked "Suppl. Ques." Both the transcription sheet and the S card contained information on an individual's work status, age, race, sex, and place of residence. There was space on each S card for information on all four sample individuals on a particular population schedule. Tabulations of these cards yielded the number of persons in each work status classified by race, sex, farm residence, and several age intervals. For each state, tabulations were made separately for (1) the rural farm and rural nonfarm areas, (2) towns and cities between 2,500 and 100,000 persons, and (3) each city of over 100,000 persons.

Tabulation

In order to rapidly obtain statistics on employment and unemployment, the punching and tabulating of S cards occurred before the schedules had been edited. The tabulations made from the S cards were, therefore, *preliminary* releases and were adjusted to the hand count of the total population for the areas for which tabulations were made (BC 1941). The results of these tabulations were released almost one year ahead of the tabulations based upon the other punch cards.

All cards other than the preliminary sample card were punched after editing had been performed. Statistics based on the remaining punch cards differed from the statistics based upon the S card. The magnitudes of changes in statistics after editing usually were not great. For state tables with small cell sizes, however, preliminary figures were sometimes changed by 20 to 25 percent. The tabulations from the later sample cards had closer controls since they were adjusted to the totals of various population classes, such as age, sex, or employment status, counted in the complete enumeration.

The first through seventh counts were made from tabulations of "Individual Cards" (A cards), a card punched for each individual enumerated on the population schedule. The A card included personal characteristics, educational information, birth and residence data, and data on labor force participation and income (see Appendix V).

The first count was a tabulation by each enumeration district. The second through sixth counts were tabulated by different geographical areas: for tracted cities by census tracts; by each ward in untracted cities of 100,000 or more; by each city of 2,500 to 100,000; by that part of the balance of each county which was included in a metropolitan district, divided by farm and nonfarm; and by that part of the balance of each county which was not in the metropolitan district, divided by farm and nonfarm.

The characteristics of the population that were tabulated varied from count to count. The first count tabulated farm residence, race and nativity by sex, and age by sex. The second count tabulated age and school attendance, education, and work status by sex, race, and nativity. The third count tabulated foreign-born Whites by country of birth and citizenship by sex and age. The fourth count tabulated for foreign-born Negroes, citizenship by sex and age, and for "minor races," race by nativity, age, and sex. The fifth count of employed workers was broad occupation and industry group by sex and race for those states where a significant proportion of the population was not White. The sixth count was the age, marital status, and citizenship of the institutionalized population that was 14 years of age and over, and education for persons 25 years and over, by color, sex and type of institution. Finally, the seventh count was for internal migration and consisted of two parts. Part one was the migrant's place of residence, April 1, 1940, by the place of residence, April 1, 1935. Part two consisted of migrant characteristics of work status, relationship to household head, education, citizenship, broad occupation group, age and color, crosstabulated with sex.

The tabulations produced by the first through fifth counts were published initially as the Second, Third, and Fourth Series of State and United States Summary Bulletins. These series bulletins were later edited, assembled, and bound together as sections of published volumes. The tabulations from the sixth count served as the basis for a special report on the institutional population. Similarly, a series of reports on migration were issued based upon the seventh count tabulations.[5]

In addition to the S card there were several other punch cards made from the 5-percent sample. The "Supplementary Individual Card" (B card) was prepared for each individual in the sample. This card included the coded responses for the supplementary (sample) items, as well as a number of items from the complete enumeration for that person. The "Fertility Card" (C card) was completed for every married woman in the sample. The C card contained items from the B card pertaining specifically to the woman (such as age at first marriage, number of children ever born, number of children living in the household, etc.), and also items pertaining to the woman's husband (age, education, and employment and occupational information). A "Sample Family Card" (D card) was prepared for each household for which the head fell on a sample line. The items on card D included some items reproduced from card B for the head and other items pertaining to other members of the family and to the entire family.

The results of sample tabulations were presented in a manner similar to the presentation of results based on regular tabulations. Additionally, each sample frequency was multiplied by an adjustment factor based upon known class totals of the population. This adjustment factor was close to the reciprocal of the sampling ratio, but varied somewhat due to the differential presence of blank lines among classifications. Almost all tabulations of the sample were published in a series of small reports.

There was a similar program for tabulation of the housing census. Tabulations were made from the three housing cards—cards E, F, and G. The "Dwelling Card" (card E) included information on the persons living in

---

5. These publications are detailed in chapter 5.

the dwelling unit, in addition to information on the occupancy status of the dwelling. The F card, called the "Household Card," included information on household items from the population schedule in addition to information from the housing schedule. Finally, the G card, or "Mortgage Card," had information on the nature of the dwelling structure and on the mortgage debt. Due to other demands for available funds, few of these data were tabulated or published (Truesdell 1965).

Since there was widespread interest in the economic situation in the country, extensive tabulations were made of the labor force and income data. The 1940 tabulation also increased the emphasis on metropolitan districts as the areal unit. The metropolitan district was deemed a more significant unit of analysis than the central city for the purpose of labor market analyses, since the larger area of the metropolitan district was seen as a more appropriate delineation of the labor market.

THE EFFECT OF WORLD WAR II ON THE 1940 CENSUS

The entry of the United States into World War II had a substantial impact on the operations of the Bureau of the Census and its work on the 1940 Census. Prior to the war, the Bureau was involved in the compilation of the census data and the preparation of final reports. All schedules had been edited and coded, punching of cards for population and housing was substantially completed, tabulations were under way, and preliminary reports for all major fields had been issued. Figure 1 in Appendix VI reports the completion dates of the major processing steps.

The Bureau had already begun activities in the area of national defense. A new Assistant Director had been appointed with the responsibility of planning and facilitating the defense activities of the Bureau. These activities centered around the preparation of information needed by agencies engaged in national defense projects. Priority was given to tabulations of 1940 Census data most needed by these agencies and a number of special tabulations were also prepared (DOC 1941, pp. 42–43).

With the United States' entry into the war, the preparation of needed statistics for defense and war agencies became the chief function of the Bureau. The Bureau was converted to a war program by the Second War Powers Act of 1942. This act authorized the Secretary of Commerce to make information on census schedules for individual respondents available to war agencies, to defer or dispense with any regular census or statistical work of the Commerce Department, and to make needed special investigations and reports of census or statistical matters that were necessary for the conduct of the war.

Since most of the information collected in the 1940 Census was needed for some aspect of war planning, the essential features of the program for completion of the census were retained. Certain aspects of the program, however, had to be abandoned.

A list of titles and tentative outlines of contemplated analytic studies had been circulated among consumers of census materials. The responses of these consumers had been reviewed, but this program of special reports had to be curtailed with the outbreak of war. The publication of a statistical atlas was also abandoned. The program for the compilation of certain population statistics was also modified. For example, family data were tabulated only on a sample basis instead of on a complete count basis as originally planned.

The results of tabulations of the population data were made available as quickly as possible through the use of sample tabulations and advance reports. War agencies received information, particularly labor force data, in advance of publication. Advance releases were issued on foreign-born Germans and Italians in the United States and on Japanese in the U.S. and Hawaii. Special releases were prepared on the potential labor supply in the nation, the reserve labor supply among women, the education level of men of military age, and the estimated number of males required to register under the Selective Service System. Data from the housing census were used to measure the fuel requirements of the country and the supply and characteristics of housing in critical defense areas (DOC 1942, pp. 15–18).

The additional demands made upon the Bureau by the war led the end of the Sixteenth Decennial Census to be extended from December 31, 1942 to June 30, 1943. By this latter date, most of the final reports had been printed. The costs of the Sixteenth Decennial Census are presented in Appendix VI, Figure 2.

5 PUBLICATIONS FROM THE 1940 CENSUS

THE PUBLICATION PROGRAM for the results of the Sixteenth Decennial Census was organized with tabulations first published as series of preliminary bulletins, many of which later became incorporated into final reports. This procedure was used both for the Population Census and for the Housing Census.

The War led to the curtailment of original plans for the distribution of 1940 Census publications. Some 150,000 groups and individual had requested inclusion on mailing lists for census bulletins. These lists were discontinued during the War and free bulletins were sent only when deemed justified. Pressures to curtail the use of paper, shortages of printing and processing capacity, and the increased costs of materials and labor made such actions necessary. To make information more readily available, some 1,600 libraries throughout the nation were designated as depository centers for Census publications (DOC 1942, p. 27).

The preliminary population results were first published in a series of state bulletins (including the District of Columbia), entitled "Sixteenth Census of the United States: 1940, Population, First Series, Number of Inhabitants." A United States Summary Bulletin and separate bulletins for the territories and possessions were also published. These bulletins were completed between August 1940 and April 1941. They provided population counts by counties and minor civil divisions (such as townships, districts, and precincts), with separate figures for cities, towns, villages, and other incorporated places, for wards of incorporated places of 5,000 or more persons, and for metropolitan districts and census tracts. The bulletins were later edited and assembled together in a bound volume, *Sixteenth Census of the United States: 1940, Population, Volume I—Number of Inhabitants*, which was published in 1942 and constituted a final report of the 1940 Census of Population.

The second series of the population bulletins, "Population, Second Series, Characteristics of the Population," was produced between September 1941 and April 1942. Similar to the first series bulletins, the second series of bulletins was composed of separate bulletins for each state and the summary bulletin for the United States. These second series bulletins were also edited and assembled in a bound volume for publication. Published in 1943, this final report was entitled *Sixteenth Census of the United States: 1940. Population, Volume II—Characteristics of the Population* and it was composed of seven parts, one part devoted to a U.S. summary and the other six parts presenting data on states. Included in this volume were statistics for each state, by counties and, in varying degrees of detail, for other areas such as incorporated places with 1,000 inhabitants or more, townships or minor civil divisions, wards of cities of 50,000 or more, and metropolitan districts. The characteristics reported included residence (urban, rural-nonfarm, and rural-farm), sex, age, race, nativity, citizenship, country of birth, school attendance, highest grade completed, employment status, class of worker, major occupation group, and industry group.

In a similar manner, the third series population bulletins, "Population, Third Series, The Labor Force," were completed between July and November 1942. This series was edited, assembled and published as *Sixteenth Census of the United States: 1940. Population, Volume III—The Labor Force*, in 1943. This volume was composed of 5 parts, of which one part was devoted to the U.S. summary and the remaining parts presented data by state. The data in both the bulletins and the final report included employment status, class of worker, occupation, industry, wage or salary income in 1939, hours worked in the census week of March 24 to 30, 1940, months worked in 1939, duration of unemployment, and certain personal characteristics (age, sex, race, and marital status).

Finally, there was a fourth series of population bulletins, "Population, Fourth Series, Characteristics by

Age," which was prepared in the period from December 1942 to April 1943. This series was also assembled and published in 1943, as *Sixteenth Census of the United States: 1940. Population, Volume IV—Characteristics by Age.* This volume was composed of one part devoted to the U.S. summary and three parts of state data. The data presented were general characteristics of the population: citizenship, marital status, relationship to the head of household, school attendance, highest grade of school completed, and employment status. Each population characteristic was cross-classified by age. The data were presented for states, residence (urban, rural-nonfarm, rural-farm) within states, and urban places of 50,000 persons or more.

The results of the Census of Housing were published in a manner corresponding to the publication of population results. The first series of housing tabulations was completed between June 1941 and June 1942, and was published as a U.S. summary bulletin and a series of state bulletins, entitled "Housing, First Series, Data for Small Areas." These bulletins were edited, bound and published in 1943, as *Sixteenth Census of the United States: 1940, Housing, Volume I—Data for Small Areas.* There were two parts to this volume—one part for the U.S. summary and several states and the other part for the remainder of the states. This volume presented data for the U.S., regions of the U.S., each state, and within states for residence (urban, rural-nonfarm, rural-farm), counties, incorporated of 1,000 inhabitants or more, for wards of cities of 10,000 or more, for minor civil divisions, and for metropolitan districts. The data presented were total number of dwelling units classified by occupancy and tenure, race of occupants, number of units having more than 1.5 persons per room, state of repair, and plumbing equipment. Also, for rural and rural-nonfarm areas information was presented on number of residential structures, average monthly rent or rental value of dwelling units, and mortgage status of owner-occupied nonfarm units. Additional data presented for rural-farm areas related to electric lighting, running water, and toilet facilities.

Also published in 1943 was *Sixteenth Census of the United States: 1940. Housing, Volume II—General Characteristics.* Like the other published volumes, it was an edited compilation of a series of state bulletins and a U.S. summary bulletin, in particular, "Housing, Second Series, General Characteristics." The reports in the second series had been compiled between January and November 1942. This volume contained a part devoted to a U.S. summary and four additional parts containing data for states. The data presented in this volume encompassed most of the subjects for which information was taken in the housing census. The published subjects included occupancy and tenure status, value of home or monthly rent, size of household and race of head, type of structure, exterior material, year built, conversion, state of repair, number of rooms, housing facilities and equipment, and mortgage status. These general characteristics were presented for states; within states for area (urban, rural-nonfarm, rural-farm), cities of 50,000 inhabitants or more, metropolitan districts, and counties; and within counties for urban places and rural areas.

The third series of housing bulletins, "Housing, Third Series, Characteristics by Monthly Rent or Value," was completed between October 1942 and March 1943. After editing and assembling, the series was released in 1943, as *Sixteenth Census of the United States: 1940. Housing, Volume III—Characteristics by Monthly Rent or Value,* consisting of 3 parts—a U.S. summary and two parts devoted to state data. The statistics presented in this volume were cross-classifications of monthly rent or value of homes by type and age of structure, state of repair, number of rooms, size of household and race of head, persons per room, housing facilities and equipment, and mortgage status. The data were presented for states and within states by area (urban, rural-nonfarm, rural-farm), cities of 50,000 or more inhabitants, and larger metropolitan districts.

The final series of housing data, "Housing, Fourth Series, Mortgages on Owner-Occupied Nonfarm Homes," was also completed between October 1942 and March 1943. Under the title, *Sixteenth Census of the United States: 1940. Housing, Volume IV—Mortgages on Owner-Occupied Nonfarm Homes,* this series was also edited and published in 1943. It also consisted of three parts, a U.S. summary and two parts of data by state. Also included in the published volume were two supplements to the fourth series of bulletins: "Supplement A, Homes Built in 1935–1940," and, "Supplement B, Homes Occupied by Nonwhite Owners." The data presented on first mortgages included the amount of outstanding indebtedness, type of payment, frequency and amount of payment, interest rate, and holder of mortgage; data on all mortgages included value of the property, estimated rental value, year built, and race of occupants. Also shown are data on properties with junior mortgages and the outstanding indebtedness on first and junior mortgages. The data are presented for the United States, each state, and within states for cities of 50,000 inhabitants or more and large metropolitan districts.

In addition to these bulletins which were incorporated into the final reports, there was a bulletin which was not incorporated into the final reports, "Population and Housing, Statistics for Census Tracts." This bulletin consisted of 58 pamphlets, issued between 1941 and 1943, which covered 60 tracted cities. The data presented in this bulletin included such population data as

Final Reports

sex, age, race, nativity, citizenship, country of birth, education, employment status, class of worker, and major occupational group; housing data included occupancy status, tenure, value or rent, type of structure, state of repair and plumbing equipment, size of household, race of household head, persons per room, radio, refrigeration equipment, and heating fuel by type of heating equipment.

The Census Bureau also published the results of the first tabulations of the 1940 census data in several series of preliminary releases. Most of these preliminary releases were later incorporated into bulletins and final reports. Provided below are lists of (1) those preliminary releases for which the data was not presented in other reports, and (2) final reports of the 1940 Censuses of Population and Housing, other than volumes described above.[1]

Preliminary Releases

Sixteenth Census of the United States: 1940

Series P–3:

No. 23. Population. Japanese population of the United States and its territories and possessions. December 6, 1941. Three pages.

No. 24. Population. Japanese population by nativity or citizenship in selected cities in the United States: 1940. December 10, 1941. One page.

No. 25. Population. Japanese population in the Pacific coast states by sex and nativity or citizenship, by counties: 1940. December 11, 1941. Five pages.

Series P–9:

No. 1. Population. Foreign-born Germans and Italians in selected cities of the United States. December 12, 1941. Two pages.

No. 4. Population. Citizenship of the foreign-born white population in selected cities of the United States. December 16, 1941. Three pages.

No. 5. Japanese population in selected counties and cities of the United States by sex and nativity or citizenship: 1940. December 19, 1941. Forty-nine pages.

No. 8. Population. Preliminary figures on employment status, occupation, and industry for the Japanese population of the Territory of Hawaii: 1940. February 2, 1942. Three pages.

No. 9. Population. Characteristics of the Japanese population of the Territory of Hawaii: 1940. February 2, 1942. Three pages.

No. 11. Population. Trends in the proportion of the nation's labor force engaged in agriculture: 1820 to 1940. March 28, 1942. Two pages.

No. 13. Population. Reserve labor supply among women in the United States. May 11, 1942. Four pages.

Series P–10:

No. 20. Population. Racial composition of the urban and rural population of the United States, by regions, divisions, and states: 1940. November 14, 1942. Six pages.

No. 21. Population. Age, color, and sex composition of the population in urban places classified by size and in rural areas, for the United States, by regions: 1940. March 5, 1943. Eight pages.

Series P–14:

No. 13. Population. All experienced persons in the labor force by occupation and industry, for the United States: 1940. October 29, 1943. Ten pages.

Series P–15:

No. 5. Population. Foreign white stock of German and Italian Origin: 1940. September 30, 1942. Six pages.

Series H–3:

No. 2. Housing. Urban vacancy in the United States by county: 1940. May 23, 1941. One page and map.

No. 3. Housing. Housing figures for urban places classified by size of place, for the United States and geographic divisions: 1940. September 8, 1941. Four pages.

Final Reports

Sixteenth Census of the United States: 1940. Population. Characteristics of persons not in the labor force, 14 years old and over. Age, sex, color, household relationship, months worked in 1939, and usual major occupation group. 1943. vi, 117 pages.

Population. Characteristics of the nonwhite population by race. 1943. vi, 112 pages.

Population. Comparative occupation statistics for the United States, 1870 to 1940. A comparison of the 1930 and 1940 census occupation and industry classifications and statistics; a comparable series of occupation statistics, 1870 to 1930; and a social-economic grouping of the labor force, 1910 to 1940, by Dr. Alba M. Edwards. 1943. xii, 206 pages.

Population. Differential fertility, 1940 and 1910 . . . 1943–1947. 5 v.

The reports in this series are based on tabulations of samples of the census returns for 1940 and 1910. Fertility by duration of marriage, based upon tabulations from the Sixteenth and Thirteenth Censuses of the United States: 1940 and 1910. 1947. vi,

---

1. These lists were compiled from U.S. Bureau of the Census (1974), pp. 84–113, 125–26.

338 pages. (Running title, Sixteenth Census of the United States: 1940, omitted.)
Fertility for States and large cities. 1943. vii, 281 pages.
Standardized fertility rates and reproduction rates. A supplement to the report designated Fertility for States and large cities. 1944, vi, 40 pages.
Women by number of children ever born. 1945. ix, 410 pages.
Women by number of children under 5 years old. 1945. ix, 265 pages.

Population. Education . . . 1943–1947. 3 v.
Educational attainment by economic characteristics and marital status based upon tabulations from the Sixteenth Census of the United States: 1940. 1947. vi, 226 pages. (Running title, Sixteenth Census of the United States: 1940, omitted.)
Educational attainment of children by rental value of home. 1945. iv, 50 pages.
Education, occupation and household participation of males 18 to 44 years old. Prepared by the Division of Population, Bureau of the Census, of the Department of Commerce, in cooperation with the Special Services Division of the War Department. 1943. vi, 23 pages.

Population. Estimates of labor force, employment, and unemployment in the United States, 1940 and 1930. 1944. vi, 18 pages.

Population. Internal migration, 1935 to 1940 . . . 4 v. 1943–1946.
Age of migrants. 1946. iv, 382 pages.
Color and sex of migrants. 1943. vii, 490 pages.
Economic characteristics of migrants. 1946. v, 223 pages.
Social characteristics of migrants. 1946. vi, 270 pages.

Population. The labor force (sample statistics) . . . 1943. 6 v.
The reports in this series are based on tabulations of samples of the 1940 census returns.
Employment and family characteristics of women. vi, 212 pages.
Employment and personal characteristics. vi, 177 pages.
Industrial characteristics. iv, 174 pages.
Occupational characteristics. vi, 256 pages.
Usual occupation. iv, 63 pages.
Wage or salary income in 1939. vi, 194 pages.

Population. Nativity and parentage of the white population . . . 1943. 3 v.
The reports in this series are based in whole or in part on tabulations of samples of the population returns of the 1940 census.
Country of origin of the foreign stock by nativity, citizenship, age, and value or rent of home, for States and large cities. iv, 122 pages.
General characteristics, age, marital status, and education, for States and large cities. iv, 279 pages.
Mother tongue, by nativity, parentage, country of origin, and age, for States and large cities. v, 58 pages.

Population. Special report on institutional population 14 years old and over, characteristics of inmates in penal institutions and in institutions for the delinquent, defective, and dependent. 1943 iv, 361 pages.

Population. State of birth of the native population. 1944. viii, 78 pages.

Population. Unincorporated communities, United States, by States. Total population of unincorporated communities having 500 or more inhabitants for which separate figures could be compiled. 1943. iv, 32 pages.

Population. Families . . . 1943–1944. 4 v.
Employment status; regions and cities of 1,000,000 or more. 1943. v, 110 pages.
Family wage or salary income in 1939; regions and cities of 1,000,000 or more. 1943. iv, 156 pages.
Size of family and age of head; regions and cities of 1,000,000 or more. 1944. iv, 127 pages.
Types of families; regions and cities of 1,000,000 or more. 1943. vi, 221 pages.

Population and housing. Families. Characteristics of rural-farm families. Regions and divisions. 1943. iv, 82 pages.

Population and housing. Families. General characteristics. States, cities of 100,000 or more, and metropolitan districts of 200,000 or more. 1943. vi, 332 pages.

Population and housing. Families. Income and rent. Regions, cities of 1,000,000 or more, and metropolitan districts of 1,000,000 or more. 1943. v, 237 pages. (Subtitle should read: For regions and for metropolitan districts of 1,000,000 or more . . . Slip attached to title page.)

Population and housing. Families. Tenure and rent. Regions, cities of 1,000,000 or more, and metropolitan districts of 500,000 or more. 1943. iv, 141 pages.

Territories and Possessions

The following final reports were to have been published in a single bound volume entitled "Sixteenth Census of the United States: 1940. Territories and Possessions," but such volume was never issued.

Alaska
Population. Characteristics of the population (with limited data on housing). Alaska. 1943. iv, 20 pages.

Territories and Possessions

Hawaii
Population. Second series. Characteristics of the population. Hawaii. 1943. iv, 35 pages.
Housing. General characteristics. Hawaii. 1943. v, 27 pages.

American Samoa
American Samoa. Population, agriculture. 1941. iv, 12 pages.

Guam
Guam. Population, agriculture. 1941. iv, 18 pages.

Panama Canal Zone
Panama Canal Zone. Population. 1941. iv, 28 pages.

Puerto Rico
Puerto Rico. Population. Bulletin no. 1–4. 1942–1946. 4 pts.
Puerto Rico. Housing. General characteristics. 1943. vii, 121 pages.

Virgin Islands (U.S.)
Population and housing. General characteristics. Virgin Islands of the United States. 1943. iv, 22 pages.

6 EVALUATION OF THE 1940 CENSUS

Available documents indicate that the Census Bureau conducted a post-census evaluation of the questions and procedures used in conducting the 1940 Censuses of Population and Housing.[1] While the evaluation covered the entire schedule and procedures, the available documents emphasize the questions which obtained information on labor force participation and income.

Analysis of Employment Status Questions

The evaluation documents noted a "considerable amount of error" in the employment status questions. Due to this error, coding clerks had been required to check schedules for consistency among the employment status items. In addition, the Census Bureau hired a special group of editors to check the returns. Based upon analysis of the 1940 procedures, it was recommended that future censuses have fewer and more simple questions, with correspondingly shorter instructions. Recommendations were also made to improve the data presented in tabulations.

A common error was found to be the failure of enumerators to record employment status answers for scattered individuals within an enumeration district (E.D.). In these cases, a code of "employment status not reported" was assigned. Cost considerations prevented the imputation of such missing data. However, when there were entries omitted for large groups of persons, the specially trained editors provided imputed codes. The final count for the category "employment status not reported" was 1,987,140. The evaluation noted that the Bureau had come under criticism for this large number. Critics suggested that it included many unemployed persons. The evaluation provided some suggestions for reducing the size of the unknown group, including extending the imputation procedure to the scattered instances of omissions and making a category to the effect of "presumed to be in the labor force, but particular category unknown."

Among particular items, there was large-scale misreporting of public emergency workers. The number of these workers reported on census returns was 2,400,000, while the number indicated by records of emergency work agencies was 3,500,000. It was found that many public emergency workers were reported as having nonemergency work, seeking work, or in school. Special coders reexamined the data returns, raising the final census total of public emergency workers to 2,529,606. This corrected figure still represented a large undercount when compared with the agency figures. These errors of misclassification caused error in the total number of employed and unemployed workers for each area and errors in the relation between unemployment status and other characteristics. Corrected data on employment status by age and sex based upon estimates were published in a final report (BC 1944).

Additional errors were found in the reports of seasonal workers, who were reported as not in the labor force if they were not at work or seeking work during the census week. It was recommended that future censuses make it possible to identify such workers.

There were also difficulties in obtaining correct reports of unpaid family workers due to discrepancies in enumerator interpretations. These problems were considered to be particularly acute in rural areas where there was a lack of any clear distinction in the typical farm household between workers in the family enterprise and homemakers or dependents.

Coding difficulties were also found in the returns of

---

1. U.S. Bureau of the Census, "A Critical Analysis of the Questions Used in the Sixteenth Decennial Census of Population and Housing." These evaluative documents, most of which are unsigned, were unpublished, internal memoranda of the Bureau of the Census. This author obtained copies of the documents from the library of the Census History Staff.

persons who had jobs but who were not at work during the census week. Persons in this category could have been temporarily out of work for up to four weeks and still have been considered to be in the labor force. A large number of the persons returned in this category had in fact been out of work for a longer period of time. About 300,000 persons were reassigned by the special coders into other categories, producing a corrected total for the category of 1,120,000.

Another problem identified in the evaluation of the employment status questions was the status of those persons identified as "not in the labor force." Persons in this category were determined by successive elimination on the basis of answers to the employment status questions (see Appendix I, questions 21–26, on the population schedule). The evaluation argued that this procedure introduced uncertainty into the determination of the "not in the labor force" category. Difficulties with this category included enumerators returning children who performed chores at home and housewives as "at work." In addition, the evaluation found that some of the codes used to classify those not in the labor force were ambiguous. Recommendations were made to eliminate ambiguity in future censuses.

The category of "inmates of institutions" also provided difficulties. It was found that enumerators' entries for institutional inmates were not reliable. Many enumerators failed to distinguish between employees of institutions and their families, on the one hand, and residents of institutions, on the other hand. Institutions were often not identified and frequently quasi-households, such as monasteries, convents, and other homes, were identified as institutions. It was also found that there was inconsistency in the exclusion of inmates of various types of institutions from the labor force. Several recommendations were made to correct these problems.

Analysis of Class of Worker Questions

While class of worker data had been collected since 1910, the first attempt at publishing these data was made in 1940. Efforts were made to improve the 1940 data by giving more extensive instructions to enumerators and spending more time editing the data. One of the central reasons for collecting these data was to be able to distinguish among wage or salary workers, employers, own-account workers, and unpaid family workers. Unfortunately, the evaluation indicated that most enumerators had not clearly understood these distinctions. Recommendations were made to change the terminology used on the schedules and to instruct enumerators.

Other problems found in the class of worker data included the failure of enumerators to distinguish clearly between government and private workers. There was also confusion over the distinction between employers and own-account workers, resulting in a combination of these categories in the published reports.

Omitted entries were also a problem for the class of worker question. In a large number of E.D.'s, no reports were made for this question. Moreover, in many E.D.'s, the column had been left blank for a large proportion of workers. Such omissions were most common in E.D.'s made up almost entirely of one or another class of worker groups. In these cases, the enumerators apparently only filled in the class of worker column for the exceptional groups. In cases for which the class of worker data were missing, coders were instructed to determine the most probable entry on the basis of the occupation and industry codes, the wage or salary income entry, and personal characteristics. When no definite indication was obtainable, coders were instructed to classify the person "private wage or salary worker." Only in cases in which neither occupation nor industry was reported was the category "class of worker not reported" entered in the column.

Analysis of Occupation and Industry Questions

Based upon the problems which occurred in the coding of 1940 returns, the evaluation made various recommendations related to occupation and industry coding. These suggestions included specific recommendations for developing the alphabetical index of occupations and industries, for providing instructions to enumerators, for operating the research center, for special coding problems, and for occupation and industry classification.

The suggestions for developing the alphabetical index of occupations and industries were oriented toward obtaining maximum consistency between the two indices and obtaining in advance information necessary for specific codes, in particular codes for various types of governmental activities. The suggestions for providing instructions to enumerators largely concerned specific distinctions the enumerators needed to make in coding and occupations and industries which needed special instructions to the enumerators.

The research center contained directories and other materials used in the editing and coding of occupations and industries. Six clerks from the coding operations worked in the research center, with one acting as the section chief. These clerks were responsible for obtaining the information necessary to resolve problems in editing and coding. The evaluation made suggestions about directories, lists, and other materials that would be useful in future operations of the research center.

Suggestions for the occupation and industry classifications generally were recommendations that specific items be given more attention. These recommendations usually attempted to reduce the ambiguity of categories. In addition, one general recommendation was made that there should be a determination of the characteristics (age, sex, education, income, etc.) to be used in the elimination of persons from certain occupations. It was argued that the criteria for restriction be made on the basis of information on the requirements in effect at that time for an individual occupation.[2]

Analysis of Income Questions

In 1940, the first attempt was made to obtain income data in the population census. Difficulties in obtaining this information were anticipated, and attempts were made to reduce these difficulties and minimize any opposition.[3] One concession which had been made in order to minimize opposition had been to ask only if the amount of income from sources other than wages or salary had exceeded $50 rather than asking the exact amount. The evaluation noted that failure to obtain the amount of other income limited the value of the census data as an indicator of economic well-being. It was further argued that this lack of information limited the analysis of the relationship between economic data and personal characteristics. As a result, the evaluation maintained that the data on value or rental of home provided a better indication of economic status than did the income data. It was recommended that future economic inquiries should be directed toward obtaining data on total income rather than just wage and salary income.

Despite concerns over public reluctance to report income data, the evaluation indicated a general completeness in reporting for those groups for whom wage or salary income was most significant. On the wage or salary income question, the incidence of no report among wage and salary workers was 2.3 percent; among other persons in the labor force, 14.1 percent failed to report; and, among persons not in the labor force, 17.9 percent failed to report. On the "other income" question, the only category for which the evaluation was able to determine the incidence of no report was wage or salary workers, of whom 2.1 percent had no report.

In the coding operations, no attempt was made to de-

---
2. It is possible that this is a reference to the problems encountered in coding children and women in "unusual" occupations; see list, p. 51, and Conk (1981).

3. Problems with the inclusion of income questions and the attempts by the Census Bureau to overcome opposition are described more fully above; see pp. 12–13.

termine the proper entries for persons with missing income data. In the transcription of family income data, however, certain missing income reports were eliminated in order to avoid having a family income listed as unknown when members who were housewives or students failed to report income. Families were only classified as wage or salary income not reported if a report on wage or salary income was missing for one or more members who were in the labor force and classified as a wage or salary worker or who were not in the labor force but worked one or more weeks in 1939. In cases in which the question on wage or salary income was not answered for employers, own-account workers, unpaid family workers, new workers, or persons not in the labor force (except housewives and students), the coders assumed the person had no wage or salary income. The evaluation maintained that many enumerators had assumed that the question was inappropriate or the answer was obvious for such persons and, therefore, left the wage or salary income column blank.

Errors in the income data were often difficult to detect. Some were recurrent, however, and could be easily detected and eliminated by the group of special editors. The evaluation provided three examples of such easily detected errors:

(1) There frequently occurred a combination of entries of a report of wage or salary income and "no" in the other income column for the majority of employers and own-account workers in particular E.D.'s. The presumption was made that the enumerators had considered profits as wage income in these cases. Some 240,885 such combinations were cancelled in special editing.

(2) There were returns for which there was a consistent "yes" in the other income column for unpaid family workers, housewives, and students living at home. In these cases it was assumed that the enumerator or respondent considered housing and board supplied to the family member by the head as other income. The special editors cancelled 73,807 such entries.

(3) In institutional households, such as convents, monasteries, labor camps, etc., there was often a failure on the part of workers to report nonwage income. It was assumed that enumerators or respondents did not regard room and board furnished to employees as other income. In 5,247 cases, the other income column was edited to "yes."

The evaluation made some recommendations with regard to the tabulations of the income data. First, on the assumption that the income questions remained the same in future censuses, it recommended that counts of persons with no report of "other income" be made separately for all groups in the labor force and for persons

General Population Questions

not in the labor force. The 1940 tabulation program had only made such a count for the category of wage or salary workers. Second, it was recommended that a special code be assigned to persons with no income. It was argued that such a code would facilitate tabulations and the presentation of data on such persons. Third, it was argued that future censuses utilize common intervals in income tabulations for all subdivisions of the population in order to facilitate the presentation of summary data. Finally, it was urged that future censuses tabulate family income distributions for areas as small as possible, i.e., if not individual cities, at least city-size groups. Such tabulations had been planned for 1940. A shortage of funds restricted the family tabulations to the five percent sample, however, and, thus, made it impossible to provide data for small areas.

Analysis of Other Labor Force Questions

The evaluation indicated that the question concerning number of hours worked during the week prior to the census provided little difficulty, except for nonwage workers who did not follow regular schedules. It was noted, however, that the instructions for such workers seemed clear and concise and required no modifications. It was suggested that these data might have been put to greater work in distinguishing part-time workers from both the fully employed and those completely idle.

There were greater problems with the question concerning the duration of unemployment. Responses to this question were frequently not reported, especially for emergency workers, new workers, and persons seeking work who had last been employed as nonwage workers. The nonresponse rate was also significant for wage or salary workers. Furthermore, the evaluation suggested that the reports were largely approximations and that the duration of unemployment was often exaggerated.

Despite these weaknesses, the evaluation concluded that the data on duration of unemployment were valuable when related to characteristics that allowed the determination of differences in the severity of unemployment by various types of workers. Thus, the evaluation urged inclusion of the question in any future censuses taken at times when unemployment presented serious problems. The evaluation further argued that a sample question would probably be sufficient for the purposes. It was also recommended that in the future the instructions to enumerators be shortened and simplified.

An additional problem with the data on duration of unemployment was also shared by the data on number of weeks worked in 1939. There was a marked tendency for returns to concentrate on multiples of four weeks. The evaluation felt that this concentration indicated that enumerators had determined the number of months unemployed or worked and multiplied by four. The use of four, rather than four and one-third, weeks per month introduced a bias for which an allowance had to be made. In the published tables, the data were presented in terms of months rather than weeks. The evaluation recommended that in the future these questions be asked in terms of months rather than weeks.

There were also difficulties with nonresponse for the questions on weeks worked. Of about 10,000,000 persons not in the labor force, over 20 percent of the class failed to report on this question. Of those who did report, only 2,600,000 indicated that they had worked one week or more in 1939. The evaluation argued that there was evidence which indicated this latter number should have been considerably larger. Among those persons in the labor force, reliable data was obtained only on wage or salary workers and detailed statistics were tabulated on a 100-percent basis only for this group. The evaluation recommended that this question be asked in the future only if the wage or salary income question were also asked, since the main purpose of the weeks worked question was to provide data for cross-classification for wage or salary income. If the question were asked, it was recommended that it be changed to months worked and that the instructions to enumerators be simplified.

Analysis of General Population Questions

The document pertaining to the evaluation of the general population questions did not review all the questions on the population schedule. Questions which had appeared consistently on the schedule in past censuses do not appear to have been evaluated. Whether these were deliberate omissions rather than a result of different criteria for evaluation is impossible to determine.

The evaluation indicated that there were problems with age bias in the 1940 returns. It was suggested that there had been a "large scale over-statement of age by persons 55 to 64 years old, particularly Negroes and Southern whites." Details of this over-statement were not provided in the evaluation document. It was suggested that the problem of age bias be made the subject of a complete investigation. It was also recommended that future censuses supplement the question on age at last birthday with a question on date of birth.

The evaluation only briefly examined the question of country of birth. Recommendations were made with regard to a few coding difficulties, and a classification used in publication. The evaluation also noted that the results obtained for the mother tongue questions were not the same for the second generation in 1940 as they had been for that generation in 1920 and 1910. In the 1940 census, many native white persons of foreign or mixed parentage reported their mother tongue to be English. It was thought that many persons of foreign mother tongue were being missed. Coding procedures used in 1920 and 1910 had assigned the mother tongue of the parents to the children. The evaluation stressed that this method probably overstated the existence of some foreign mother tongues. The evaluation thought it was necessary to resolve the discrepancy between the earlier procedure and the 1940 responses and recommended that suggestions be solicited on the proper system to use in future censuses.

With regard to the 1935 place of residence questions, the evaluation maintained that the term "same place" had been confusing to the enumerators. In particular, it had been confused with "same house" and "same farm." As a result, problems of distinguishing among the various types of nonmigrants—same house, same farm, and same county—arose in the special editing operation. It was suggested that if these questions were used in the next census, the term "same city or town" be substituted for "same place."

The evaluation also indicated that there was bias in the migration data. As an example, it was maintained that the number of out-migrants was always too large for urban areas and for cities. It was also argued that there were some difficulties with reports on urban or rural residence of origin. The evaluation maintained that while the absolute numbers on origin were not right, there would still be a correlation with various characteristics, making some generalizations worthwhile. It was suggested that in order to obtain a good classification on the question, it would be necessary for the enumerator to return the exact place where the informant was found or to have precisely worded questions which stress the limits of incorporated places. An alternative raised by the evaluation suggested that if there was only need to know the county of origin, there would be no need to ask for the city of origin, and the problems with classifying the place of origin would be reduced.

Recommendations on the organization of special editing for the migration questions were also made. These suggestions concerned the use of roving editors to assist the editing process. It was also suggested that migration coding be arranged so that sorting could be done on the basis of a single column rather than the two columns required in 1940.

The 1940 census had included a question on the sample line asking each person 14 years of age and over questions about social security coverage. Comparison of the tabulations on these questions with estimates of the total number of persons living with account numbers indicated that the census reports for social security account number holders were seriously deficient. Social Security Board estimates indicated that there were about 47,000,000 persons with social security or railroad retirement numbers at the time of the census. Only 33,500,000 persons, however, were reported in the census as having account numbers. In addition, about 20,000,000 persons failed to report on the questions. Enumerators were reported to have had difficulty obtaining accurate reports from persons no longer in the labor force and from those who had received account numbers at one time but were no longer engaged in employment covered by the social security law. The serious deficiencies in the data prohibited publication of the tabulations on social security status, except for persons not in the labor force—cases for which the presence of an account number was used as an indication of previous labor market participation. The evaluation concluded that it would be unwise to attempt a similar inquiry in future censuses.

Underenumeration

The evaluation document indicated that attempts were made to estimate underenumeration by using the preliminary sample data (S-card). These estimates were made for the total population by age. The results were called "rather approximate," however, and were not reported. A suggestion was made that the subject, along with a closely related problem of age bias, be given thorough examination. It was also suggested that particular attention should be given to underenumeration of children under 5 years of age.

One attempt to estimate the extent of underenumeration in 1940 was made by Daniel O. Price (1947). He compared adjusted 1940 census figures with records from Selective Service registration to obtain the underenumeration estimate. The Selective Service Registration figures of June 30, 1941, showed the number of males 21–35 years old on October 16, 1940. Price assumed that this registration had been 100 percent complete. For comparison, he adjusted the census figures by "aging" the population by 6.5 months and by eliminating the number of deaths in the period. Comparisons were then made for both the total population and the Negro population in the age-sex group.

Price found that census figures for the total population in the age-sex group had an undercount of 2.8 percent. This figure rose slightly, to 3.1 percent, when adjusted for those in the armed forces (who were not subject to the compulsory registration). He maintained that this figure did not cause "great concern." The figures for the Negro age-sex group, however, indicated an adjusted estimate for underenumeration of 13 percent, a number which was cause for concern. In addition, he noted that there were significant variations in underenumeration of Negroes by state. While his analysis indicated that migration between the Census date and the Selective Service date accounted for much of the variation by state, this cause could not be separated from an assumption that Negroes in urban areas were less completely enumerated than were Negroes in rural areas.

In addition to these estimates of underenumeration, Price also calculated correlations between the discrepancies and population characteristics, such as density, percent urban, education, and telephones per 1,000 population. He reported that the correlation between the discrepancies and education was on the borderline of significance. Statistically significant correlations, however, were found between the discrepancies and net male migration, 1935–40 ($R = .50$), and between the discrepancies and the percentage population change, 1940–41 ($R = .59$). Price concluded that the variations by state in the discrepancies for the total population were made of two components: (1) the actual underenumeration, and (2) migration between the two periods. Since these effects could not be separated, however, it was not possible to obtain accurate estimates of underenumeration by states.

**APPENDICES
REFERENCES
INDEX**

**APPENDIX I
1940 CENSUS POPULATION AND
HOUSING SCHEDULES**

Figure 1: Population Schedule

State .... Incorporated place .... Ward of city .... Unincorporated place ....
(Name of unincorporated place having 100 or more inhabitants)

County .... Township or other
division of county .... Block Nos. .... Institution .... Name of institution and lines on which entries are made)

U S GOVERNMENT PRINTING OFFICE

DEPARTMENT OF COMMERCE—BUREAU OF THE CENSUS
SIXTEENTH CENSUS OF THE UNITED STATES: 1940
POPULATION SCHEDULE

16-100 A

S. D. No. .... E. D. No. .... Sheet No. **A**

Enumerated by me on ...., 1940. ...., *Enumerator.*

Figure 2: Heading Information Section of Population Schedule

73

Figure 3: "Basic Line" Section of Population Schedule

Figure 4: "Supplementary Lines" Section of Population Schedule

Figure 5: Housing (Occupied Dwelling) Schedule

**APPENDIX II
ORIGINAL INSTRUCTIONS AND ADDENDA
FOR GENERAL POPULATION CODING
(OPERATION 7)**

POPULATION
Form P-327A

REVISED EDITION
JULY 31, 1940

OPERATION 7

INSTRUCTIONS FOR GENERAL POPULATION CODING

GENERAL INSTRUCTIONS

1. The purpose of the general coding of the Population Schedules is two-fold: (1) to translate specified non-numerical entries on the Population Schedules into number codes, and (2) to edit specified items for consistency. Although a careful examination of entries for individual persons or households may reveal a number of inconsistencies, you are not to spend time in either finding or correcting any inconsistencies other than those specified in the instructions that follow. Other inconsistencies can be corrected more accurately and efficiently in later mechanical operations.

2. Before you begin the work of coding the schedules, study carefully the question headings and the symbols and explanatory notes that are printed in the bottom margin of the schedule, and read carefully the "Instructions to Enumerators," with particular attention to pars. 413 to 627, which will indicate how the schedules should have been filled out. Note, however, that you are not to correct any of the mistakes the enumerator may have made because he did not follow the printed and oral instructions, except those specified below.

3. Read also the "Instructions for Punching Population Individual Cards A and B," which will show how the puncher will use the various code numbers and corrections that you are to place on the schedule.

4. Make all corrections and code figures with red pencil.

5. <u>Cancelations</u>. Where it is necessary to cancel completely any item on the schedule, draw a single horizontal line through it, continuing the line for approximately the full width of the column in which the entry appears. Be careful not to extend any line further than necessary. Superfluous marking of the schedules is to be avoided. For example, if the enumerator has written "Na" in col. 16 for a person reported in col. 15 as born in the United States, draw a line through the "Na." Col. 16 will then be read as blank by the puncher.

6. <u>Corrections</u>. Where a correction is required in any column, first draw a single horizontal line through the original entry, placing the line somewhat below the center of the space between the lines on the schedule, and make the correct entry in the upper part of this space. Since the correction will always be made in red, it may, in part, be written over the original entry made in black. Make the new entry as legible as possible for the puncher. These corrections must be made within the space between the lines, since the schedule holder used by the puncher permits only one line to be visible at a time.

7. Where any entry is, at first glance, illegible or difficult to read, cross it out and rewrite it, as indicated above. For example, if the age in col. 11 is written so poorly that at first glance it might be read either "33" or "35," cancel the entry and rewrite it.

8. <u>Codes in columns with entries</u>. Special columns have been provided for most of the code numbers required, but occasionally it is necessary to write a code number in the same column as the enumerator's entry. For example, the entry "M" in col. 12 (Marital status) is sometimes to be coded "7." Handle all these cases as corrections, that is, first draw a horizontal line through the original entry and then write the code figure in the same space, at one side of the original entry if possible, otherwise above or below it.

9. Before beginning the editing and coding, check the sheet number in the upper right-hand corner of each schedule to make sure that the sheets are arranged in consecutive order and that the "A" side of each sheet is up. There may be four series of sheet numbers:

-2-

  a. Nos. 1, 2, 3, etc. for households enumerated in regular order.
  b. Nos. 51, 52, etc. for sheets originally numbered 100 or more, but changed in Operation 3.
  c. Nos. 61, 62, etc. for households and persons (except transients) not enumerated in regular order.
  d. Nos. 81, 82, etc. for transients enumerated as of the night of April 8.

10. Within each of these series there should be no sheet numbers omitted. There must be no sheets numbered 100 or more. If you find a sheet number missing in any one of the series, or a sheet numbered 100 or more, refer the portfolio to your Section Chief. On some sheets you may find that the enumerator's entry for sheet number has been changed in green or red pencil by the Population and Housing matching clerk. Accept such changes as correct. Do not change any sheet numbers.

11. No coding is to be done at the present time on cols. 1 to 5, 7, 28 to 30, 34, 35, or 45 to 50. You are to make no entries in code cols. F, J, and U. "In some cases a Problem Referral Slip will have been attached to the portfolio and will contain additional instructions on which columns are not to be coded. Follow the instructions given on this Referral Slip."

12. Each line of entries that has not been canceled must be coded in the columns specified, and in accordance with the instructions which follow. Canceled lines are those on which the line number in the extreme left-hand column of the schedule has been canceled in either red or green pencil. If a line has been incorrectly canceled and then restored, the line number will be encircled: such lines are to be coded as if they were uncanceled. When a whole side of a schedule is blank, cols. 1 to 34 are not to be coded. "However, cols. 36 to 44, even though blank, are always to be coded and the proper codes entered in code cols. K to T and V to Y unless the supplementary line has actually been canceled. Any uncanceled line which you find it impossible to code, such as one bearing the notation 'Here ends block _____,' should be referred to your Section Chief."

13. **Confidential Report on Wage or Salary Income.** Before proceeding with the general coding of the Population Schedules, arrange the Confidential Reports on Wage or Salary Income (Form P-16) in sheet and line number order, and transfer the information to col. 32 ("Amount of money wages or salary received") and col. 33 ("Did this person receive income of $50 or more from sources other than money wages or salary?"). These reports will be in the portfolio. Omit any dollar signs and cents. If the amount is over $5,000, enter "5000+" in col. 32 on the schedule. If the answer to question 33 is "Yes," or an amount equal to or greater than $50, enter "1" in col. 33 on the Population Schedule; if the answer to question 33 is "No," or an amount less than $50, enter "0"; if question 33 is unanswered, leave col. 33 blank.

CODING OF COLUMNS 6 TO 33

<u>Farm Residence</u>

14. <u>Col. 6. Does this household live on a farm?</u> Where the enumerator has entered "Yes" in col. 6 for the head, to indicate that the household lives on a farm, enter "1" in this column for all other members of the household, since farm residence must be punched on the cards for all members of the household (not merely on the card for the head). Do not change a "Yes" to "1." Do not make any entries in this column for members of households where the enumerator's entry for the head is "No," as blanks in this column will be punched as "No."

15. In the case of a city district where the enumerator has made a statement on the schedule that there are no farms in the district, he should have made no entries in col. 6. If there are none, do no coding in col. 6; but if the enumerator has made the general statement that there are no farms and has then entered "Yes" in col. 6 for one or more households, disregard the general statement and code the column as directed in par. 14.

16. If the enumerator has made <u>no entries whatever</u> in col. 6 for a household nor indicated <u>there are no farms</u> in his district, write "1" in col. 6 for each member of the household if a farm schedule number (indicating that a farm schedule was filled out) appears in col. 34 for <u>any</u> member of the household. Otherwise leave col. 6 blank.

17. If the enumerator has entered either "Yes" or "No" in col. 6 for the head of a household, you are <u>not</u> to change his entry, regardless of what may be entered in col. 34.

-3-

18. You must be particularly careful when you are coding col. 6 for persons enumerated on sheets numbered 61, 62, etc. (These were used by the enumerator for households and persons enumerated out of order.) If col. 6 has been left blank for a person enumerated out of order, you must refer (by means of the household visitation number shown in col. 3) to the entry in col. 6 for the head of the household of which the person is a member to determine whether you should write "1" in col. 6. But if the enumerator has entered either "Yes" or "No" opposite the name of a person enumerated out of order, you need not refer to the entry for the head of the household. When a whole household is enumerated out of order, col. 6 should, of course, be coded as if the household had been enumerated in regular order.

Relationship

19. <u>Col. 8, Relation of this person to the head of the household</u>. There should be an entry in this column for every person, designating his relationship to the head of the household. If the entry has been omitted, determine the probable relationship on the basis of the entry of the name in col. 7, the sex in col. 9, the age in col. 11, and the marital status in col. 12. Enter in col. A the code symbol for the relationship as follows:

Relationship	Code for Col. A
Head, either male or female, except head of a hotel, institution, etc.	0
Wife (of head)	1
Child (either son or daughter, including stepchild, but not including son-in-law or daughter-in-law)	2
Parent (including father-in-law, mother-in-law, stepfather, and stepmother)	3
Grandchild	4
Other relative of head (including son-in-law, brother-in-law, nephew, niece, brother, sister, uncle, aunt, grandparent, etc.)	5
Lodger, roomer, boarder, or partner, (wife, son, or daughter of a lodger, boarder, etc.)	6
Servant, maid, chauffeur, butler, housekeeper, etc.	7
Servant's wife, son, daughter; hired hand's wife, son, daughter; any other employee's wife, son, or daughter; or any other person not covered by other codes	8
Hired hand or other employee who is <u>not</u> a domestic servant	X

Resident in a hotel, institution, prison, school, household with 11 or more lodgers, etc. (except an employee and the members of his family who occupy a detached house or structure and are returned as a separate household in accordance with par. 427, Instructions to Enumerators):

Head (that is, manager, officer, superintendent, or warden) of hotel, institution, etc.--usually the first person listed	V
Any other person in a hotel, institution, etc.	9

20. You will encounter cases where the relationship entry in col. 8 has been edited in a previous operation. If an entry of "Head" has been canceled, code the person and all following persons in the household as members of the preceding household, determining their relationship to the head of the preceding household as best you can on the basis of the entries in cols. 7, 9, 10, 11, and 12. If the entry in col. 8 has been canceled and "Head" has been entered in either red or green pencil, code "0" in col. A on the line on which the

-4-

change has been made, and code the remaining persons in the new household (i. e., the household created by the editor's entry of "Head") on the basis of the entries in cols. 7, 9, 10, 11, and 12. Whenever you find, that the relationship has been edited, refer to the series of schedules beginning with sheet number 61, and code the relationship for each person of the household that is affected by the editor's change, before you proceed with the coding of other columns.

21. Whenever it is necessary for you to determine the relationship code for col. A on the basis of entries other than those in col. 8, do not cancel or correct the entry in col. 8. Simply enter the proper code in col. A.

22. If the person enumerated as the head of a household is a female whose husband is enumerated as a member of the same household, again do not change the enumerator's entries, but code the husband as the head (code 0), and his wife (whom the enumerator has entered as "Head") as wife (code 1). Note that this procedure is not to be followed in hotels and institutions (see par. 23 below).

23. For persons in institutions and hotels for whom the enumerator has made entries in col. 8 in accordance with the instructions in pars. 449 and 450 of the Instructions to Enumerators, the code "V" is to be entered in col. A for the person who is most probably the head of the household (manager, superintendent, principal, etc.) and the code "9" is to be entered for all other persons, whether they be inmates, employees, or guests, of the institution or hotel.

24. Also enter the code "V" in col. A for the head of any household in which there are 11 or more lodgers. Assign the code "9" to all other members of such a household whether they are related to the head or not.

25. Enumerators were instructed to return as a separate household an officer or employee and members of his family, if any, who live in separate quarters (in a detached home or structure, containing no inmates) on the grounds of an institution. (See par. 427 in Instructions to Enumerators.) The members of households so returned should be coded in the same manner as the members of households not living on institution grounds. If all of the resident employees of an institution live in separate quarters and are returned as separate households, you must assign to some inmate of the institution (usually the first inmate enumerated) the code "V," and to all of the other inmates, the code "9." Likewise, if a household contains 11 or more lodgers and all members of the household are lodgers, code the first lodger "V" and all of the other lodgers "9."

26. Note that the code "7" (servant) is to be used for employees who perform personal services for the household or some of its members, and the code "X" (hired hand, etc.) is to be used for employees whose labors contribute in some manner to the family income. Thus, a child's nurse should be coded "7" since her duties are not performed in connection with the operation of the family business or agricultural enterprise; a farm hand (a hired hand, or farm helper) should be coded "X" since his duties are performed in connection with the operation of the family farm.

27. Persons who have the entry of "servant," "housekeeper," or other domestic servant in col. 8 of the Population Schedule should have an entry of "Yes" in col. 21 or 24. If a person with such a relationship has the entry of "No, No, No, No, H" in cols. 21 to 25, code "1" in col. E. If there are no entries in cols. 28 and 29, enter the occupation "servant," "housekeeper," etc., as the case may be, in col. 28, and "private family" in col. 29.

28. Note also that persons returned as relatives (wife, son, daughter, etc.) of servants, of hired hands, or of other employees of the head are to be coded "8" in col. A, although the domestic servants themselves are to be coded "7" and the hired hands are to be coded "X."

29. Whenever you code "6" or "9" in col. A for a lodger, you must determine the total number of lodgers in the household. If there are 5 or more lodgers:
    a. Inspect col. 33 and if there is no entry of "Yes" in this column for some related member of the household, cancel the entry in col. 33 and enter "Yes" for the head of the household.

-5-

b. Inspect cols. 28 and 29 and if no related member of the household is reported as a lodginghouse proprietor or housekeeper:

(1) Enter "1" in col. E, and "Lodginghouse keeper" and "Lodginghouse" in cols. 28 and 29, respectively, for that <u>one</u> related member, if any, for whom "No" appears in cols. 21 to 24 and "H" has been entered in col. 25.

(2) If there are two or more related persons for whom there is "No" in cols. 21 to 24 and "H" has been written in col. 25, enter "1" in col. E, "Lodginghouse keeper" in col. 28, and "Lodginghouse" in col. 29, for the related person who, it appears, has the major housekeeping responsibility in the lodginghouse.

(3) If there is no related member of the household for whom "No" has been entered in cols. 21 to 24 and for whom "H" has been written in col. 25, make no entries in cols. E, 28, nor 29.

<u>Personal Description</u>

30. <u>Col. 9, Sex</u>. In col. 9 there must be an entry of "M" for every male person enumerated, and an entry of "F" for every female person enumerated. If col. 9 has been left blank for any person, an entry must be supplied. Determine the sex of the person from the name in col. 7 and the relationship in col. 8, and make the proper entry. Watch for possible inconsistencies in the enumerator's returns for sex. If he has entered "M" for both John Smith and his wife, Mary, the second entry is obviously wrong and should be corrected.

31. <u>Col. 10, Color or race</u>. There must be an entry in col. 10 for every person enumerated. If no entry has been made for a person, determine the race from the entries made for other persons in the same household. If col. 10 is blank for a whole household, enter for every person the color abbreviation of the head of the preceding household.

32. No coding of the entry in col. 10 will be required when it is "W" or "Neg." Any other entries in col. 10 are to be canceled and a code entered as follows:

Entry in Col. 10	Code
Mex	1 (white)
Col or C	2 (Negro)
In	3
Chi	4
Jp or Jap	5
Fil	6
Hin	7
Kor	8
Any other entry	Refer to Section Chief

33. <u>Col. 11, Age</u>. There should be an entry of a whole number or a fraction in col. 11 for every person enumerated. If col. 11 has been left blank or is illegible, or if it contains an entry of "Un," you must immediately make the required entries on Form P-306 (Persons of Unknown Age). This form must be securely fastened in the upper right-hand corner on the outside of the portfolio, when you return it to the control desk. No coding is necessary, in this operation, for persons who are 100 years old or over.

34. Pay particular attention to the enumerator's entries in col. 11 for children under one year of age. These entries are fractions (twelfths of a year; see footnote on schedule) and <u>must be written</u> within the space between the lines. There should be no possibility that the puncher will see only the numerator or denominator of the fraction and, for example, punch "11" instead of "11/12." (Should this happen, the infant who was actually only 11 months old would be counted as an 11-year-old person.) If you find any fraction that is not within the space between the lines, cancel the fraction, and code as follows:

-6-

Fraction	Code
0/12	V0
1/12	V1
2/12	V2
etc., to:	
9/12	V9
10/12	VX
11/12	VV

Note that you are to code the ages of infants under one year of age only when the fraction does not appear within the space between the lines in col. 11.

35. <u>Col. 12, Marital status</u>. There must be an entry in col. 12 for every person enumerated. If no entry has been made, supply the abbreviation for marital status (according to the heading of col. 12 of the schedule), on the basis of the other information on the schedule, especially col. 8 (Relationship) and col. 11 (Age). If it is impossible to determine what the marital code should be, enter "S" for "Single."

36. For every person whose marital status is reported as "M" (for married) but whose husband or wife was not enumerated as a member of the household, cancel the "M" in col. 12 and code "7" to indicate "Married, husband or wife not present."

Education

37. <u>Col. 13, Attended school</u>. If "Yes" or "No" has been entered in col. 13 by the enumerator, you are to accept that entry as correct. If the enumerator has left col. 13 blank, first inspect col. 25. If "S" (Student) is entered in col. 25, enter "Yes" in col. 13. If there is not an entry of "S" in col. 25, inspect the age given in col. 11 and enter "Yes" in col. 13 if the person is within the compulsory school ages of the State in question, and "No" for persons outside the compulsory school ages. The compulsory school ages in the various States are shown at the end of these instructions.

38. <u>Col. 14, Highest grade of school completed</u>. The entry in col. 14 is to be coded in col. B as follows:

Entry in col. 14	Code in col. B
0 or "None"	leave blank
1	1
2	2
3	3
4	4
5	5
6	6
7	7
8	8
H-1 or 9	9
H-2 or 10	10
H-3 or 11	20
H-4 or 12	30
C-1 or 13	40
C-2 or 14	50
C-3 or 15	60
C-4 or 16	70
C-5 or over, or 17 or over	80
Blank or Un:	
For a person under 6 years of age	leave blank
For a person 6 years old or over	90

Place of Birth and Citizenship

39. **Col. 15, Place of birth.** The place of birth entered in col. 15 is to be coded in col. C, according to the code schemes for States and countries given on the attached pages. When the name of a foreign country is entered in col. 15 and "Am Cit" is entered in col. 16, enter "X0" (American citizen born abroad) in col. C, rather than the code for the foreign country.

40. There must be a code symbol entered in col. C for every person. If the place of birth is omitted for some member of a household, determine it, if possible, from the entries for other members of the same household. (Do not write the name of the place of birth in col. 15 in such cases; simply enter the code in col. C.) If the enumerator could not find out with certainty in which country a person's birthplace was located on January 1, 1937, he was instructed to enter the name of the province, state, or city in which the person was born. In cases, therefore, where such place names are entered in the "Country of birth" column, refer to pages 18ff on which are listed foreign provinces, cities, and states with the correct code. If col. 15 is blank, and the code can not be determined from entries for other members of the household, proceed as follows:

    a. If the entry in col. 16 (Citizenship) is "Am Cit" or is blank, code "99" (for United States, State, Territory, or possession unknown);

    b. If "Na," "Pa," or "Al" is written in col. 16 (Citizenship), code "V8" (for foreign born, country of birth unknown).

41. If the entry "Indian Territory" appears on schedules for Oklahoma and adjacent States code it with the symbol for Oklahoma (86).

42. For a person born at sea ("At sea" entered in col. 15), if the entry in col. 16 (Citizenship) is "Am Cit," or if this column is blank, code X9 in col. C; if the entry in col. 16 is "Na," or "Al," code V9 in col. C.

43. The codes for persons of unknown or undeterminable birthplace and for persons born at sea can be summarized as follows:

Col. 15	Col. 16	Code for Col. C	Meaning of Code
Blank	Blank	99	(United States, State unknown)
Blank	Am Cit	99	(United States, State unknown)
Blank	Na	V8	(Foreign born, country unknown)
Blank	Pa	V8	(Foreign born, country unknown)
Blank	Al	V8	(Foreign born, country unknown)
At sea	Blank	X9	(Born at sea, American citizen)
At sea	Am Cit	X9	(Born at sea, American citizen)
At sea	Na	V9	(Born at sea, foreign)
At sea	Pa	V9	(Born at sea, foreign)
At sea	Al	V9	(Born at sea, foreign)

44. **Col. 16, Citizenship of the foreign born.** There should be an entry of "Na," "Pa," "Al," or "Am Cit" in col. 16 for every person born in a foreign country. All entries of "Am Cit" are to be canceled, but if "Am. Cit." appears frequently for foreign-born persons, refer the schedule to your Section Chief.

45. Check the correctness of the entries in col. 16, and, if possible, supply the missing entries. The two following rules will assist you in both of these processes:

    a. For all foreign-born children under the age of 18 both of whose parents either are alien (Al) or have their first papers (Pa), the entry should be "Al" (for Alien).

    b. For all foreign-born children under the age of 21, one of whose parents has been naturalized (Na), the entry should be "Na" (for Naturalized).

If you are unable to supply a missing entry for a foreign-born person, enter "4" (for unknown) in col. 16. (The code "4" should _never_ be entered in col. 16 for a person reported in col. 15 as born "At sea," see par. 43 above.)

46. If an entry has been made in col. 16 for a person born in the United States or one of its territories or possessions (coded in col. C from 50 to 99 or from X1 to X9), cancel the entry.

-8-

Instructions For Coding Migration
Cols. 17-20, Residence April 1, 1935

47. *General.* Every combination of entries in cols. 17-20 must be given a four-digit code in col. D except the following:
    a. An entry of "Same house," which is not to be coded.
    b. A dash in col. 17 for a child under 5 years old for which a dash (-) is to be entered in col. D.

Each of the four-digit codes represents a specifically named place of residence in 1935 except for the general codes that are assigned the following classes of persons:
    a. Those having an acceptable entry of "Same place," which is coded XOXO.
    b. Those who lived in the <u>same county</u> in 1935 as in 1940 but not in the same house or the same place. Entries for such persons, unless they involve a city of 100,000 or more, are coded XOV for the first 3 digits and given a fourth digit indicating the population group, such as "rural farm" or "city of 10,000 to 25,000."

Persons with acceptable entries of the categories listed above are classified as nonmigrants. The conditions under which such entries are accepted are given in paragraphs 49 to 57. Codes for specifically named places of residence in 1935 are given in code lists 1-7. These codes have been constructed on the following general principles:
    a. For cities of 100,000 or more there is a simple four-digit code, always beginning with 4, and ending with 7 as 4147 for Cincinnati.
    b. In all other codes, the first 2 digits represent the State, the third digit the subregion within the State, and the fourth digit the population group within the subregion.

Persons for whom acceptable entries indicate a specifically named place of residence in 1935 are called migrants. That is, if cities of 100,000 or more and independent cities are considered as equivalent to counties, migrants are all persons who are now living in a different "county" from that in which they lived in 1935.

48. In what follows it is assumed that entries are made in the proper order on the schedule. Where there are transpositions (such as State in col. 18 and county in col. 19), be governed by the nature of the entry and not by the number of the schedule column. When the place in col. 17 is not located in the county in col. 18 or the county in col. 18 is not located in the State in col. 19, you are to call the case to the attention of your Section Chief. Do not correct the enumerator's entries in cols. 17-20 unless directed to do so by your Section Chief.

49. <u>Same house.</u> Leave col. D blank for all entries of "Same house."

50. <u>Children under 5 years old</u>. For children under 5 years old there should be a dash in col. 17 and cols. 18-20 should be blank. If there are only blanks or dashes in cols. 17-20, check the age of the person as entered in col. 11:
    a. If the person is reported as under 5, enter a dash (-) in col. D.
    b. If the person is reported as 5 years old or over, determine in accordance with the instructions in paragraph 70 whether he should be given the same code as the head or should be coded XX09 for "unknown."

51. <u>Entries of "Same place" in col. 17</u>. "Same place" is to be accepted only for persons whose residence in 1940 was in an incorporated place. No enumeration district consists partly of incorporated and partly of unincorporated territory. You need inspect the heading of only the first sheet to see if the name of an incorporated place has been entered.
    a. If it has, write XOXO for all entries of "Same place."
    b. If it has not, treat all entries of "Same place" as if they represented an "R" in col. 17 with an entry of the same county in col. 18 as in the heading of the schedule. The procedure for coding is given below in paragraphs 55 to 57. Do <u>not</u> accept entries of "Same place" when the name of an <u>unincorporated</u> place is entered in the heading of the schedule.

52. A few minor civil divisions were classified as urban in 1930 under a special rule. Before you receive portfolios from such areas, they will be stamped "Urban--1930: Note in coding cols. 17-20" on line 16 of the Portfolio Memorandum. If the portfolio you are coding bears this notation, disregard the instructions in paragraph 51 and code all entries of "Same place" XOXO.

-9-

53. Where the enumerator should have written "Same place," he may occasionally have entered the name of the city, town, or village. Therefore you should keep in mind the name of the place in which the enumeration district on which you are working is located and code XOXO any cases where this incorporated place is reported in col. 17.

Residence in Same County in 1935 as in 1940

54. *Entries that are not to be coded same county.* As indicated in paragraph 47, cities of 100,000 or more are considered as distinct from counties. Therefore persons who now live in a city of 100,000 or more must never be coded XOV for "Same county." Likewise, persons who in 1935 lived in a city of 100,000 or more must never be coded XOV for "Same county." (If the person lived in the same city of 100,000 or more in 1940 as in 1935, he would, of course, be given the code XOXO for "Same place.") Cities of 100,000 or more are shown in List 4.

55. *Procedure for coding same county.* When col. 17 contains an entry other than "Same house" or other than an acceptable entry of "Same place", compare the county and State reported in cols. 18 and 19 with the county and State shown in the heading of the schedule, that is, the county in which the enumeration district on which you are working is located. If the county of 1935 residence is the same as the county of 1940 residence, enter XOV for the first three digits of the code in col. D. Note that, as stated in paragraph 51, an entry of "Same place" for a person not now living in an incorporated place is to be treated as if there were an "R" in col. 17 and the same county in col. 18.

56. Determine the fourth digit as follows: If a place that appears in the List of Urban Places (List 1), is entered in col. 17 disregard the entry in col. 17 and enter as the fourth digit of the code, the fourth digit of the code for that place as given in this list. Hence the complete code will be XOV4, XOV5, or XOV6. For example, if the place in col. 17 were Frederick, Frederick County, Maryland, it would be seen from the List of Urban Places that the usual code would be 7225. Therefore, if the enumeration district on which you are working is an area elsewhere in Frederick County, Maryland, you must write XOV5 for a person living in Frederick city in 1935.

57. If the entry in col. 17 is "R" or a place not in the List of Urban Places (that is, a place that had a population of less than 2,500 in 1930), the fourth digit of the code should be determined by the entry in col. 20 as follows:
If "No" in col. 20, code 1 (rural nonfarm)
If "Yes" in col. 20, code 2 (rural farm)
If col. 20 is blank:
    a. Code "1" (rural nonfarm) if an incorporated place of less than 2,500 in 1930 is entered in col. 17, just as if "No" were entered in col. 20. Rural incorporated places of 1,000-2,500 inhabitants in 1930 are given in List 2, and those of less than 1,000 are given in State table 5, of *Population, Volume I, 1930*.
    b. Code "3" (rural, farm residence unknown) if the entry in col. 17 is "R" or a place not on any of the lists of incorporated places.
The complete code will then be XOV1, XOV2, or XOV3.

Procedure for Migrants

58. *General procedure.* The above instructions cover entries representing nonmigrants (including persons who moved simply from one location to another within the same county). The remaining entries in cols. 17-20 are to be given codes representing geographic locations as indicated below. The first two digits, which represent the State, are usually the same as the codes for col. 15 (place of birth). The third digit represents the subregion of the State. These subregions are composed of groups of counties whose populations had similar characteristics in 1930. When there are more than 9 subregions in a State, an additional State code is used with the extra subregions. For example, the first two digits for a locality in Oneida County, New York, outside Utica city (which was a city of 100,000 or more) are not 56 but 5V. The proper State code is given in connection with the subregion code for each county in the List of Counties (List 3).

86

59. If the city or other place shown in col. 17 appears in the List of Urban Places (List 1), disregard the entry in col. 20 and enter the code given in the list except that if the city reported in col. 17 happens to be the city in which the person now lives, as shown in the heading of the schedule, the code should be XOXO for "Same place." (See paragraph 53 above.) Thus, a return of 1935 residence as Frederick, Frederick County, Maryland, found in any enumeration district outside Frederick County, would receive the code shown for Frederick in List 1. (See paragraph 56 above for the exceptional procedure of using only the last figure of the city's code in coding moves from a city to other parts of the county in which the city is located.)

60. If the entry in col. 17 is "R" or a place not in the List of Urban Places, get the first three digits of the code from the County List and supply the fourth digit on the basis of the entries in col. 20 as follows:
If "No" in col. 20, code 1 (rural nonfarm)
If "Yes" in col. 20, code 2 (rural farm)
If col. 20 is blank:
    a. Code "1" (rural nonfarm) if an incorporated place of less than 2,500 in 1930 is entered in col. 17, just as if "No" were entered in col. 20. Rural incorporated places of 1,000-2,500 inhabitants in 1930 are given in List 2, and those of less than 1,000 are given in State table 5, of Population, Volume I, 1930.
    b. Code "3" (rural, farm residence unknown) if the entry in col. 17 is "R" or a place not on any of the lists of incorporated places.

61. Cities of 100,000 or more. Cities of 100,000 or more in 1930 have codes which always begin with 4 and end with 7 and hence are in a different series from those for other places in the same State. Such cities are given alphabetically in a special list (List 4) as well as in the complete list of urban places. For a person living in one of these cities in 1935, simply write the code for the city. Disregard the entry in col. 20.

62. The independent cities in Virginia, given both in the County List and in the List of Urban Places, are not a part of any county. The enumerator, however, occasionally may have entered in col. 18 the name of the county that surrounded the independent city. Regard a move between an independent city and a county that surrounds it as a change of residence from one county to another. Hence, follow the procedure in paragraphs 58 to 60 above and not the procedure in paragraphs 55 to 57.

63. Places in two States or in two or more counties. Some places are located partly in one State or county and partly in another. The code lists show a separate code for each part of such places. The code to be supplied will therefore be based on the entry for the State or county as well as the name of the place. The parts of places located in two or more areas will be followed by a single asterisk (*) or a double asterisk (**). If the identifying information on State or county is missing, write the code for the part marked with a double asterisk (**). This part included a plurality of the population of the place in 1930. The procedure just described affects not only the determination of State or subregion but also the determination of whether or not the person lived in the same county in 1935 as in 1940. If the place entered in col. 17 is located both in the county of 1940 residence and in an adjacent county and if col. 18 is blank, you must make use of the double asterisk (**) designation to determine the county of residence in 1935. If the double asterisk (**) indicates that a plurality of the population of the place in col. 17 lived in the county of the person's 1940 residence, you must adopt the procedure of paragraphs 55 to 57. If, however, the double asterisk (**) indicates that a plurality of the population of this place lived in the adjacent county, you must adopt the procedure of paragraphs 58 to 60.

64. 1935 residence in foreign countries or outlying possessions. If the person lived in 1935 in a foreign country or an outlying possession of the United States, there should be an entry of the name of the country or possession in col. 19. Disregard entries in other columns, refer to the Code List for Foreign Countries and Outlying Possessions (List 5), and enter the code given there for the country or possession reported.

-11-

Incomplete Entries

65. If a place of less than 2,500 in 1930 (and hence one not in the List of Urban Places) is entered in col. 17 and there is no county given in col. 18, you may find the county with the first three digits of the code by referring to the List of Incorporated Places of 1,000 to 2,500 (List 2). If the place is not in this list, refer the case to your Section Chief. For a 1935 residence in a New England State, the name of a town (not an incorporated place but a minor civil division) may be entered in col. 17. If the county is not entered in col. 18, determine the first three digits of the code from the List of New England Towns not Classified as Urban (List 7). With such a minor civil division entered in col. 17, the fourth digit of the code must always be one for a rural population group, never 4, 5, or 6.

66. If the county but not the State is given, assume that the State is the one in the heading of the schedule if there is a county of this name in the State. (See County List.) If there is not such a county in the State, refer the case to your Section Chief.

67. If only the county and State are given with no entry in col. 17 or 20, determine the first three digits by reference to the County Code List. To determine the fourth digit, see if the county is marked with an asterisk in the County Code List. Counties so marked contained no urban places in 1930. If the county contained no urban places (i. e., was purely rural), you will know that the entry in col. 17 should have been "R". In such a case, write "3" for the fourth digit to indicate rural, farm residence unknown. If the county was not purely rural, write "8" for the fourth digit. If the county in col. 18 is the same as that in the heading of the schedule and the county was purely rural, code X0V3. If the county was not purely rural, code X0V8.

68. Where col. 17 is blank, with county and State, State alone, or county alone given, and there is an entry of "Yes" in col. 20 write "2" for the fourth digit (regardless of whether the county is purely rural or not). For a "No" in col. 20 with the county given in col. 18, write "1" for the fourth digit only if the county is found to have been purely rural. (See paragraph 67.) Otherwise, write "8" for the fourth digit, just as if col. 20 were blank.

69. If there is no county in col. 18, an "R" in col. 17, and a State in col. 19, determine the first two digits of the code from the State codes given for col. 15 (Place of birth) and write "0" for the third digit. (An entry of "0" for the third digit indicates that the sub-region is unknown.) Write 1, 2, or 3 for the fourth digit according to the entry in col. 20. If col. 17 is blank and there is an entry in col. 20, determine the fourth digit according to the procedure in paragraph 68. If col. 17 and col. 20 are both blank, write "8" for the fourth digit.

70. Some enumerators systematically left blanks or entered dashes in cols. 17-20 for members of the household other than the head if their 1935 residence was the same as that of the head. Give these persons the same code as the head. When these columns are only occasionally left blank, give only related persons the same code as the head, and for unrelated persons write XX09 for "Unknown." If the entries for a related person are only partially complete and those for the head are more complete and if all the entries made by the enumerator for the related person agree with those for the head, give the same code to the entries for the other member of the family as was given to the head.

71. Code XX09 if there is no information whatever in cols. 17-20 for a person 5 years old or over and the code cannot be determined on the basis of the entries made for the head of the household (paragraph 70). Also write XX09 if it is impossible to determine from the entries the State in which the person was living.

72. **Illustrative coding of incomplete entries.**

Col. 17	Col. 18	Col. 19	Col. 20	Code	Paragraph
R	Barbour	Alabama	---	8273	60
Clayton	Barbour	Alabama	---	8271	60
Blue Springs	Barbour	Alabama	---	8271	60
---	Autauga	Alabama	---	8233	67
---	Barbour	Alabama	---	8278	67
---	Barbour	Alabama	Yes	8272	68
---	---	Alabama	Yes	8202	68
---	Autauga	Alabama	No	8231	68
---	Barbour	Alabama	No	8278	68
---	---	Alabama	No	8208	68
---	---	Alabama	---	8208	69
R	---	Alabama	No	8201	69
R	---	Alabama	Yes	8202	69
R	---	Alabama	---	8203	69
R	---	---	Yes	XX09	71

73. **Summary of Migration Code.** Some of the more important parts of the Migration Code scheme may be summarized as follows:

```
Blank   Same house
 --     Children under 5
XOXO    Same place
XOV     First three digits of the code for "Same county."
XX09    No entry
```
Fourth digit indicates population group, thus:
1. Rural nonfarm
2. Rural farm
3. Rural, farm residence unknown
4. Urban place of 2,500 to 10,000
5. Urban place of 10,000 to 25,000
6. Urban place of 25,000 to 100,000
7. City of 100,000 or more
8. Incomplete entries: foreign country or outlying possession
9. No entry

MIGRATION CODE LISTS

List 1. Urban places in 1930.
List 2. Incorporated places of 1,000-2,500 in 1930.
List 3. Counties.
List 4. Cities of 100,000 or more in 1930.
List 5. Foreign countries and outlying possessions.
List 6. States. (Cities of 100,000 or more have separate codes. See List 4.)
List 7. New England towns not classified as urban in 1930.

-13-
Employment Status

74. **Cols. 21 to 25, Work Status, week March 24-30.** The entries in cols. 21-25 are to be coded in col. E. If there is a "Yes" in cols. 21-24, the code for col. E will be the last digit of the number of the column in which the first "Yes" appears (that is, "1" for col. 21, "2" for col. 22, etc.) with the following exception: When there is a "Yes" in both cols. 21 and 22, disregard the "Yes" in col. 21, and code "2" in col. E for the "Yes" in col. 22. If the entry "Inst." appears in col. 21, disregard all other entries in cols. 21-25, and code the entry "9" in col. E. If "Yes" does not appear in cols. 21-24, the code for col. E is to be based on the entry in col. 25 in accordance with the code scheme below. If "Yes" has not been entered in cols. 21-25, and col. 25 is blank, code as follows:

    a. If there is a number in col. 26, and no entry of 1 or more in col. 27, code "1" in col. E.

    b. If there is an entry of 1 or more in col. 27, and no entry of 1 or more in col. 26, code "3" in col. E.

    c. If there is no entry in either col. 26 or col. 27, or if there is an entry of 1 or more in both columns, leave code col. E blank.

If a code has been entered in col. E for a person enumerated on a line marked "Suppl. Quest.", accept the entry as correct.

75. The code scheme for col. E can be summarized as follows:

Schedule Entries	Code for Col. E
If there is any "Yes" in cols. 21-24:	
If the "Yes" is in col. 21	1
If the "Yes" is in col. 22	2
If "Yes" occurs in col. 21 and col. 22 both	2
If the first "Yes" is in col. 23	3
If the first "Yes" is in col. 24	4
If "Inst." is entered in col. 21	9
If there is no "Yes" in cols. 21-24 and no "Inst." in col. 21, and:	
If "H" occurs in col. 25	5
If "S" occurs in col. 25	6
If "U" occurs in col. 25	7
If "Ot" occurs in col. 25	8
If no "H," "S," "U," or "Ot" occurs in col. 25, and:	
If "1" or more in col. 26	1
If "1" or more in col. 27	3
If "1" or more in both cols. 26 and 27	blank
If blank in both cols. 26 and 27	blank

76. All men reported as residing in CCC Camps should be returned as engaged in Public Emergency Work, and therefore are to be coded "2" in col. E, even though cols. 21-24 are blank or a "Yes" has been entered in a column other than 22. If an E.D. for a CCC Camp contains the names of any women, refer the portfolio to your Section Chief.

77. Before you enter the code "9" in col. E (that is, when "Inst." is entered in col. 21), see whether you have coded the head of the household "V" in col. A; if not, refer the household to your Section Chief. If you enter the code "9" in col. E, you must cancel any entries that appear in cols. 26 and 27 and enter a code in col. 26 to identify the type of institution, as follows:

Type of Institution	Code in Col. 26
State prison, penitentiary, prison farm or camp, reformatory	01
Local jail, workhouse, house of correction, county penal farm or camp	02
Mental institution (institution, home or colony for mentally diseased or defective or epileptic)	03
Home for the aged, infirm, or needy (including orphanages)	04
Other and unknown (refer to Section Chief)	05

- 14 -

The enumerators were instructed to identify the type of institution in the heading of the schedule, and in the case of an inmate of a penal institution to enter either his prison number, or "prisoner," in col. 8. (See pars. 410 and 449, Instructions to Enumerators.) Refer to your Section Chief cases where the type of institution is indefinite or unknown.

78. <u>Col. 26, Hours worked</u>. If the code in col. E is not "1," cancel any entry in col. 26 other than the entry you made in accordance with par. 77. If col. 26 is blank, leave it blank. If the code in col. E is "1" and the entry in col. 26 is 100 or more, cancel the entry in col. 26 and write "99."

79. <u>Col. 27, Duration of unemployment</u>. If the code in col. E is neither "2" nor "3" and there is an entry in col. 27, cancel the entry in col. 27. If col. 27 is blank, leave it blank. If the code in col. E is "2" or "3" and the entry in col. 27 is 100 or over, cancel the entry and code according to the following scheme:

Entry in col. 27	Code
100-124 weeks	V0
125-149 weeks	V1
150-199 weeks	V2
200-249 weeks	V3
250 weeks or more	V4

80. <u>Cols. 28, 29, 30, and col. F</u>. Cols. 28, 29, 30, and col. F are not to be coded at this time.

81. <u>Col. 31, Weeks worked</u>. If there is an entry in this column of more than 52 weeks, cancel and write "52."

82. <u>Col. 32, Money wages or salary</u>. If col. 32 is blank, leave it blank, unless the entry in col. 31 is "0," in which case you must enter "0" in col. 32. If a fraction of a dollar has been entered in col. 32, cancel the fraction. If the entry in col. 32 is 6000 or over, cancel the entry and write "5000+."

83. <u>Col. 33, Other income</u>. If an amount has been entered in col. 33, cancel the amount and enter "1" (for "Yes") if the amount is $50 or more, or enter "0" (for "No") if the amount is less than $50. If no entry has been made in col. 33, leave the column blank. If the enumerator has consistently entered "No" in col. 33 for persons returned as residing in a CCC Camp or on an NYA resident project, you should cross out the reply of "No" and enter "1" (for "Yes") for all persons reporting seven or more weeks of employment in 1939.

84. <u>Col. 34, Number of Farm Schedule</u>. No coding is to be done in col. 34.

Supplementary Questions

85. Uncanceled supplementary lines are to be coded in accordance with the instructions in pars. 86 to 111, even when cols. 35 to 50 are completely blank. Enter the code symbol "8" in col. I if cols. 36-50 for that person are completely blank, or have been completely canceled.

86. <u>Col. 35, Name</u>. No coding is to be done in this column.

87. <u>Cols. 36 and 37, Place of birth of father and mother</u>. The place of birth of father and mother are to be coded in col. G. When cols. 36 and 37 are blank, it may be that either or both of the parents of the supplementary person were enumerated on the main schedule, in which case the code for col. G may be determined from col. 15. It is not necessary to fill in the entries for cols. 36 and 37. Select the country of birth to be coded, as shown below, and supply the symbol from the list of countries on the attached pages.
    a. Leave col. G blank if the entries in cols. 36 and 37 indicate that both parents of the person were born in the United States, its territories, possessions, at sea, or in a place that cannot be determined.
    b. If the entry in col. 36 indicates that the person's father was born in a foreign country, enter in col. G the code for the country specified in col. 36, and disregard the entry for the mother.

91

- 15 -

  c. If the entries in cols. 36 and 37 indicate that the person's father was born in the United States, its territories, possessions, at sea, or in a place that cannot be determined, and that his mother was born in a foreign country, enter in col. G the code for the country of birth of the mother.

  88. <u>Col. 38, Mother tongue (or native language)</u>. Code the entries in col. 38 in code col. H in accordance with the symbols for mother tongue on the coding scheme attached. If the entry in col. 38 is English, leave code col. H blank. If col. 38 is blank code 49 in col. H.

  89. <u>Cols. 39, 40, and 41, Veterans</u>. Cols. 39 to 41 are to be coded in col. I according to the code scheme shown below. It will be noticed that when "S," "R," or "Ot" is entered in col. 41, it is not necessary to inspect cols. 39 and 40.
    a. If the entry in col. 41 is "S" code "3" in col. I.
    b. If the entry in col. 41 is "R" code "5" in col. I.
    c. If the entry in col. 41 is "Ot" code "6" in col. I.
    d. If the entry in col. 41 is "W" inspect col. 40:
     (1) If the entry in col. 40 is "No" or if this column is blank, code "1" in col. I.
     (2) If the entry in col. 40 is "Yes" code "2" in col. I.
    e. If the entry in col. 41 is "SW" inspect col. 40:
     (1) If the entry in col. 40 is "No" or if this column is blank, code "4" in col. I.
     (2) If the entry in col. 40 is "Yes" code "2" in col. I.
    f. If col. 41 is blank inspect col. 39:
     (1) If the entry in col. 39 is "Yes," code "7" in col. I.
     (2) If the entry in col. 39 is "No" or if this column is blank, leave col. I blank.

  90. The code for col. I can be summarized as follows:

Col. 39	Col. 40	Col. 41	Code for Col. I	Meaning of Code
Disregard	Disregard	S	3	Spanish American
Disregard	Disregard	R	5	Regular Establishment
Disregard	Disregard	Ot	6	Other Veteran
Disregard	No or blank	W	1	World War
Disregard	Yes	W or SW	2	Child-World-Father dead
Disregard	No or blank	SW	4	Spanish and World
Yes	Disregard	Blank	7	Veteran-Service Unknown
No or blank	Disregard	Blank	Leave Blank	Not veteran

  91. <u>Cols. 42, 43, and 44, Social Security</u>. If "Yes" is entered in both cols. 42 and 43 and "1," "2," or "3" is entered in col. 44, no coding of these questions will be necessary. For other combinations of entries in cols. 42, 43, and 44, the entry in col. 44, if there is one, must be canceled and the combination coded in accordance with the following scheme:

Col. 42	Col. 43	Col. 44	Code for Col. 44	Meaning of Code
No	No or blank	None or blank	0	Does not have S.S.No.
Yes	No	Blank	4	Has S.S.No. No deductions
Yes	Yes	Blank	5	Has S.S.No., amount of deductions unknown
Yes	Blank	Blank	6	Has S.S.No., unknown whether deductions
Any other combinations			Leave blank	Unknown S.S. status

  92. <u>Cols. 45, 46, 47, and code col. J, Usual occupation, industry, and class of worker</u>. Cols. 45, 46, and 47, and code col. J, are not to be coded at this time.

  93. <u>Cols. 48, 49, and 50, For all women who are or have been married</u>. Cols. 48, 49, and 50 are not to be coded at this time.

-16-

94. Col. K. Ten. (4). Code in col. K for each person enumerated on a supplementary line as follows:

    a. Code "0" for owned, if "O" appears in col. 4 on the line for the head of the household of which the person on the supplementary line is a related member (code 0, 1, 2, 3, 4, or 5 in col. A).

    b. Code "1" for rented, if "R" appears in col. 4 on the line for the head of the household of which the person on the supplementary line is a related member.

    c. Code "2" if the person on the supplementary line is a lodger, servant, hired hand, etc., or is a member of an institutional household (code 6, 7, 8, 9, V, or X in col. A).

95. Col. L, V-R (5). The value of an owned home ("0" in col. K) or the monthly rental of a rented home ("1" in col. K) must be coded in col. L for each person enumerated on a supplementary line according to the following scheme:

Value	Rental	Code for Col. L
Under $500	Under $5	0
$500 to $999	$5 to $9	1
$1,000 to $1,499	$10 to $14	2
$1,500 to $1,999	$15 to $19	3
$2,000 to $2,999	$20 to $29	4
$3,000 to $3,999	$30 to $39	5
$4,000 to $4,999	$40 to $49	6
$5,000 to $7,499	$50 to $74	7
$7,500 to $9,999	$75 to $99	8
$10,000 or more	$100 or more	9
Unknown	Unknown	Leave blank

96. The value or rental of the home should appear in col. 5 on the line for the head of the household of which the person is a member, but if it appears in col. 5 for some related member of the household other than the head, it may still be used. If col. 5 is blank or "Un" for all related members of the household including the head, leave col. L blank, regardless of what may be entered in col. 5 for any unrelated member of the household. Leave col. L blank for a person who has been coded "2" in col. K (that is, all those coded 6, 7, 8, 9, V, or X in col. A).

97. Col. M, Fm. res. and Sex (6 and 9). The entry for col. M is to be supplied on the basis of a combination of the entries in cols. 6 and 9 for this person. If there is a "No" or a blank in col. 6 and the person is reported as male ("M" in col. 9), enter "1" in col. M. If there is a "No" or blank in col. 6 and the person is reported as female ("F" in col. 9), code "2" in col. M. If there is a "Yes" or a "1" in col. 6 and an "M" in col. 9, code "3" in col. M. If there is a "Yes" or "1" in col. 6 and an "F" in col. 9 for this person, code "4" in col. M. Never leave col. M blank.

98. The codes for col. M can be summarized as follows:

Col. 6	Col. 9	Code for Col. M	Meaning of Code
No or blank	M	1	Nonfarm male
No or blank	F	2	Nonfarm female
Yes or 1	M	3	Farm male
Yes or 1	F	4	Farm female

99. Col. N, Color and Nativity. (10, C, 36, and 37). The code for col. N is to be supplied from a combination of the entries for the person in cols. 10, C, 36, and 37. Supply the code for col. N in accordance with the following scheme:

-17-

Col. 10	First digit of code in Col. C	Col. 36	Col. 37	Code for Col. N	Meaning of Code
W or 1	X,5,6,7,8, or 9	A state, territory or possession of the U.S., or blank	A state, territory or possession of the U.S., or blank	Leave blank	Native white, both parents native
W or 1	X,5,6,7,8, or 9	A foreign country	A foreign country	1	Native white, both parents foreign born
W or 1	X,5,6,7,8, or 9	A foreign country	A state, territory or possession of the U.S., or blank	2	Native white, father foreign born
W or 1	X,5,6,7,8, or 9	A state, territory or possession of the U.S., or blank	A foreign country	3	Native white, mother foreign born
W or 1	V,0,1,2, or 3	Disregard	Disregard	4	Foreign-born white
Neg	Disregard	Disregard	Disregard	5	Negro
3-9	Disregard	Disregard	Disregard	6	Other race

100. **Col. O, Age (11).** Transcribe the age (or the code for age if age has been coded) for the person from col. 11 to col. O. If col. 11 is blank or contains an entry of "Un," leave col. O blank; the fact that the age is unknown is already recorded on the Persons of Unknown Age form. (See par. 33 above.)

101. **Col. P, Mar. st. (12).** Enter a code in col. P for the marital status of the person according to the entry in col. 12 as follows:

```
         Entry in Col. 12   Code in Col. P
              S ................ 1
              M ................ 2
              Wd ............... 3
              D ................ 4
              7 ................ 7
```

102. **Col. Q, Gr. com. (B).** Transcribe the code which appears in col. B for the person to col. Q. If col. B is blank, leave col. Q blank.

103. **Col. R, Cit. (16).** Enter a code in col. R for the citizenship status of a person according to the entry in col. 16 as follows:

```
         Entry in Col. 16   Code in Col. R
      If blank or canceled....Leave blank
              Na ............... 1
              Pa ............... 2
              Al ............... 3
              4 ................ 4
```

-18-

104. <u>Col. S, Wrk. st. (E)</u>. Transcribe the code that appears in col. E for the person to col. S. If col. E is blank, leave col. S blank.

105. <u>Col. T, Hrs. Wkd. or Dur. Un. (26 or 27)</u>. An entry is to be made in col. T only when the entry in col. S is 1, 2, or 3. When there is any other entry (i.e., 4, 5, 6, 7, 8, 9, 0, or blank) leave col. T blank. Code the entries in cols. 26 and 27 in accordance with the following schemes. Note that where the original entry in cols. 26 or 27 was 100 or more, the entry has been coded, and the code for col. T is based on this code and not the original entry.

If 1 in Col. S		If 2 or 3 in Col. S	
Entry in Col. 26	Code for Col. T	Entry in Col. 27	Code for Col. T
0 to 13	0	Under 3	0
14 to 29	1	3 to 6	1
30 to 34	2	7 to 10	2
35 to 39	3	11 to 14	3
40	4	15 to 23	4
41 to 44	5	24 to 35	5
45 to 47	6	36 to 49	6
48	7	50 to 99	7
49 to 59	8	V0, V1	8
60 to 69	9	V2, V3	9
70 to 99	V	V4	V
Blank or canceled	Leave blank	Blank or canceled	Leave blank

106. <u>Col. U, Occupation, Industry, and Class of Worker (F)</u>. No entry is to be made in col. U at this time.

107. <u>Col. V, Wks wkd. (31)</u>. Enter a code in col. V according to the entry in col. 31 for the person as follows:

Entry in Col. 31	Code in Col. V
0	0
1 to 6	1
7 to 10	2
11 to 14	3
15 to 23	4
24 to 31	5
32 to 35	6
36 to 47	7
48 to 49	8
50 to 52	9
Blank	Leave blank

108. <u>Col. W, Wages (32)</u>. If col. 32 is blank (or if the entry in col. 32 has been canceled) for the person, leave col. W blank. If there is an entry of 1000 or more in col. 32 for the person, transcribe the first two digits of the entry to col. W. If there is an entry of any number from 100 to 999 transcribe the first digit of the number and precede by an 0 in col. W. If any number from 1 to 99 is entered in col. 32 code 0V in col. W. If the entry in col. 32 is "0" write "00" in col. W.

109. <u>Col. X, Ot. inc. (33)</u>. Transcribe the entry for the person from col. 33 to col. X as follows:

Entry in Col. 33	Code in Col. X
Blank	Leave blank
Yes or 1	1
No or 0	0

110. <u>Col. Y</u>. Transcribe the code for the relationship entered in col. A.

111. When you have completed the coding for all of the schedules in that portfolio, make the proper notation on line 6 "General coding" of the Portfolio Memorandum to indicate that the process has been completed, and return the portfolio to the control desk.

GEOGRAPHICAL CODE LIST FOR STATES

	Code
NEW ENGLAND:	
Maine	50
New Hampshire	51
Vermont	52
Massachusetts	53
Rhode Island	54
Connecticut	55
MIDDLE ATLANTIC:	
New York	56
New Jersey	57
Pennsylvania	58
EAST NORTH CENTRAL:	
Ohio	59
Indiana	60
Illinois	61
Michigan	62
Wisconsin	63
WEST NORTH CENTRAL:	
Minnesota	64
Iowa	65
Missouri	66
North Dakota	67
South Dakota	68
Nebraska	69
Kansas	70

	Code
SOUTH ATLANTIC:	
Delaware	71
Maryland	72
District of Columbia	73
Virginia	74
West Virginia	75
North Carolina	76
South Carolina	77
Georgia	78
Florida	79
EAST SOUTH CENTRAL:	
Kentucky	80
Tennessee	81
Alabama	82
Mississippi	83
WEST SOUTH CENTRAL:	
Arkansas	84
Louisiana	85
Oklahoma	86
Texas	87
MOUNTAIN:	
Montana	88
Idaho	89
Wyoming	90
Colorado	91

	Code
MOUNTAIN (Cont'd.)	
New Mexico	92
Arizona	93
Utah	94
Nevada	95
PACIFIC:	
Washington	96
Oregon	97
California	98
United States, State not reported	99
American citizen born abroad (Am. cit. in col. 16)	X0
Outlying possessions:	
Alaska	X1
Hawaii	X2
Puerto Rico	X3
Philippine Islands	X4
Virgin Islands	X5
Panama Canal Zone	X6
Guam	X7
Samoa (American)	X8
At sea (blank or Am. cit. in col. 16)	X9

ALPHABETICAL CODE LIST FOR STATES
(Includes outlying possessions)

	Code
Alabama	82
Alaska	X1
Arizona	93
Arkansas	84
California	98
Colorado	91
Connecticut	55
Delaware	71
District of Columbia	73
Florida	79
Georgia	78
Guam	X7
Hawaii	X2
Idaho	89
Illinois	61
Indiana	60
Iowa	65
Kansas	70
Kentucky	80
Louisiana	85
Maine	50

	Code
Maryland	72
Massachusetts	53
Michigan	62
Minnesota	64
Mississippi	83
Missouri	66
Montana	88
Nebraska	69
Nevada	95
New Hampshire	51
New Jersey	57
New Mexico	92
New York	56
North Carolina	76
North Dakota	67
Ohio	59
Oklahoma	86
Oregon	97
Panama Canal Zone	X6
Pennsylvania	58
Philippine Islands	X4
Puerto Rico	X3

	Code
Rhode Island	54
Samoa (American)	X8
South Carolina	77
South Dakota	68
Tennessee	81
Texas	87
Utah	94
Vermont	52
Virginia	74
Virgin Islands	X5
Washington	96
West Virginia	75
Wisconsin	63
Wyoming	90
United States, State not reported	99
American citizen born abroad (Am. cit. in col. 16)	X0
At sea (blank or Am. cit. in col. 16)	X9

GEOGRAPHIC CODE LIST FOR FOREIGN COUNTRIES: 1940

Country	Code
NORTHWESTERN EUROPE:	
England	00
Scotland	01
Wales	02
Northern Ireland	03
Irish Free State (Eire)	04
Norway	05
Sweden	06
Denmark	07
Iceland	0V
Netherlands (Holland)	08
Belgium	09
Luxemburg	0X
Switzerland	10
France	11
CENTRAL EUROPE:	
Germany	12
Poland	13
Danzig	1V
Czechoslovakia	14
Austria	15
Hungary	16
Yugoslavia	17

Country	Code
EASTERN EUROPE:	
Russia (Soviet Republic - U.S.S.R.)	18
Lithuania	19
Latvia	1X
Estonia	20
Finland	21
Rumania	22
Bulgaria	23
Turkey in Europe	2V
SOUTHERN EUROPE:	
Greece	24
Albania	25
Italy	26
Spain	27
Portugal	28
EUROPE (not specified)	2X
ASIA:	
Palestine	29
Syria	30
Turkey in Asia	31
China	32

Country	Code
ASIA (Cont'd.):	
Japan	33
India	3V
Other Asia	3X
AMERICA:	
Canada-French	34
Canada-English	35
Newfoundland	36
Mexico	37
Cuba	38
Other West Indies[1]	39
Central America	V0
South America	V1
ALL OTHER:	
Africa	V2
Australia	V3
Azores	V4
Other Atlantic Islands	V5
Pacific Islands	V6
Country not specified (Na, Pa, or Al in col. 16)	V8
At sea (Na, Pa, or Al in col. 16)	V9

[1] Except possessions of the United States: Puerto Rico and Virgin Islands.

ALPHABETICAL CODE LIST FOR FOREIGN COUNTRIES

	Code
Africa	V2
Albania	25
Asia (not specified)	3X
Australia	V3
Austria	15
Azores	V4
Belgium	09
Bulgaria	23
Canada-French	34
Canada-English	35
Central America	V0
China	32
Cuba	38
Czechoslovakia	14
Danzig	1V
Denmark	07
England	00
Estonia	20
Europe (not specified)	2X
Finland	21
France	11
Germany	12

	Code
Greece	24
Holland	08
Hungary	16
Iceland	0V
India	3V
Irish Free State (Eire)	04
Italy	26
Japan	33
Latvia	1X
Lithuania	19
Luxemburg	0X
Mexico	37
Netherlands	08
Newfoundland	36
Northern Ireland	03
Norway	05
Palestine	29
Poland	13
Portugal	28
Rumania	22
Russia	18
Scotland	01

	Code
South America	V1
Spain	27
Sweden	06
Switzerland	10
Syria	30
Turkey in Asia	31
Turkey in Europe	2V
U. S. S. R.	18
Wales	02
West Indies (except Cuba, Puerto Rico, and Virgin Islands)	39
Yugoslavia	17
Atlantic Islands (except Azores, Iceland, and West Indies)	V5
Pacific Islands	V6
Country not specified (Na, Pa, or Al in col. 16)	V8
At sea (Na, Pa, or Al in col. 16)	V9

MINIMUM AGE PERIODS OF COMPULSORY SCHOOL ATTENDANCE, BY STATES

(This table is based on both the compulsory school attendance laws and the child labor laws permitting exemptions for employment.)

State	Age (both years inclusive)	State	Age (both years inclusive)	State	Age (both years inclusive)
Alabama	7 to 13	Louisiana:		North Dakota	7 to 13
		Orleans Parish	8 to 13		
Arizona	8 to 13	Bal. of State	7 to 13	Ohio	6 to 15
Arkansas	7 to 13	Maine	7 to 14	Oklahoma	7 to 13
California	8 to 14	Maryland	7 to 13	Oregon	7 to 13
Colorado	8 to 13	Massachusetts	7 to 15	Pennsylvania	8 to 15
Connecticut	7 to 15	Michigan	7 to 14	Rhode Island	7 to 15
Delaware	7 to 13	Minnesota	8 to 13	South Carolina	7 to 15
Dist. Columbia	7 to 13	Mississippi	7 to 13	South Dakota	8 to 13
Florida	7 to 13	Missouri	7 to 13	Tennessee	7 to 13
Georgia	8 to 13	Montana	8 to 15	Texas	7 to 14
Idaho	8 to 13	Nebraska	7 to 13	Utah	8 to 15
Illinois	7 to 13	Nevada	7 to 13	Vermont	8 to 13
Indiana	7 to 13	New Hampshire	8 to 13	Virginia	7 to 13
Iowa	7 to 13	New Jersey	7 to 13	Washington	8 to 13
Kansas	7 to 13	New Mexico	6 to 13	West Virginia	7 to 15
Kentucky	7 to 13	New York	7 to 15	Wisconsin	7 to 15
		North Carolina	7 to 15	Wyoming	7 -- No minimum

May 11, 1940
8951

SIXTEENTH CENSUS
POPULATION
Form P-327A-1

ADDENDUM 1

INTREPRETATIONS AND ADDITIONAL INSTRUCTIONS FOR OPERATION 7

1. <u>Cols. 4 and 5</u>. These cols. are to be edited only for those households in which some member appears on a supplementary line (See paragraph 22, Operation 7, Instructions for General Population Coding). When you code as head a person other than the one originally returned as head do not transfer the household data appearing in cols. 4 and 5 from the original head (as entered by the enumerator) to the present head.

2. In nonfarm districts ("No" in col. 6) entries in Col. 5 of $100 or more for rented homes are acceptable and should not be referred for special editing if the entry in col. 32 is $5,000+ or if the person has an occupation usually commanding a high income and has an entry of "Yes" in col. 33.

3. Values of owned homes in the same range as the rentals for a farm district should be referred for special editing.

4. <u>Col. 6</u>. Paragraph 14. If the enumerator has entered "Yes" or "No" for each member of the household, the second and consecutive entries should not be canceled or coded. "No" in col. 6 is not to be changed to "Yes" even though there may be a Farm Schedule entered in col. 34. If "Yes" and "No" have been entered for members of the same family refer the folio to your Section Chief.

5. <u>Col. 8</u>. Paragraph 19. Read carefully paragraph 20 of the General Instructions for Operation 7. If the word "head" has been canceled in an earlier operation, follow the instructions given in paragraph 20. If there is a group of persons which you believe constitutes a separate household but for which there is no entry of "head," consult your Section Chief to see whether the first person should be coded "head" and the household marked "NH" in the left-hand margin of the schedule.

6. <u>Coding Relationship of Persons Enumerated Out of Order</u>. The following types of situations may be encountered on sheets 61, 61, etc., reserved for persons in households enumerated out of order. For these proceed as follows:

(a) If an entire household is enumerated on the out of order sheets, code the entries in the usual way as instructed in paragraphs 19-29.

(b) For a person enumerated out of order, for whom the number of the household of which he is a member has been clearly specified, code the relationship of the person to the head in accordance with the instructions in paragraphs 19-29.

(c) For a person enumerated out of order, for whom no relationship has been specified, and for whom the household visitation number is not given, try to find a household at the same address, and if one is found, code the person's relationship to the head of the household at that address in accordance with the instructions in paragraphs 19-29.

(d) If there are a number of persons enumerated on sheet 61 with the same address but with no relationship specified, the first person in the group should be coded as head and the remaining persons as members of the same household in accordance with the instructions in paragraphs 19-29.

(e) If there are a number of persons listed consecutively for whom neither the relationship nor the address is specified, code the first person in the group as head and the remaining persons as members of the same household in accordance with the instructions in paragraphs 19-29.

- 2 -

(f) If sheet 61 contains names of a number of persons not necessarily listed consecutively for whom no relationship and no address has been specified, but each of whom has been marked as head of an NH household, cancel the entries of "head" and "NH" for all but the first such person and code the remaining persons as members of the same household in accordance with the instructions in paragraphs 19-29.

7. Households in which the first person is always to be coded "V" and the succeeding persons "9," include the following:

(a) A household including 2 or more unrelated keepers in lighthouses;

(b) ~~A household including 2 or more coast guard attendants;~~

(c) ~~A group of 2 or more unrelated persons in a college dormitory;~~

(d) ~~A group of 2 or more unrelated religious workers;~~

(e) CCC Camps; if an E.D. for a CCC Camp contains a private household refer the folio to your Section Chief;

(f) Masters and crews of vessels;

(g) Institutional households which include 1 or more inmates.

8. <u>Other Instructions for Coding Col. A.</u> In the following instances the head of the household is always to be coded "0" and the succeeding persons in accordance with their relationship to the head:

(a) A household consisting of one religious worker and his family with or without servants, such as a minister and his family, a priest and a housekeeper.

(b) A head with a common law wife. The common law wife should be coded "1."

(c) A related group of persons living on a boat or vessel, such as a mate living alone or with his family.

9. In the following instances the first person in the household is always to be coded "0" and the succeeding persons "6" or "X" <u>unless</u> there are 11 or more persons, in which case the first person will be coded "V" and the succeeding persons "9."

<u>The code "6" is to be assigned to persons other than the head in the following cases:</u>

(a) Households consisting of a group of servants, such as a butler, housekeeper, maid, chauffeur, etc.

(b) Persons in construction camps.

(c) Persons living in private convalescent homes.

<u>The code "X" is to be assigned to persons other than the head in cases like the following:</u>

(a) Waitresses in restaurants, secretaries, or garage attendants who live in the household of the proprietor.

(b) A nurse or attendant in a doctor's or dentist's office who lives in his household.

(c) Persons in bunk houses (usually found on sheep and cattle ranches).

10. An institutional family, even though the institution consists of several dormitories, should be coded as one household; that is, the head should be coded "V" and all inmates or employees not

- 3 -

comprising a separate household should be coded "9" in col. A. Follow this rule even though a private household has been enumerated between two groups of inmates (coding the private household 0, 1, 2, etc.).

11. To paragraph 19 add the following:

Relationship to head: Code in col. A

  Adopted child 2
  Step-grandchild 4
  Great-grandchild 5
  Orphan, ward, foster child 6
  A divorced spouse living in the household with the head 6
  A "Guest" (paying guest) 6
  A gardner 7
  Companion:
    If working in the household 7
    If not working in the household 8
  Friend 8
  Godson, Godmother, Foster Mother 8
  "Helpers" (who are not helpers in domestic service.
    Helpers in domestic service should be coded "7.") X
  A groom X

12. An entry of two wives is to be accepted, each wife to be coded "1."

13. Paragraph 27. The second sentence of this paragraph should read: "If a person with such a relationship has an entry other than "Yes" in cols. 21 or 24, code "1" in col. E.

14. Paragraph 29. Where the first person in a household of 11 or more lodgers was originally listed as a lodger, paragraph 29 of the Instructions for Operation 7 does not apply.

15. <u>Col. 9</u>. Paragraph 30. An *f* (written through the line) must be changed to a capital F between the lines.

16. <u>Col. 10</u>. Paragraph 31. Where "N," "C," or "B" intended for "Negro" appears, cancel the entry and code "2."

17. Paragraph 32. If the entry is Hawaiian, Malay, Siamese (Thian), or Samoan, assign the code "9" in col. 10. If the race entry is other than these (and other than those specified in paragraph 32), refer the portfolio to the Assistant Operations Chiefs.

18. Sons and daughters of a Negro head or Negro wife must be edited "Neg" even if they have been enumerated as "W" for white. Sons and daughters of all mixed white and colored are to be edited according to the color or race of the nonwhite parent <u>except</u> in the case of Indians. An entry of "W" for sons and daughters of Indian-white parents is acceptable, and should not be changed.

19. <u>Col. 11</u>. Paragraph 33. If age is given in months for persons over one year old, correct it to the last full year.

20. If an entry of "0," "0/12," "1/12," "2/12," or "3/12" years is discovered in col. 11 for a person after whose name there is no red or green check or "X," an Infant Card should be filled out for that person and in the "Date of birth" space should be written "Age reported as 0, 0/12, 1/12, 2/12, or 3/12 years," as the case may be. After filling out the Infant Card, enter a red "X" after the name of the child. The Infant Cards should then be delivered to your Section Chief, who will see that they are returned to Operation 6 for transmission to the Division of Vital Statistics.

19898

- 4 -

21. If age is given in fractions other than twelfths of a year, cancel the entry and code "V-1," "V-2," etc.

22. <u>Col. 12</u>. Paragraph 35. When "W" appears for widowed, cancel the entry and write Wd. Coding is not acceptable in this column.

23. Be sure to check the out-of-order sheets before changing "M" to "7."

24. Portfolios containing numerous entries of "married" with spouse absent (7) and without entries of "Wd" in col. 12 are to be referred to your Section Chief.

25. When col. 12 is blank for a person whose relationship in col. 8 indicates that he is a parent do not enter "S" in col. 12. If the marital status cannot be determined on the basis of the other information on the schedule, enter a "Wd" for a person 55 years of age or over; for a person under 55 years of age, enter the code "7."

26. <u>Col. 13</u>. Paragraph 37. Entries in this column must be either "Yes" or "No." Coding is not acceptable in this column. Folios containing "Yes" for all persons should be referred to the Assistant Operations Chiefs.

27. If "No" has been entered in col. 13 for all persons in the enumeration district, accept the entries. Editing of col. 13 is to be done only when it is blank.

28. <u>Col. 14</u>. Paragraph 38. When numerous entries of "No," blanks, or dashes appear, refer the portfolio for special editing.

29. If entries of "H-6," "H-7," "H-8," "H-9," "H-10," "H-11," or "H-12" appear, disregard the H and code accordingly. H-5 should be coded "30."

30. If "K" (kindergarten) appears in col. 14 leave column B blank.

31. When an entry of "H-C" appears, regard the entry as "C-1" and code "40" in col. B.

32. If the enumerator has occasionally entered "H" in col. 14 instead of "H-1," "H-2," etc., code the entry "9" for "H-1." Code an entry of "C" in col. 14, "40" for "C-1."

33. <u>Cols. 15 and 16</u>. Paragraphs 39-46. All persons born in territories or possessions of the United States, including Alaska, American Samoa, Guam, Hawaiian Islands, Panama Canal Zone, Phillipine Islands, Puerto Rico, and the Virgin Islands of the United States are to be regarded as citizens, and entries of "Al," "Na," etc. for people born in these territories or possessions are to be canceled.

34. Portfolios containing blanks in col. 16 for foreign-born persons or consistent entries of "Na," "Pa," "Al," "Am cit," etc., are to be referred to the Assistant Operation Chief, who will either advise you of the manner in which these cases are to be handled, or refer the folio to your Section Chief for special editing.

35. On page 26 of the index of foreign countries, provinces, cities, etc. with code numbers, strike through the entry

    Santa Cruz ....39 W. Ind.

If the only entry in col. 15 is Santa Cruz, refer the portfolio to your Section Chief in order that he may obtain a special ruling on the code number to be entered in code column C.

36. When the entry of "Ireland" appears, code for Irish Free State.

37. When the entry of "Turkey" appears, code for Turkey in Asia. (This cancels earlier instructions to code for Turkey in Europe.)

19898

38. Occasionally you may find entries of Dakota or Carolina. Ask the Assistant Operations Chiefs for instructions in these cases.

39. When the entry of "Canada" appears, code for Canada English.

40. An entry of "Al," "Pa," "Na," etc., for a person born in the United States or one of its territories or possessions, even though married to a foreign-born person, must be canceled. Thus, col. 16 must be blank for persons born in the United States or any of its territories or possessions.

41. Paragraph 49. Treat an entry of "Same Institution" in col. 17 as if it were an entry of "Same house."

42. Cols. 17-20. Paragraph 51. The reference to "incorporated places" in the first sentence of paragraph 51 means places that were incorporated on April 1, 1940. Some incorporated places have been incorporated since 1930, and some incorporated places in 1930 have since been disincorporated. If the entry in the heading of the schedule disagrees with the Geographer's description, refer the discrepancy to the Heading Review Section.

43. Paragraph 70. "Related Persons" for whom the same migration code should be given as is assigned the head do not include the following classes of persons:

　　1. Wives, daughters-in-law, sons-in-law who are without children and under 30 years of age.

　　2. Wives, daughters-in-law, and sons-in-law whose oldest child is under 5.

　　3. Blood relatives of persons in Classes 1 and 2.

44. In order to assume that the blanks or dashes in cols. 17-20 were used systematically by the enumerator for ditto marks, the folio should contain, for persons other that the head, occasional entries that are different from the entries for the head. In most cases unrelated persons and the related persons listed above should have a different entry if the entry for the head was "Same house." If it thus appears that blanks or dashes were used strictly to indicate repetition, definite entries may be extended even to unrelated persons. However, if the enumerator has left cols. 17-20 blank frequently and at random, if he has never or rarely ever made entries except for the head, or if he has made entries only for the first person on the sheet, refer the folio to the Special Editors of Migration.

45. To follow Paragraph 71. Inconsistent entries in col. 17-19. When the entries in cols. 17-19 are inconsistent, you have been instructed to refer the case to your Section Chief (paragraph 48). He may use the following rules in deciding what you are to code. When, in his judgment, these rules result in an unreasonable decision, he may refer the case to the Statistician for Internal Migration or his representative.

46. In the usual disagreement, the entry for county is most likely to be wrong. When place and county do not agree and both are in the State in col. 19, assume that the place entry is correct.

47. When entries in two of the cols. 17-19 agree and the entry in the third column disagrees with both of the others, assume that the third entry is wrong. If the wrong entry is a place in col. 17, assume that the entry in col. 17 is "R."

48. When there are entries in each of cols. 17-19 and no two agree, accept the State.

49. If place and county disagree and State is not given, accept the place.

50. If place and State disagree and county is not given, accept the State, and assume that the entry in col. 17 is "R," unless not far from the area of present residence there is a place of this name in an adjacent State.

19898

- 6 -

51. If county and State disagree and col. 17 does not contain a place, accept the State.

52. When there is an occasional "R" in col. 17 and an urban place in col. 18, treat the entry as representing the rural part of the county in which the given place is located. When there are frequent discrepancies of this nature, refer the folio for special editing.

53. Edit in red pencil all inconsistent entries to indicate the interpretation made.

54. <u>Army, Navy, CCC, etc.</u> Where a specific army post is given, the geographic location may be found in the <u>Postal Guide</u> in the list beginning on Page 941.

55. When there is an entry of "Army," "Navy," the name of a ship, "Marines," "Coast Guard," or "CCC" together with some specific geographic information, code only the specific geographic information. If "Army," "Marines," "Coast Guard," or "CCC" is the only entry, code XX09. If "Navy" or the name of a ship is the only entry, code V908.

56. <u>Cols. 21-25</u>. Paragraph 74. The code for col. E is to be determined only on the basis of the instructions in paragraphs 74 to 76 of the Instructions for General Population Coding. The entries in cols. 28-30 are not to be used in the determination of the code for col. E (employment status). The exceptions to this general rule are clearly stated in paragraphs 27, 29-b, and 74-76.

57. Occasionally you will find homes for the aged or incapacitated operated by private organizations or individuals or bearing a notation indicating that they are leased from a governmental agency. The <u>inmates</u> of these institutions are to be coded "9" in col. E.

58. Staff members and employees of institutions of any type are not to be coded "9" in col. E. If the enumerator's entry is other than "Yes" in col. 21, refer the portfolio to the Assistant Operations Chiefs.

59. If the enumerator has entered "0" in col. 26 with no entries in cols. 21 to 25 nor col. 27 leave col. E blank.

60. <u>Paragraph 76</u>. This paragraph applies only to men enumerated as residing in the CCC Camps (that is, the name of the Camp has been entered in the heading of the schedule). This paragraph does not apply to a man who is enumerated with his family, even though an "Ab" may be written after his name in col. 7.

61. <u>Col. 26. Paragraph 78</u>. An entry of "0" in col. 26 is acceptable when the code "1" has been entered in col. E.

62. Fractions of hours worked should be canceled.

63. If the enumerator has entered any figure of 100 or more, including "168 hours" for a physician, a soldier, a turnkey in a jail, etc., cancel the entry and code "99."

64. <u>Cols. 31 and 32</u>. Paragraph 82. Add the following sentence to this paragraph:

    If the entry in col. 32 is "No" or "None," cancel the "No" or "None" and enter "0" in col. 32.

65. "Unknown" or any entry other that a figure in these cols. should be canceled. If the entry in col. 31 is "one-half time," "one-quarter time," etc., refer the folio to your Section Chief.

66. If dollar signs appear in col. 32, cancel the dollar signs.

67. "C" (confidential report) in col. 32 should be canceled and col. 32 left blank if a confidential wage report has not been received.

104

- 7 -

68. Paragraph 82. An entry of a figure in col. 32 should never be canceled, even though there is a zero in col. 31.

69. Paragraph 13. If the enumerator made entries of wages in col. 32 and a "Yes" or "No" in col. 33 for a person for whom you have a Confidential Report on wages (Form P-16), accept the information on the Confidential Report if it is different from the enumerator's entry. Make certain, however, that the Confidential Report is for the proper person.

70. Col. 33. Paragraph 83. This paragraph applies only to men residing in the CCC Camps, that is, the name of the Camp has been entered in the heading of the schedule. This paragraph does not apply to a man who is enumerated with his family, even though an "Ab" may be written after his name in col. 7.

71. Paragraph 83. Add the following sentences to this paragraph:

(a) ~~Also cross out the reply, "No" and enter "1" (for yes) for all persons except commissioned officers residing on an army post.~~

(b) If cols. 32 or 33 is blank, or if "No" has been consistently entered in col. 33 for persons in the employ of any institution, or for persons in the labor force in religious institutions, refer the folio to the Assistant Operations Chief.

72. If the entry in col. 33 is not easily read, code the entry.

73. Cols. 36 and 37. Paragraph 87. If the entries on these lines differ from the information on the main lines of the schedule, the entries on the main lines are to be accepted. If the entry in either col. 36 or 37 is for a parent with an acceptable entry of "American citizen born abroad," enter "XO" above the place of birth and regard that parent as having been born in the United States.

74. Col. 38. Paragraph 88. Mother Tongue. If col. 38 has been left blank by the enumerator, leave it blank, and code "49" in col. H.

75. "Austrian" in col. 38 should be coded "German."

76. "Pennsylvania-Dutch" in col. 38 should be coded "German."

77. If the mother tongue entered in col. 38 differs from that usually spoken in the country of birth of father or mother, accept the entry as it appears.

78. If both a foreign language and "English" appear in col. 38, code the foreign language; if two foreign languages, code the first.

79. Entries of "Swiss" or "Belgian" in col. 38 are to be referred to the Assistant Operations Chiefs for determination of the code.

80. Col. I. Enter "8" in column I if:

(a) Cols. 36-50 are completely blank, except possibly for a "No" in col. 39.

(b) Cols. 36-50 have been completely canceled, even though some information has subsequently been entered in red pencil by special editors.

(c) Cols. 36-50 have been left blank by the enumerator and red pencil entries appear only in cols. 36-38. (If entries are in red ink or black ink, do not code "8.")

(d) Cols. 45-50 have been canceled and the name in col. 35 has been changed in red pencil.

- 8 -

But do not enter "8" in col. I if there is a "Yes" in col. 39 or 40, or if war service is shown in col. 41; instead enter in col. I the code for these cols. in the regular manner. (In other words col. I is to be coded in the regular manner if this person is a veteran, wife, widow, or child of a veteran, regardless of what other supplementary information may be missing or canceled.)

If there is any case to which none of these rules applies, or if there is any doubt about applying a rule, refer the folio to the Section Chief, who will bring it to the attention of Dr. Deming or his representative.

81. <u>Cols. 39, 40, and 41</u>. Paragraph 89. Extreme caution should be exercised in the interpretation of incomplete or irregular entries in cols. 39-41 (veterans). Checking the age of the person in col. 11 to determine whether the person is a World War veteran is not always enough information, since the person may have been in a regular establishment. Unless the information available is certain, use the code "7" rather than a special code.

82. If throughout the portfolio the entries in these columns appear contradictory, refer the portfolio for special editing.

83. <u>Cols. 42, 43, and 44, Social Security</u>. Cancel paragraph 91, and substitute the following: The entries in cols. 42, 43, and 44 are to be coded in col. 44. For certain combinations of entries the enumerator's entry in col. 44 is the code; in these cases, you need not make any entry. For other combinations of entries the enumerator's entry in col. 44 must be canceled; sometimes a code is then to be entered in col. 44, and at other times no code will be required.

84. The entries (either enumerator's or coder's) that should appear in col. 44 after coding, are summarized below:

Col. 42	Col. 43	Col. 44	Code for Col. 44		Meaning of code
Yes	Yes or blank	1	No coding to be done	Has S.S. No.	Deductions from all
Yes	Yes or blank	2	No coding to be done	Has S.S. No.	Deductions from one-half or more
Yes	Yes or blank	3	No coding to be done	Has S.S. No.	Deductions from less than half
Yes	Yes	Yes	Cancel "Yes" and code "5."	Has S.S. No.	Amount of deductions unknown
Yes	Yes	Blank	code "5."	Has S.S. No.	Amount of deductions unknown
No	No or blank	None or blank	Cancel "None" and code "0."	Does not have S.S. No.	

If there is an entry of "No" in col. 42, "Yes" in col. 43, and "1" in col. 44, <u>and the person is definitely working at an occupation in the railway industry, do not cancel the entry in col. 44.</u>

Yes	No	Blank	code "4."	Has S.S. No.	No deductions
Yes	Blank	Blank	code "6."	Has S.S. No.	Unknown whether deductions
Any other combinations.			Cancel entry in col.44 if there is one, and leave blank.		Unknown S.S. status

85. <u>Col. K. Paragraph 94</u>. Correct (a) to read as follows:

    a. Code "0," for owned, if "0" appears in col. 4 on the line for the head (or for a person related to the head) of the household of which the person on the supplementary line is a related member (code 0, 1, 2, 3, 4, or 5 in col. A).

    b. Leave col. K blank if there is no entry in col. 4 for the head or any related member of the household and no unrelated member of the household has an entry of "0" in col. 4.

- 9 -

86. <u>Col. L.</u> Paragraph 95. If the entry in col. 5 affecting the supplementary line is "1/3 of crop" etc., leave col. L blank.

87. <u>Paragraph 96.</u> If col. 4 has been left blank for all members of the household, leave col. L blank even though a figure may appear in col. 5.

88. <u>Col. N.</u> Paragraph 99. If the person to be coded in col. N is an American citizen born abroad, consider the person as native.

89. This addendum (No. 1) supersedes all previous addenda to the Instructions for General Population Coding - Operation 7.

CORRECTIONS AND ADDITIONS TO INSTRUCTIONS FOR CODING MIGRATION

(1) Paragraph 56, line 2 "col. 17" should read "col. 20"

(2) Paragraph 70a. If any or all of the entries in cols. 17-20 are lacking for a child, age 5-13 inclusive, give the child the same code as its mother, or if the mother is not a member of the household, as its father.

(3) An entry of "Long Island, New York" with no county or place mentioned should be given the code 5V7 for Nassau County, New York.

(4) List 1, page 43   IOWA   Valley Junction city   Polk "8554" Name changed to West Des Moines

(5) List 1, page 44   LOUISIANA   New Orleans   Orleans "8547" should read "4547"

(6) List 1, page 62   PENNSYLVANIA   "Morristown"   should read "Norristown"

(7) List 2, page 72   DELAWARE   Delmar*   Sussex "712" should read "711"

(8) List 2, page 83   NEW JERSEY   Riverside   Bergen "574" Name changed to River Edge

(9) List 2, page 91   TEXAS   Devine   Medina "870" should read 8X1"

(10) List 3, page 100, footnote Coextensive with New Orleans city, "Code 8547" should read "Code 4547."

List 3, - Georgia. Milton and Campbell Counties were annexed to Fulton County in 1932. If the name of one of these two counties appears in col. 18, code 787, for Fulton.

(11) List 5, page 111 "Canada-French 3408"   should read "Canada 3408"
                       "Canada-English 3508"

(12) List 7, page 115 MAINE   Delete Gardiner Kennebec 502

(13) List 7, page 117 MASSACHUSETTS "Brinfield"   should read "Brimfield"

(14) List 7, page 119 NEW HAMPSHIRE "Corydon"   should read "Croydon"

(15) List 7, page 120 NEW HAMPSHIRE "Louden"   should read "Loudon"

(16) List 7, page 120 NEW HAMPSHIRE "Oxford"   should read "Orford"

Approved:

Leon E. Truesdell
Chief Statistician for Population

November 12, 1940

SIXTEENTH CENSUS
POPULATION
Form P-327A - 2

ADDENDUM NO. 2 TO OPERATION 7

REVISED INSTRUCTIONS FOR GENERAL POPULATION CODING

Hereafter, all coders whose work is eligible for sample verification, that is, those coders who have been instructed to write the letter "Q" in the right hand margin of the line for general population coding on the Portfolio Memorandum, are to code column by column (in some cases, a group of columns) rather than line by line. General rules to be followed are:

1. Follow the instructions for Operation 7 as now written, making only those checks for consistency between columns specified in the instructions.

2. Complete the "A" side of the schedule before beginning the "B" side, etc.

Proceed as follows for the coding of the specific columns:

1. Code Column 6 in accordance with the instructions in Paragraphs 14-18.

2. Code in Column A the entries in Column 8 in accordance with the instructions in Paragraphs 19-29.

3. Check Column 9 to be sure there is an entry of M or F for every person and that this is consistent with the name and relationship.

4. Code the entries in Column 10 and supply any missing entries in accordance with the instructions in Paragraphs 31-32.

5. Check the entries in Column 11 in accordance with the instructions in Paragraphs 33-34.

6. Proceed in like manner to code the entries in Column 12 in accordance with the instructions in Paragraphs 35 and 36; the entries in Column 13 in accordance with the instructions in Paragraph 37; the entries in Column 14 in accordance with the instructions in Paragraph 38; the entries in Column 15 in accordance with the instructions in Paragraphs 39-43; and the entries in Column 16 in accordance with the instructions in Paragraphs 44-46.

7. Columns 17-20 will be treated as one section and the code for Column D supplied on the basis of the entries in these columns in accordance with the instructions in Paragraphs 47-73.

8. Columns 21-25 should also be treated as a unit and the entries in these columns coded in Column E in accordance with the instructions in Paragraphs 74-77.

9. Proceed to code Columns 26, 27, 31, 32 and 33 column by column.

10. Code the supplementary lines, line by line as heretofore, in accordance with the instructions in Paragraphs 85-110.

Approved: Leon E Truesdell
Chief Statistician for Population.

November 14, 1940.
20067

APPENDIX III
AGE ALLOCATION TABLES USED
IN 1940 CENSUS[1]

TABLE 9. ESTIMATION OF AGE FROM HIGHEST GRADE OF SCHOOL COMPLETED

Highest grade of school completed	Age to be assigned
0	6
1	7
2	8
3	9
4	10
5	11
6	12
7 or 8	*13
7 or 8	*14
9 (H-1)	15
10 (H-2)	16
11 (H-3)	17
12 (H-4)	18
One year of college (C-1)	19
Two years " " (C-2)	20
Three " " " (C-3)	21
Four " " " (C-4)	22

* Grades 7 and 8 indicate age 13 if the enumerator gave no information on employment or occupation, and age 14 if he did give information on employment or occupation (in which case the employment and occupation entries would show the person to be in school).

3-30564

Figure 1: Age-Education Relationship Table

TABLE 10. THE RELATIONSHIP BETWEEN THE AGES OF HUSBANDS AND WIVES, ON THE BASIS OF SPIEGELMAN'S FIGURES

To find age of husband				To find age of wife			
Wife's age	Husband's age	Wife's age	Husband's age	Husband's age	Wife's age	Husband's age	Wife's age
15	20	53	55	15	14	57	53
16	21	54	56	16	15	58	53
17	22	55	57	17	16	59	54
18	22	56	58	18	17	60	55
19	23	57	59	19	18	61	56
20	24	58	60	20	19	62	57
21	25	59	61	21	20	63	58
22	26	60	62	22	21	64	59
23	27	61	63	23	22	65	60
24	28	62	64	24	23	66	61
25	29	63	65	25	23	67	62
26	30	64	66	26	24	68	62
27	31	65	67	27	25	69	63
28	32	66	68	28	26	70	64
29	33	67	69	29	27	71	65
30	34	68	70	30	28	72	66
31	35	69	71	31	29	73	67
32	36	70	72	32	30	74	68
33	37	71	72	33	31	75	69
34	38	72	73	34	32	76	70
35	39	73	74	35	33	77	71
36	39	74	75	36	34	78	72
37	40	75	76	37	34	79	73
38	41	76	77	38	35	80	73
39	42	77	78	39	36	81	74
40	43	78	79	40	37	82	75
41	44	79	80	41	38	83	76
42	45	80	81	42	39	84	77
43	46	81	82	43	40	85	78
44	47	82	83	44	41	86	79
45	48	83	84	45	42	87	80
46	49	84	85	46	43	88	81
47	50	85	86	47	43	89	82
48	51	86	87	48	44	90	83
49	52	87	88	49	45	91	83
50	53	88	89	50	46	92	84
51	54	89	90	51	47	93	85
52	55	90	90	52	48	94	86
				53	49	95	87
				54	50	96	88
				55	51	97	89
				56	52	98	90

* Mortimer Spiegelman, "Mortality in relation to widowhood," Proc. Amer. Philos. Soc. vol. 80, 1939; pp. 541-558. See also the Statistical Bulletin of the Metropolitan Life Insurance Co. for April 1939, for remarks on the age differentials of husband and wife at high ages.

Figure 2: Husband-Wife Age Relationship Table

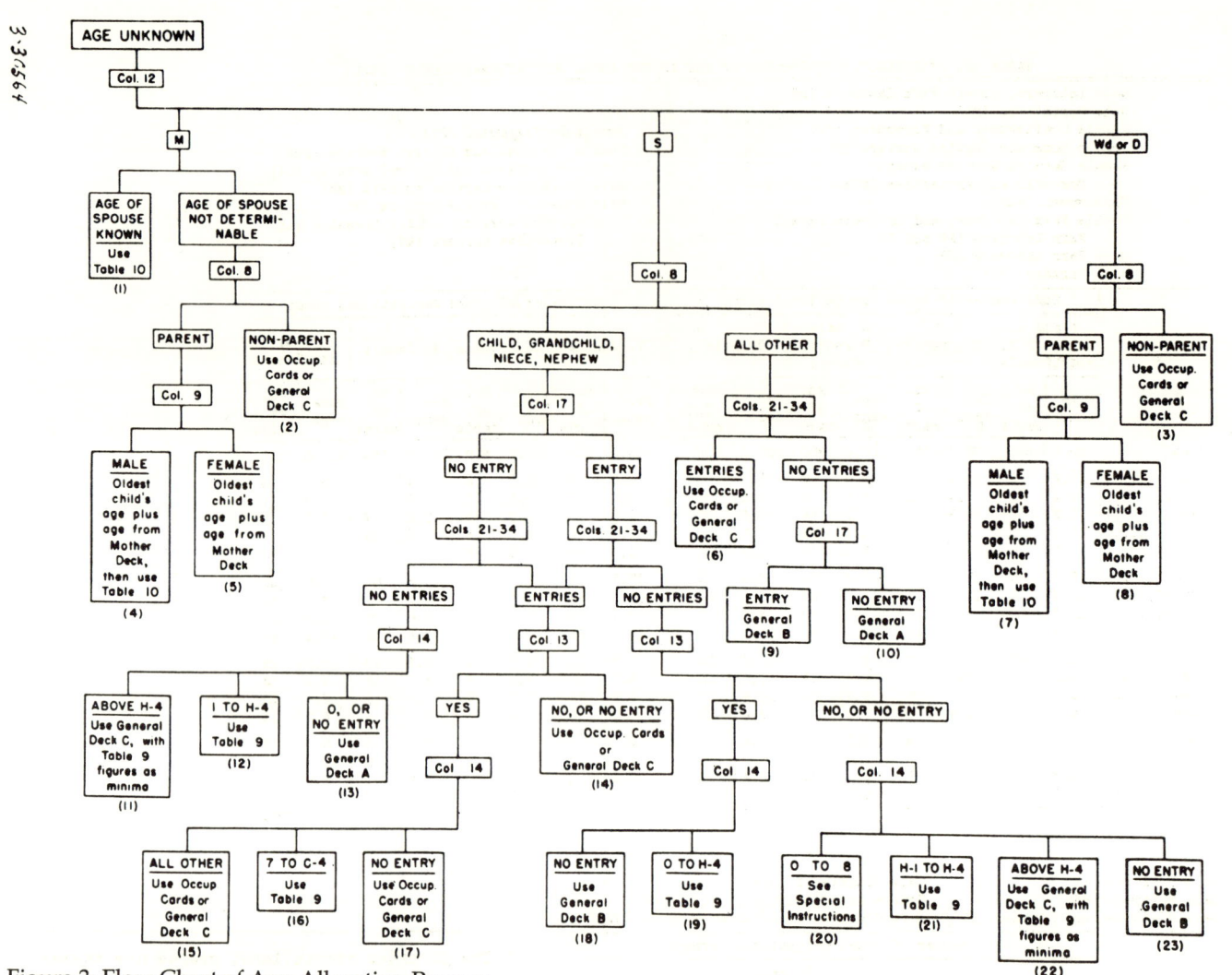

Figure 3: Flow Chart of Age-Allocation Process

TABLE 12. FREQUENCY DISTRIBUTION OF AGE IN THE BROAD OCCUPATIONAL GROUPS (1930)

Male Laborers, except Farm Laborers (M9)
Male Operatives (M4)
Female Craftswomen and Forewomen (F3)
Female Domestic Service Workers (F5)
Female Service Workers except Domestic and Protective (F7)
Saleswomen (F2b)
Female Farm Laborers, and Laborers except Farm Laborers (F8 and F9)
Male Farm Laborers (M8)
Male Farmers (M0)

Female Professional (FV)
Female Clerical and Kindred Workers (F2a)
Female Operatives and Kindred Workers (F4)
Male Protective Service Workers (M6)
Male Domestic Service Workers (M5)
Male Service Workers, except Domestic and Protective Workers (M7)

Age	4 and 9, male - 3,5, and 7,female Percent	No. of cards	2b, female Percent	No. of cards	8, male - 8 and 9, female Percent	No. of cards	0, male Percent	No. of cards	V, female Percent	No. of cards	2a, female Percent	No. of cards	4, female Percent	No. of cards	5, 6, and 7, male Percent	No. of cards
14 and over..	100.0	250	100.0	250	100.0	250	100.0	250	100.0	250	100.0	250	100.0	250	100.0	250
14.........	0.2	0	0.1	0	2.6	7	0.0	0	0.0	0	0.0	0	0.4	1	0.1	0
15.........	0.4	2	0.4	1	3.5	9	0.0	0	0.0	0	0.2	1	1.3	3	0.3	1
16.........	1.3	3	1.6	4	5.5	14	0.0	0	0.1	0	1.2	3	3.6	9	0.7	2
17.........	2.0	5	3.0	8	6.6	16	0.0	0	0.3	1	3.2	8	5.1	13	1.2	3
18-19......	5.7	14	9.0	23	13.1	33	0.8	2	4.7	12	13.0	32	11.5	29	3.7	10
20-24......	15.8	40	19.5	49	22.0	55	5.9	15	27.7	69	33.0	83	20.9	52	11.8	29
25-29......	13.9	35	13.0	33	11.2	28	8.6	21	19.1	48	18.7	47	12.7	32	12.3	31
30-34......	11.7	29	11.3	28	7.1	18	9.9	25	12.3	31	11.0	28	9.8	25	11.8	30
35-39......	11.8	29	11.7	29	6.1	15	11.9	30	10.3	26	7.7	19	9.6	24	12.1	30
40-44......	10.0	25	9.9	25	4.9	12	11.7	29	7.8	20	4.9	12	7.7	19	10.5	26
45-49......	8.7	22	8.0	20	4.5	11	11.8	30	6.1	15	3.2	8	6.1	15	9.3	23
50-54......	6.8	17	5.7	14	3.9	10	11.4	29	4.9	12	1.9	5	4.5	11	8.1	20
55-59......	4.8	12	3.4	9	3.0	8	9.4	24	3.2	8	1.0	2	3.0	8	6.3	16
60-64......	3.4	9	1.8	4	2.5	6	7.6	19	2.0	5	0.5	1	2.0	5	5.2	13
65-69......	2.1	5	0.9	2	1.8	4	5.4	13	1.0	2	0.2	1	1.1	3	3.6	9
70-74......	0.9	2	0.3	1	1.1	3	3.4	8	0.4	1	0.1	0	0.5	1	2.0	5
75 and over	0.4	1	0.1	0	0.7	1	2.1	5	0.2	0	0.0	0	0.2	0	0.9	2

Male Professional (MV)   Male Proprietor (M1)
Male Salesmen (M2b)   Female Proprietor (F1)
Male Craftsmen and Foremen (M3)   Male Clerical and Kindred Workers (M2a)

Age	V and 2b, male Percent	No. of cards	3, male Percent	No. of cards	1, male 1, female Percent	No. of cards	2a, male Percent	No. of cards
14 and over..	100.0	250	100.0	250	100.0	250	100.0	250
14.........	0.2	0	0.0	0	0.0	0	0.1	0
15.........	0.2	1	0.0	0	0.0	0	0.6	2
16.........	0.4	1	0.0	0	0.0	0	1.6	4
17.........	0.7	2	0.2	0	0.1	0	2.6	6
18-19......	2.4	6	2.1	5	0.6	2	7.3	18
20-24......	11.4	29	10.0	25	5.0	13	19.8	50
25-29......	14.8	37	12.6	32	9.3	23	15.5	39
30-34......	14.3	36	13.2	33	12.5	31	12.7	32
35-39......	13.4	33	14.1	35	15.1	38	10.7	27
40-44......	11.1	28	12.8	32	14.3	36	8.1	20
45-49......	9.2	23	11.0	28	12.7	32	6.5	16
50-54......	7.7	19	8.7	22	10.8	27	5.3	13
55-59......	5.7	14	6.4	16	8.0	20	3.9	10
60-64......	4.1	10	4.5	11	5.7	14	2.8	7
65-69......	2.4	6	2.6	7	3.4	8	1.5	4
70-74......	1.3	3	1.2	3	1.6	4	0.7	2
75 and over	0.7	2	0.5	1	0.8	2	0.3	0

3-30564

[6] The 13 broad occupational groups are these:

Code	Occupation
V	Professional and semiprofessional workers
	a. Professional workers
	b. Semiprofessional workers
0	Farmers and farm managers
1	Proprietors, managers, and officials, except farm
2	Clerical, sales, and kindred workers
	a. Clerical and kindred workers
	b. Salesmen and saleswomen
3	Craftsmen, foremen, and kindred workers
4	Operatives and kindred workers
5	Domestic service workers
6	Protective service workers
7	Service workers, except domestic and protective
8	Farm laborers and foremen
9	Laborers, except farm

Figure 4: Age-Occupation Relationship Table

1. Source: U.S. Department of Commerce, Bureau of the Census, *The Elimination of Unknown Ages in the 1940 Census*, prepared by W. Edwards Deming, January 1942. Figure 1: p. 11; Figure 2: p. 12; Figure 3: p. 8; Figure 4: pp. 13, 15.

**APPENDIX IV
INSTRUCTIONS FOR CODING OCCUPATION,
INDUSTRY, AND CLASS OF WORKER
(OPERATION 9)**

SIXTEENTH CENSUS
POPULATION
Form P-329

OPERATION 9

INSTRUCTIONS FOR CODING OCCUPATION, INDUSTRY, AND CLASS OF WORKER

THE OCCUPATION INDEX

1. In preparation for coding the occupation, industry, and class of worker returns in cols. 28, 29, and 30 of the Population Schedule, an occupation index was prepared. The occupation index is printed in two forms--classified and alphabetical--and a separate volume is devoted to each form. In the Classified Index, the 25,000 or more occupational designations of which the index is composed are arranged in classified form, with each designation under its proper occupation or occupation group, and with each occupation or occupation group preceded by its code symbol. In the Alphabetical Index, the occupational designations are arranged alphabetically, and each designation is followed by a symbol indicating to which of the 451 occupations and occupation groups of the classification it belongs. The Alphabetical Index also includes approximately 9,500 industry designations. These designations are arranged alphabetically and each is followed by a symbol indicating to which of the 132 titles of the census industry classification it belongs.

GENERAL CODING PROCEDURE

2. Each occupation coding clerk will have a copy of the Alphabetical Index of Occupations and Industries and a large card entitled "List of Principal Occupations and Industries with their Symbols" on which a number of the principal occupations and a number of the principal industries contained in the index have been printed. In the case of each return of an occupation in col. 28 and an industry in col. 29, look up the same occupation and industry in the index and enter in the first two sections of col. F of the schedule the symbol given in the index.

3. Following the instructions relating to the class of worker, printed on pages 7 and 8 of the Alphabetical Index, and the supplementary instructions on this topic (see paragraphs 13 to 15 hereof), enter in the last section of col. F the correct code for the class of worker returned in col. 30.

4. Code the occupation, industry, and class of worker entries in cols. 45, 46, and 47 of the "Supplementary Questions" section of the schedule in accordance with the instructions for coding the corresponding entries in cols. 28, 29, and 30 of the main part of the schedule. In case there is no entry in cols. 45, 46, and 47, or in case "None" has been entered in col. 45, enter the figure 7 in the third section of col. J.

5. Copy in col. U of the "Supplementary Questions" section of the schedule the codes, if any, entered for the same person in col. F of the main part of the schedule.

GENERAL INSTRUCTIONS

6. On receiving a portfolio for coding, consult the portfolio memorandum on the front cover to see whether or not the portfolio is to be examined (according to paragraphs 16 to 23) for industrial home workers.

7. Before beginning the coding, check the sheet number in the upper right-hand corner of the schedule to make sure that the sheets are arranged in consecutive order and that the "A" side of each sheet is up. There may be four series of sheet numbers:

   a. Nos. 1, 2, 3, etc. for households enumerated in regular order.

   b. Nos. 51, 52, etc. for sheets originally numbered 100 or more, but changed in Operation 3.

   c. Nos. 61, 62, etc. for households and persons (except transients) not enumerated in regular order.

   d. Nos. 81, 82, etc. for transients enumerated as of the night of April 8.

10295

- 2 -

8. Within each of these series there should be no sheet numbers omitted. There must be no sheets numbered 100 or more. If you find a sheet number missing in any one of the series, or a sheet numbered 100 or more, refer the portfolio to your Section Chief. On some sheets you may find that the enumerator's entry for sheet number has been changed in green or red pencil by the Population and Housing matching clerk. Accept such changes as correct. Do not change any sheet numbers.

9. Enter all codes with red pencil.

SPECIFIC INSTRUCTIONS

10. Most of the specific instructions for coding occupation, industry, and class of worker returns are contained in the Alphabetical Index of Occupations, under the title "Instructions for Using the Occupation Index" (pp. 6-15), under the title "Instructions for Using the Industry Index" (pp. 16 and 17), and under the title "Instructions for Using the List of Principal Occupations and Industries" (p. 18). In addition to these instructions, there are the following supplementary instructions:

Coding "Not Specified" Industry Returns

11. County data have been prepared on the number of establishments or wage earners in the selected industries or types of work listed below. These data are to be used as aids (1) in classifying specifically certain types of "not specified" industry returns that otherwise would have to be classified in "not specified" industries, and (2) in distinguishing between returns for certain types of establishments or industries which are difficult to differentiate. Consult your Section Chief before assigning codes to indefinite returns of the industries covered by these data. From these data your Section Chief may be able to suggest the codes that are most likely to be correct.

12. Following are the industries, types of establishments, or types of work for which county data have been prepared:

Automobile factories
Blast furnaces, steel works, and rolling mills
Cloth glove factories, knitted glove factories, and leather glove factories
Cut stone and stone products (manufacturing) and stone quarrying
Fur goods factories and fur dressing and dyeing factories
Hat body factories and hat trimming and millinery factories
Iron and steel foundries and nonferrous metal foundries (copper, brass, etc.)
Knitted outerwear (manufacturing)
Leather tanneries and leather product factories
Lumber industries (selected)
Mining industries
Navy yards
Nonferrous metal primary products and miscellaneous nonferrous metal industries
Oil and petroleum industries
Paper and pulp mills
Paper bag factories and bag factories other than paper
Paper box factories and wooden box factories
Railroad car building shops and repair shops operated by steam or street railroads
Rayon chemical factories and rayon textile mills
Rubber boot and shoe factories
Textile mills
Underwear knitting mills and other underwear factories
W.P.A. projects
Wire mills
Wrought pipe mills

10295

Checking and Coding "Class of Worker" Entries in Col. 30

13. These instructions are supplementary to the basic instructions for checking and coding the entry in col. 30 of the Population Schedule, which are presented on pages 7 and 8 of the "Alphabetical Index of Occupations and Industries." You should become thoroughly familiar with the basic instructions. You should also review paragraphs 569-575 of "Instructions to Enumerators," which explain the entries in col. 30 of the schedule. The following supplementary instructions deal with (a) rules for coding "class of worker" when the enumerator has omitted the "class of worker" entry in col. 30 of the schedules; and (b) rules for detecting incorrect entries in col. 30 and for supplying the correct codes for such entries. Note that in case of missing or incorrect entries in col. 30, you are not to make entries or corrections in that column--merely enter the proper codes in the third space in col. F.

14. Rules for coding "Class of Worker" when there is no entry in col. 30. (For any case which does not appear to be covered by one of the following rules, consult your Section Chief.)

   a. Code as "2" (GW) any person coded "2" (public emergency worker) in col. E.

   b. Code as "2" (GW) any person coded "95" (Postal service), "96" (National defense), "97" (Federal government n.e.c.), or "98" (State or local government) in the second (industry) space in col. F.

   c. Code as "2" (GW) any other person who, according to the occupation-industry entry in cols. 28 and 29, is employed by any governmental agency (Federal, State, county, municipal, etc.).

   d. A farmer for whom a Farm Schedule is returned (a number in col. 34) should be coded as "3" (E), provided that he is the head of the household or related to the head of the household (0, 1, 2, 3, 4, or 5 in code col. A) and there is an unrelated member of the household (6, 7, 8, or X in code col. A) who is a farm worker or farm laborer and is reported as "PW"; if no unrelated member of the household is a farm worker or farm laborer reported as "PW" the code for the related person for whom a Farm Schedule was returned should be "4" (OA).

   e. A farm worker or farm laborer for whom a Farm Schedule was not returned (no entry in col. 34) should be coded as "1" (PW); except that a related member of the household, other than the head (1, 2, 3, 4, or 5 in code col. A) with an entry of "1" or more in col. 31 (weeks worked) and "0" or blank in col. 32 (wages) should be coded "5" (NP) if the head or another related member is a farmer.

   f. Code as "3" (E) the proprietor or owner of any establishment or enterprise which usually requires the assistance of employees (e.g., factory, mill, newspaper, etc.).

   g. Code as "4" (OA) the proprietor or owner of any establishment or enterprise about which there is considerable doubt as to whether it requires the assistance of employees (e.g., retail grocery store, gas filling station, physician or lawyer with private practice, etc.).

   h. Code as "1" (PW) an officer, supervisor or any other employee of any non-governmental establishment or enterprise which is entered as "corporation" in col. 29.

   i. Any person for whom the industry entry in col. 29 includes "at home" (when there is no indication that the person is employed by an outside commercial employer) should be coded "4" (OA) if an adult, and "5" (NP) if a child under 18 years old.

   j. Code as "1" (PW) all other persons for whom there is no evidence in the schedule to the contrary.

10295

- 4 -

15. **Rules for detecting and coding "inconsistent" class of worker entries in col. 30.** (Note that some of the rules listed above in paragraph 14 for coding class of worker when the entry in col. 30 has been omitted are repeated below, while others are not. Do not use any of the above rules which are not listed below to make corrections in entries in col. 30. If any case of apparent inconsistency arises to which the following rules do not apply, consult your Section Chief).

Inconsistent Entries in Col. 30	Correct Entry	Correct Code (in 3rd space of col. F)
a. Any entry other than "GW" for a person coded "95" (Postal service), "96" (National defense), "97" (Federal government n.e.c.), or "98" (State or local government) in the second (industry) space in col. F	GW	2
b. Any entry other than "GW" for any other person who, according to the occupation-industry entry in cols. 28 and 29, is employed by any governmental agency (Federal, State, county, municipal, etc.)	GW	2
c. An entry of "OA" for a farmer who is the head, or related to the head, of a household (0, 1, 2, 3, 4, or 5 in code col. A) and for whom a Farm Schedule was returned (a number in col. 34) if there is a farm laborer or farm worker in the household for whom the entry in code col. A is "X" and who is reported as "PW" in col. 30	E	3
d. An entry of "OA" for a person working in his own home for a commercial employer (see paragraphs 16 to 19 below)	PW	1
e. Any entry other than "PW" for an officer, supervisor or other employee of any non-government establishment or enterprise which is entered as "corporation" in col. 29	PW	1
f. An entry of "PW" or "NP" for the proprietor or owner of any establishment or enterprise which typically requires the assistance of employees (e.g., factory, mill, newspaper, etc.)	E	3
g. An entry of "PW" or "NP" for the proprietor or owner of any establishment or enterprise about which there is considerable doubt as to whether it requires the assistance of employees (e.g., retail grocery store, gas filling station, etc.)	OA	4
h. An entry of "NP" for a clergyman, pastor, etc.	PW	1
i. An entry of "NP" for the head of the household or for an unrelated member of the household (0, 6, 7, 8, 9, or X in code col. A)	(Code according to other evidence on the schedule, especially occupation entries.)	

10295

- 5 -

INSTRUCTIONS FOR INDUSTRIAL HOME WORKER TRANSCRIPTION SHEET

16. Some portfolios are to be examined for <u>industrial home workers</u>, and certain information for such persons is to be transcribed from the schedules to a special "Industrial Home Worker Transcription Sheet" (Form P-358). Each portfolio to be examined is identified on the portfolio memorandum. There must be a Transcription Sheet for each of these portfolios. If no industrial home worker is found in an E.D., fill out the heading of the Transcription Sheet and write "None" across the face of the sheet.

Identifying Industrial Home Workers

17. <u>Definition</u>. An industrial home worker is one who works in his or her own home for a <u>commercial</u> employer who, in turn, furnishes the materials or products on which the person works. The employer usually is a manufacturing concern.

18. <u>Proper form of returns</u>. A proper return for an industrial home worker should include the words "at home" in the occupation column of the schedule, following the occupation title, and should state, in the industry column, the kind of business or factory by which the person was employed (see Instructions to Enumerators, paragraph 564). Examples follow:

Occupation	Industry
28	29
Sewer at home	Dress factory
Button carder at home	Button factory
Lace maker at home	Lace factory

19. <u>Distinction between industrial home workers and other workers at home</u>. Care must be exercised in distinguishing between industrial home workers, who work for commercial employers, and persons who work in their own homes for themselves, other members of their families, or for individual customers (see Instructions to Enumerators, paragraphs 564 and 565). For some industrial home workers the words "at home" may be entered in error in the industry column instead of an industry designation. Industrial home workers should have been returned only as wage workers (PW) or as unpaid family workers (NP), whereas home workers <u>not</u> working for commercial employers <u>usually</u> should have been returned as working on their own account (OA) or as unpaid family workers (NP). The following procedures should be followed in distinguishing between industrial home workers and other persons working in their own homes:

a. Any person working in his own home, for whom the class of worker returned is "PW", should be considered as an industrial home worker if there is evidence that the person is working for a <u>commercial</u> employer and is not merely working in some <u>home</u> enterprise (as a store, dressmaking shop, or filling station).

b. Any person working in his own home, for whom the class of worker returned is "OA" should <u>not</u> be considered as an industrial home worker unless the occupation or industry return indicates that the person is working for a commercial employer.

c. Any person reported as an unpaid family worker (NP) should be considered as an industrial home worker only if another related member of the same household--particularly a parent--is engaged in the same kind of work and is returned or is classified as an industrial home worker.

10295

- 6 -

20. **Most common types of industrial home work.** The following list, presented as an aid in identifying industrial home workers, includes some of the common types of industrial home work. Industrial home workers will be found in other lines of work, but the list suggests the types of returns for which to watch:

Bunching safety pins	Making collars
Carding bobby pins	Making doll dresses
Carding buttons	Making gloves
Crocheting	Making handbags and purses
Cutting embroidery	Making infants' and children's wear
Cutting lace	
Drawing threads from lace	Making lamp shades
Embroidering	Making samples of art needlework
Hemming handkerchiefs	
Knitting	Sewing garments
Making artificial flowers	Stringing greeting cards
Making bedspreads	Stringing tags

Filling out Transcription Sheet (Form P-358)

21. For each person identified as an industrial home worker, fill out a line on the Industrial Home Worker Transcription Sheet (Form P-358), being careful to record each code symbol, abbreviation, or other entry for which provision is made on the sheet.

22. All entries on the Transcription Sheet, except the third, are to be transcribed directly from the schedules. For the third entry, "Number in household," enter "1" for the first (or only) person in a household engaged in industrial home work, enter "2" for the second person in the same household so engaged, enter "3" for the third person, etc. With the exception of schedules on which the sheet numbers are 61, 62, etc. the members of a household can be identified by the codes in col. A. In this column, the code "0" for head will represent the beginning of a household and the codes 1-8 or X will appear for the other members of this household on the immediately following lines. If you find any industrial home worker for whom either V or 9 is entered in col. A, refer the portfolio to your Section Chief.

23. Industrial home workers may appear on one of the sheets numbered 61, 62, etc. In such cases, refer, by means of the household visitation number entered in col. 3, to the entries for the other members of the household on the preceding sheets, in order to determine the proper entry for the "Number in household" column on the Transcription Sheet.

SIGNING THE PORTFOLIO MEMORANDUM

24. When you have completed coding a portfolio, make the proper entries on the portfolio memorandum on the front cover to show that you have done the coding and that, if called for, you have made the transcription of data relating to industrial home workers.

June 7, 1940
10295

APPENDIX V
DESCRIPTION OF PUNCH CARDS (A–S) USED IN 1940 CENSUS OF POPULATION AND HOUSING

DEPARTMENT OF COMMERCE
Bureau of the Census
Washington

POPULATION: 1940
Form P-471

PUNCH CARDS USED IN THE 1940 CENSUSES OF POPULATION AND HOUSING

The various punch cards being used in the Population Census and Housing Census of 1940 are presented and described below. The required statistics are obtained by sorting and tabulating these cards on machines which are operated through electrical contacts made through the holes in the cards.

All of these cards are of the 45-column type. In general, this type of card is adequate for the unit (person, household, family, or dwelling unit) that the card represents. The use of a greater number of cards with 45 columns, rather than fewer cards with more columns, makes possible greater flexibility in the tabulation program. Also, special census tabulating machines called "unit tabulators" have been developed that make possible very rapid counts of the characteristics represented by the punches in the card.

In general, the number of the schedule or transcription sheet columns from which the information is taken, are printed across the top of the card, and the card column numbers and description of the information across the bottom of the card. Where additional information is helpful, this is printed on the card either in italics, or is underscored. The symbols, such as "Hd" for "Head", are printed on the card rather than the number of the position on the card which represents that characteristic.

The following punch cards are described in more detail on the pages that follow.

Card S. This card is punched for individuals included in the 5% sample, that is, each person enumerated on the line marked "Suppl. Quest." of the Population Schedule. Each card provides space for the entry of information for 4 such persons.

Card A. This card is punched for each individual enumerated on the Population Schedule.

Card B. This card is punched for each individual included in the 5% sample, that is, each person enumerated on the line marked "Suppl. Quest." of the Population Schedule.

Card C. This card is punched for each woman, 15 years of age or over, included in the 5% sample.

Card D. This card is punched for each household included in the 5% sample, that is, each household whose head was enumerated on a line marked "Suppl. Quest." of the Population Schedule.

Card E. This card is punched for each dwelling unit enumerated on the Occupied Dwelling Schedule or the Vacant Dwelling Schedule.

Card F. This card is punched for each household enumerated on the Population Schedule. Information regarding the dwelling unit occupied by the household is obtained from the Occupied Dwelling Schedule.

Card G. This card is punched for each mortgaged owner-occupied nonfarm property enumerated on the Occupied Dwelling Schedule.

December 18, 1940

DEPARTMENT OF COMMERCE
Bureau of the Census
Washington

Population: 1940
Form P-471-A

PUNCH CARD A
Population Individual Card 1940

A Card A, like the one shown below, is punched for each individual enumerated on the Population Schedule.

The items presented in the various columns of Card A, and the categories included for each item, are indicated below.

Columns 1-6. Gang punch. Designates State, county, metropolitan region, city size, city or minor civil division, ward or census tract, and enumeration district. This code is mechanically punched into all cards for an enumeration district as a separate operation.

Columns 7 and 8. Sheet number. Columns 9 and 10. Line number. The sheet and line number on which the individual was enumerated.

Column 11. Farm residence. Whether living on a farm.

Column 12. Relationship to the head of the household. Including head; wife; child; parent; grandchild; other relative; lodger; servant; other unrelated persons; hired hand; other employee (X position); heads of institutions or other quasi-households (V position); inmates of institutions and other members of quasi-households.

Column 13. Sex.

Column 14. Color or race. White, Negro, Indian, Chinese, Japanese, Filipino, Hindu, Korean, other races.

Columns 15 and 16. Age. By months for persons under 1 year of age and for others by single years from 1 to 108, 109 or more.

Column 17. Marital status. Single; married, spouse enumerated as a member of the household; widowed; divorced; married, spouse not enumerated as a member of the household.

Column 18. Has this person attended school since March 1, 1940? Yes or No.

Columns 19 and 20. Highest grade of school successfully completed. Single grades from the first through four years of college, five years of college or more.

Columns 21 and 22. Birthplace. State or country of birth.

Column 23. Citizenship of the foreign-born. Naturalized, first papers, alien, unknown.

Columns 24-27. Migration. Place of residence on April 1, 1935. For nonmigrants: same house or different house but same place. For migrants: State, subregion of State, and classification of place, as "City of 100,000 or more," "Urban, 25,000-100,000," "Urban, 10,000-25,000," "Urban, 2,500-10,000," "Rural nonfarm," "Rural farm," "Rural farm residence unknown."

Population: 1940
Form P-471-A (cont.)

Column 28. Work status during the week of March 24-30.

    Persons in the labor force:
      At work
      Engaged in emergency work
      Seeking work
      With a job
    Persons not in the labor force:
      Housewives
      Students
      Unable to work
      Not in the labor force for other reasons
    Inmates of specified institutions
    Unknown work status

Columns 29 and 30. Time. For persons at work, number of hours worked week of March 24-30. For persons seeking work or engaged in emergency work, number of weeks since the last full-time job in private or nonemergency government employment.

Columns 31-36. Occupation, industry, and class of worker. The major occupational group; the specific occupation; the industry in which the occupation is pursued; the class of worker, that is, wage worker in private employment, government wage worker, employer, own-account worker, unpaid family worker, new worker, or unknown.

Columns 37 and 38. The number of full-time weeks worked during 1939.

Columns 39-42. The amount of wages or salary received during 1939.

Column 43. Other income. Received $50 or more from sources other than money wages or salary during the year 1939. Yes or No.

Column 44. Whether the person was enumerated on a line marked "Suppl. Quest." and, hence, included in the five percent sample for whom additional information was obtained.

Column 45. The symbol "2" is punched as a control of punching.

December 18, 1940

22901

DEPARTMENT OF COMMERCE
Bureau of the Census
Washington

Population: 1940
Form P-471-B

PUNCH CARD B
Population-Supplementary Individual Card 1940

A Card B, like the one shown below, is punched for each individual included in the five percent sample, that is, each person enumerated on a line marked "Suppl. Quest."

The items presented in the various columns of Card B, and the categories included for each item, are indicated below.

Columns 1-6. Gang punch. Designates State, county, metropolitan region, city size, city or minor civil division, ward or census tract, and enumeration district. This code is mechanically punched into all cards for an enumeration district as a separate operation.

Columns 7 and 8. Sheet number. Columns 9 and 10. Line number. The sheet and line number on which the individual was enumerated.

Columns 11 and 12. Parents' birthplace. For a native-born person, one of whose parents was born abroad, the country of birth of the foreign-born parent. If both parents were foreign-born, the country of birth of the father.

Columns 13 and 14. Mother tongue. The language spoken in the person's home during his childhood.

Column 15. Veteran. Veterans, and wives, widows, and under 18-year-old children of veterans classified by the war or service in which the veteran participated, as follows:

    World War
    Child of deceased World War veteran
    Spanish and World War
    Spanish-American War
    Regular establishment (peace-time service only)
    Other war or service
    War or service unknown.

Column 16. Social Security. Part of wages and salary from which deductions were made for Old Age Insurance or Railroad Retirement during 1939:

    No Social Security account
    Deductions from all wages or salary
    Deductions from one-half or more of wages or salary
    Deductions from less than one-half of wages or salary
    Has Social Security account but no deductions
    Has Social Security account but amount of deductions unknown
    Has Social Security account, unknown whether deductions made.

Columns 17-22. Usual occupation, industry, and class of worker. The major occupational group; the specific occupation in which the person is usually engaged; the industry in which the usual occupation is pursued; the usual class of worker, that is, wage worker in private employment, government wage worker, employer, own-account worker, unpaid family worker, new worker, or unknown.

Population: 1940
Form P-471-B (cont.)

- 2 -

Column 23. Tenure. Home owned or rented.

Column 24. Value or monthly rent. If the home is rented, the rental is shown as: Under $5, $5-$9, $10-$14, $15-$19, $20-$29, $30-$39, $40-$49, $50-$74, $75-$99, $100 or more. If the home is owned, the value of the home is shown as: Under $500, $500-$999, $1000-$1499, etc.

Column 25. Farm residence and sex. Not living on a farm: males, females; living on a farm: males, females.

Column 26. Color and nativity. Native white, both parents native; native white, both parents foreign; native white, father foreign; native white, mother foreign; foreign-born white; Negro; other races.

The items presented in columns 27-45 of Card B correspond to the items presented in various columns of Card A, as follows:

Card B column	Item	Corresponding Card A column
27-28	Age	15-16
29	Marital status	17
30-31	Highest grade of school successfully completed	19-20
32	Citizenship of the foreign-born	23
33	Work status during the week of March 24-30	28
34	Time (coded)	29-30
35-40	Occupation, industry, and class of worker	31-36
41	The number of full-time weeks worked during 1939 (coded)	37-38
42-43	The amount of wages or salary received during 1939	39-40
44	Other income	43
45	Relationship to the head of the household	12

December 18, 1940

DEPARTMENT OF COMMERCE
Bureau of the Census
Washington

Population: 1940
Form P-471-C

PUNCH CARD C
Population-Fertility Card 1940

A Card C, like the one shown below, is punched for each woman 15 years of age and over enumerated on a line marked "Suppl. Quest." Items in columns 1-20 and 45 are mechanically reproduced from Card B. The remaining items are punched from the Fertility Transcription Sheet prepared from the Population Schedule.

The items presented in columns 1-20 are mechanically reproduced from the various columns of Card B as indicated below.

Card C column	Item	Reproduced from Card B column
1-6	Gang punch	1-6
7-8	Parents' birthplace	11-12
9	Tenure	23
10	Value or monthly rent	24
11	Color and nativity	26
12-13	Age	27-28
14-15	Highest grade of school successfully completed	30-31
16	Relationship to the head of the household	45
17-18	Sheet number	7-8
19-20	Line number	9-10
45 (part)	Farm residence and sex	25

The items presented in columns 21-45 and the categories included for each item are indicated below. The items are punched from the Fertility Transcription Sheet.

Columns 21-34 refer to the woman

Column 21. **Marital status.** The categories shown are: Single; widowed; divorced; married once, husband present; married more than once, husband present; married unknown times, husband present; and married, husband absent.

Columns 22 and 23. **The age of the woman at first marriage.**

Column 24. **The number of children ever born to the woman.**

Column 25. **Mother tongue.** English, Scandinavian, French, German, Polish, Yiddish, Southeast Slovak, Italian, Spanish, Russian, other.

Column 26. **Number of this woman's children under 5 years of age living in the household.**

Column 27. **Number of this woman's children 5-9 years of age living in the household.**

Columns 28 and 29. **Place of birth.** Same as columns 21-22 of Card A.

Columns 30-33. **Migration.** Place of residence on April 1, 1935. Same categories as shown in columns 24-27 of Card A.

129

Population: 1940
Form P-471-C (cont.)

- 2 -

Column 34. Work status and occupation of this woman.

    Not in the labor force
    Employed at home
    Employed away from home:
      Professional or semiprofessional
      Clerk, saleswoman, etc.
      Craftsman, operative, etc.
      Service worker, except protective
      Other occupation
    On public emergency work
    Seeking work, with experience
    Seeking work, new worker.

The items presented in columns 35-42 refer to the husband of the woman and correspond to the items presented in various columns of Card A, as follows:

Card C column	Item	Corresponding Card A column
35-36	Age	15-16
37-38	Highest grade of school successfully completed	19-20
39	Work status during the week of March 24-30	28
40	Occupation, industry, and class of worker	31
41	The number of full-time weeks worked during 1939 (coded)	37-38
42	The amount of wages or salary received during 1939 (coded)	39-40

Column 43. Family wages. The total wages received in 1939 by persons who were enumerated as members of the household and who are related to the woman.

Column 44. Other income. Whether the husband, or if not the husband, whether some other member of the household received income amounting to $50 or more from sources other than wages or salary in 1939.

Column 45. Color-nativity of the husband of the woman. Native white, foreign-born white, Negro, other.

December 18, 1940

22401

DEPARTMENT OF COMMERCE
Bureau of the Census
Washington

Population: 1940
Form P-471-D

PUNCH CARD D
Sample Family Card-1940

A Card D, like the one reproduced below, is punched for each family whose head is enumerated on a line marked "Suppl. Quest." Items presented in columns 1-18 and part of columns 19 and 35 are mechanically reproduced from the Card B for the head of the family. The remaining items are punched from the Sample Family Transcription Sheet, which is prepared from the Population Schedule.

The items presented in columns 1-18, 19 (part), and 35 (part) are reproduced from the Card B as indicated below.

Card D column	Item	Reproduced from Card B column
1-6	Gang punch	1-6
7	Veteran	15
8	Social Security	16
9	Value or monthly rent	24
10	Color and nativity	26
11-12	Age	27-28
13	Work status during the week of March 24-30	33
14	Occupation, industry, and class of worker	35
15-16	Sheet number	7-8
17-18	Line number	9-10
19 (part)	Marital status	29
35 (part)	Tenure	23

The items presented in column 19 (part) and columns 20-45, and the categories included for each item, are indicated below.

Column 19 (part). Persons 65 years of age and over. No persons; 1 male and 1 female; 1 male and no females; 1 female and no males; 2 males and no females; 2 females and no males; 3 or more persons regardless of sex.

Column 20. Highest grade completed by the head of the household. None; 1-4 grades; 5-6 grades; 7-8 grades; 1 year of high school; 2-3 years of high school; 4 years of high school; 1 year of college; 2-3 years of college; 4 or more years of college; unknown.

Columns 21 and 22. Age of the wife of the head of the household.

Column 23. Work status and occupation of the wife of the head of the household. (Same as column 34 of Card C.)

Column 24. Number of children under 10 years of age related to the head of the household.

Column 25. Number of related single children under 18 years of age.

Population: 1940
Form P-471-D (cont.)

- 2 -

Column 26. Number of children 14-17 and whether in the labor force.

    No children 14 to 17 years of age
    One or more children 14 to 15, but no children 16 to 17:
      One or more in labor force
      None in labor force
    No children 14 to 15, but one or more children 16 to 17:
      One or more in labor force
      None in labor force
    One or more children 14 to 15 and one or more children 16 to 17:
      One or more 14 to 15 and one or more 16 to 17 in labor force
      One or more 14 to 15, but none 16 to 17 in labor force
      None 14 to 15, but one or more 16 to 17 in labor force
      None in labor force.

Column 27. The least duration of unemployment of related workers. The smallest number of weeks since the last full-time job reported by any worker related to the head is coded in this column in the following groups: No workers on emergency work or seeking work (or no duration reported), under 3 weeks, 3-6, 7-10, 11-14, 15-23, 24-35, 36-49, 50-99, 100-149, 150 or over.

Column 28. Class of worker composition of related workers.

    No workers
    1 or more wage workers:
      All wage workers or all wage and new workers:
        Head wage worker
        Head not a wage worker
      Some wage workers and some workers other class of worker
        Head wage worker
        Head not a wage worker
    No wage workers:
      1 or more employers, own account workers, unpaid family
        workers, with or without new workers or unknown workers
      All new workers and/or unknown class of worker.

Column 29. Weeks worked by related earners.

    No earners
    Head earner, 50 weeks or more:
      Every earner 50 weeks or more
      Some earners 50 weeks or more, and some under 50 or unknown
    Head earner, 36-49 weeks:
      Some earners 50 weeks or more, and some under 50 or unknown
      Every earner less than 50 weeks or unknown
    Head earner, 24-35 weeks:
      Some earners 50 weeks or more, and some under 50 or unknown
      Every earner less than 50 weeks or unknown
    Head earner, less than 24 weeks or unknown:
      Some earners 50 weeks or more, and some under 50 or unknown
      Every earner less than 50 weeks or unknown
    Head not earner, but some other earners in the family:
      Every earner 50 weeks or more
      Some earners 50 weeks or more, and some under 50 or unknown
      Every earner less than 50 weeks or unknown.

Columns 30 and 31. Wages of first earner. The amount reported in hundreds of dollars of wages or salary received in 1939 by the head of the household or, if he was not a wage earner, by the wife or first person listed who was a wage earner.

Columns 32 and 33. Amount of money wages or salary received by second earner.

Column 34. Number of related earners.

Column 35 (part). Relationship of earners. No earners; head earner, wife not an earner; wife earner, head not an earner; head and wife both earners; neither head nor wife earner.

Column 36. Other related persons' other income. Whether the head or some other member of the family had an income of $50 or more from sources other than wages or salary.

Column 37. Lodgers and sub-families (a married couple with or without children not including the head of the household).

    No lodgers:
      No sub-families
      1 sub-family:
        Father as sub-head
        Son as sub-head
        Other relative as sub-head
      2 or more sub-families

Population: 1940
Form P-471-D (cont.)

Column 37. Lodgers and sub-families (cont.).

    1 or more lodgers:
     No sub-families
     1 sub-family:
      Father or son as sub-head
      Other relative as sub-head
      Lodger as sub-head
     2 or more sub-families:
      1 related sub-head
      2 or more related sub-heads
      All lodger sub-heads

Column 38. Number of related persons.

Column 39. Number of related workers.

Column 40. Number of related workers at work or with a job during the week of March 24-30.

Column 41. Number of related workers on emergency work.

Column 42. Number of related workers seeking work.

Columns 43 and 44. Family wage. Total wages or salary received in 1939 by workers related to the head reported in hundreds of dollars.

Column 45. Farm residence and sex. Same as column 25 on Card B.

December 18, 1940

DEPARTMENT OF COMMERCE
Bureau of the Census
Washington

POPULATION: 1940
Form P-471-E

PUNCH CARD E
Housing-Dwelling Card

A Card E, like the one shown below, is punched for each of the dwelling units enumerated on the Occupied-Dwelling Schedule and on the Vacant-Dwelling Schedule.

[Punch card image]

The items presented in the various columns of Card E, and the categories included for each item, are indicated below.

Column 1-6. Gang punch. Designates State, county, metropolitan region, city size, city or minor civil division, ward or census tract, and enumeration district. This code is mechanically punched into all cards for an enumeration district as a separate operation.

Column 7-8. Sheet number. Represents sheet number of the Occupied-Dwelling Schedule which is the same as the sheet number of the Population Schedule for the head of the household occupying the dwelling unit.

Column 9. Dwelling unit number within structure.

Column 10-11. Population line number. Represents the line number on the Population Schedule for the head of the household occupying the dwelling unit.

Column 12-13. Block number. Shown only for cities of 50,000 or more.

Column 14. Color or race of head: White, Negro, Other race.

Column 15. Number of persons in household: 1 person, 2 persons, etc., to 10 persons, 11 or more persons.

Column 16 (upper). Live on farm? Yes, No.

Column 16 (lower). Persons per room: .50 or less; .51 to .75; .76 to 1.00; 1.01 to 1.50; 1.51 to 2.00; 2.01 or more.

Column 17. Home tenure or occupancy status:

    Owned
    Rented
    Vacant, for sale or rent, ordinary
    Vacant, for sale or rent, seasonal
    Vacant, held for occupancy of absent household, ordinary
    Vacant, held for occupancy of absent household, seasonal
    Occupied by nonresident household, ordinary
    Occupied by nonresident household, seasonal

POPULATION: 1940
Form P-471-E
Page 2

Column 18-20. Value or rent. Value of home in $100 intervals for owners; monthly rent in $1 intervals for renters.

Column 21-23. Estimated or gross rent. Estimated monthly rent for nonfarm owners; gross monthly rent (unfurnished rent plus utility costs) for nonfarm renters in $1 intervals.

Column 24. Type of structure:

    1-family detached
    1-family attached
    2-family side-by-side
    2-family other
    3-family, no business
    4-family, no business
    1-4 family, with business
    5-9 family, with or without business
    10-19 family, with or without business
    20-family or more, with or without business
    Other dwelling place

Column 25 (part). Originally built as:

    Residential structure, same number of dwelling units
    Residential structure, different number of dwelling units
    Nonresidential structure

Column 25 (part). Type of other dwelling place. Not used.

Column 26. Exterior material: Wood, brick, stucco, other.

Column 27 (part). Structure in need of major repair? Yes, No.

Column 27 (part). State of repair and plumbing equipment:

    Not needing major repair
        With private bath, private flush toilet and running water
        With private flush toilet and running water, no private bath
        With running water, no private flush toilet
        No running water in dwelling unit
    Needing major repair
        With private bath, private flush toilet and running water
        With private flush toilet and running water, no private bath
        With running water, no private flush toilet
        No running water in dwelling unit
    Unknown major repair or plumbing

Column 28-29. Year originally built: 1850-1940 by single years; 1849 or before.

Column 30. Number of rooms: 1 room, 2 rooms, etc., to 10 rooms, 11 or more rooms.

Column 31. Water supply:

    Running water in dwelling unit
    Hand pump in dwelling unit
    Running water within 50 feet
    Other supply within 50 feet
    No water supply within 50 feet

Column 32. Toilet facilities:

    Flush toilet in structure, exclusive use
    Flush toilet in structure, shared
    No flush toilet in structure
    Outside toilet or privy
    No toilet or privy

Column 33. Bathtub or shower with running water in structure: Exclusive use, shared, none.

Column 34. Principal lighting equipment: Electricity, gas, kerosene or gasoline, other.

Column 35. Principal refrigeration equipment: Mechanical, ice, other, none.

Column 36. Radio in dwelling unit? Yes, No.

Column 37. Heating equipment:

    Steam or hot water system
    Piped warm air system
    Pipeless warm air furnace
    Heating stove
    Other or none

POPULATION: 1940
Form P-471-E
Page 3

Column 38. <u>Principal fuel used for heating:</u>

    Coal or coke
    Wood
    Gas
    Electricity
    Fuel oil
    Kerosene or gasoline
    Other or none

Column 39. <u>Principal fuel used for cooking:</u>

    Coal or coke
    Wood
    Gas
    Electricity
    Kerosene or gasoline
    Other or none

<u>For Nonfarm Renters</u>

<u>Column 40-43.</u> Total monthly cost of utilities and fuel. In dollars and cents.

<u>Column 44.</u> Is furniture included in rent? Yes, No.

<u>For Nonfarm Owners</u>

<u>Column 40-42.</u> Value of property. In $100 intervals.

<u>Column 43.</u> Number of dwelling units included in value.

<u>Column 44.</u> Mortgage on property? Yes, No.

<u>For All Dwelling Units</u>

<u>Column 45.</u> Control punch. Code X is punched as a control of punching and tabulation.

22901

DEPARTMENT OF COMMERCE
Bureau of the Census
Washington

POPULATION: 1940
Form P-471-F

PUNCH CARD F
Household Card

A Card F, like the one shown below, is punched for each household enumerated on the Population Schedule. Items relating to the dwelling unit occupied by the household, as enumerated on the Occupied-Dwelling Schedule, are mechanically reproduced from Card E. The remaining items, relating to the population characteristics of the household and of the head of the household, are punched from the household transcription sheet which is prepared from the Population Schedule.

[Punch card image]

The items presented in columns 1 to 23, and parts of columns 22 and 45 of Card F are mechanically reproduced from the various columns of Card E, as indicated below.

Card F Column	Item	Reproduced from Card E Column
1-6	Gang punch	1-6
7-9	Estimated or gross rent (nonfarm only)	21-23
8	Water supply (farm only)	31
9	Toilet facilities (farm only)	32
10	Type of structure	24
11 (part)	Structure in need of major repair?	27
11 (part)	State of repair and plumbing equipment	27
12	Number of rooms	30
13	Home tenure	17
14-16	Value or rent	18-20
17 (part)	Live on a farm?	16
17 (part)	Persons per room	16
18-19	Sheet number	7-8
20-21	Population line number	10-11
22 (part)	Principal lighting equipment	34
45 (part)	Furniture included in rent? (nonfarm renters only)	44
45 (part)	Mortgage on property? (nonfarm owner only)	44

The items presented in columns 23-45 and parts of columns 22 and 45 of Card F, and the categories included for each of these items are indicated below. These columns are punched from information transcribed from the Population Schedule to the household transcription sheet for each household.

Column 22 (part). Sex of head of household.

Column 23. Color or race of head of household. White, including Mexican; Negro; Indian; Chinese; Japanese; Filipino; Hindu; Korean; other.

Column 24-25. Age of head of household. By single years to 108, 109 or more.

Column 26. Marital status of head of household. Single; married, spouse enumerated as a member of the household; widowed; divorced; and married, spouse not enumerated as a member of the household.

137

POPULATION: 1940
Form P-471-F
Page 2

Column 27. **Citizenship of head of household:**

    Native born
    Foreign born, naturalized citizen
    Foreign born, having first papers
    Foreign born, alien
    Foreign born, unknown citizenship

Column 28. **Migration of head of household.** Designates place of residence on April 1, 1935 as:

    Same house
    Same county, different house
    Outside same county:
        Rural-nonfarm
        Rural-farm
        Rural-farm residence unknown
        Urban, 2,500 to 10,000
        Urban, 10,000 to 25,000
        Urban, 25,000 to 100,000
        Urban, 100,000 or more
        Population group unknown or foreign
    Unknown

Column 29. **Work status during the week of March 24 to 30 of head of household:**

    At work in private industry or nonemergency government work
    At work in public emergency work
    Seeking work
    Not at work but with a job
    Home housework
    In school
    Unable to work
    Other
    Unknown

Column 30. **Occupation group of head of household:**

    Professional or semi-professional work
    Farmer or farm manager
    Proprietor, manager, or official, except farm
    Clerical, sales, or kindred worker
    Craftsman, foreman, or kindred worker
    Operative or kindred worker
    Domestic service worker
    Protective service worker
    Service worker, except domestic or protective
    Farm laborer or foreman
    Laborer, except farm
    Unknown

Column 31-32. **Full-time weeks worked during 1939 by head of household.**

Column 33. **Lodgers and sub-families** (a married couple with or without children, not including the head of the household.)

    No lodgers:
        No sub-families
        1 sub-family:
            Father or father-in-law as sub-head
            Son or son-in-law as sub-head
            Other relative as sub-head
        2 or more sub-families
    1 or more lodgers:
        No sub-families
        1 sub-family:
            Father, father-in-law, son or son-in-law as sub-head
            Other relative as sub-head
            Lodger as sub-head
        2 or more sub-families:
            1 related sub-head
            2 or more related sub-heads
            All lodger sub-heads

Column 34. **Total persons in household.** 1 person, 2 persons, etc., to 11 persons, 12 or more persons.

Column 35. **Number of related persons.** 1 person, 2 persons, etc., to 11 persons, 12 or more persons.

Column 36. **Number of related children under 21 years of age.** No children, 1 child, 2 children, etc., to 8 children, 9 or more children.

POPULATION: 1940
Form P-471-F
Page 3

Column 37. Number of related workers. No workers, 1 worker, 2 workers, etc., to 8 workers, 9 or more workers.

Column 38. Number of related workers employed in private or nonemergency government work. No workers, 1 worker, 2 workers, etc., to 8 workers, 9 or more workers.

Column 39. Number of related workers employed in emergency government work. No workers, 1 worker, 2 workers, etc., to 8 workers, 9 or more workers.

Column 40. Number of related workers seeking work. No workers, 1 worker, 2 workers, etc., to 8 workers, 9 or more workers.

Column 41. Class of worker. Composition of related workers.

> No workers
> 1 or more wage workers:
> > All wage workers or all wage and new workers
> > Some wage workers and some workers of other class
> No wage workers:
> > 1 or more employers, own account workers, or unpaid family workers
> > All new workers of class of workers unknown

Column 42-43. Related persons wage income. Total wage and salary income in 1939 of related persons 14 years old or over. Presented in $100 intervals.

Column 44. Related persons other income. Indicates whether or not any of the related persons had income of $50 or more from sources other than wages or salary, in 1939.

Column 45. Supplementary question. Indicates whether the head of the household was enumerated on a line marked "Suppl. Quest." and hence included in the 5 percent sample for whom additional information was obtained.

DEPARTMENT OF COMMERCE
Bureau of the Census
Washington

POPULATION: 1940
Form P-471-G

PUNCH CARD G
Mortgage Card

A Card G, like the one shown below, is punched for each mortgaged, owner-occupied nonfarm property without business that contains not more than four dwelling units. Items relating to the characteristics of home mortgage finance are obtained from the Occupied-Dwelling Schedule. General housing and population characteristics are mechanically reproduced from Card F.

The items presented in columns 1 to 33, and the categories included for each of these items are indicated below. These columns are punched from information on the Occupied-Dwelling Schedule.

Column 1-6. *Gang punch.* Designates State, county, metropolitan region, city size, city or minor civil division, ward or census tract, and enumeration district. This code is mechanically punched into all cards for an enumeration district as a separate operation.

Column 7-8. *Sheet number.* Represents sheet number of the Occupied-Dwelling Schedule which is the same as the sheet number of the Population Schedule for the head of the owner's household.

Column 9-10. *Population line number.* Represents the line number on the Population Schedule for the head of the owner's household.

Column 11. Type of structure:

    1-family detached
    1-family attached
    2-family side-by-side
    2-family other
    3-family, no business
    4-family, no business

Column 12-13. *Year originally built.* 1850-1940 by single years; 1849 or before.

Column 14-16. *Value of property.* In $100 intervals.

Column 17. *Number of dwelling units included in value.*

Column 18-20. *Total mortgage debt.* For properties with both first mortgage and second mortgage or other junior lien. In $100 intervals.

Column 21-23. *First mortgage debt.* In $100 intervals.

140

POPULATION: 1940
Form P-471-G
Page 2

<u>Column 24. Frequency of regular payments:</u> Monthly, quarterly, semi-annual, annual, other regular payment plan, no regular payments required.

<u>Column 25-28. Amount of each mortgage payment.</u> In $1 intervals.

<u>Column 29.</u> Do payments include an amount for reduction of principal? Yes, No.

<u>Column 30.</u> Do payments include real estate taxes? Yes, No.

<u>Column 31-32. Interest rate now charged.</u> Presented as full percent, fraction less than 1/2%, exactly 1/2%, fraction more than 1/2%. From 0 to 10%.

<u>Column 33. Holder of first mortgage.</u> Building and loan association, commercial bank or trust company, mutual or stock savings bank, life insurance company, mortgage company, Home Owners' Loan Corporation, individual, other.

The items presented in columns 34 to 45 of Card G are mechanically reproduced from the various columns of Card F as indicated below. These items relate to the characteristics of the owner's household and the dwelling unit it occupies.

Card G Column	Item	Reproduced from Card F Column
34	Color or race of head of household	23
35-37	Estimated rent	7-9
38 (part)	Structure in need of major repair?	11
38 (part)	State of repair and plumbing equipment	11
39	Number of rooms	12
40	Occupation group of head of household	30
41	Total persons in household	34
42-43	Related persons' wage income	42-43
44	Related persons' other income	44
45	Lodgers and sub-families	33

December 18, 1940

22901

DEPARTMENT OF COMMERCE
Bureau of the Census
Washington

Population: 1940
Form P-471-S

PUNCH CARD S
Population-Preliminary Sample Card 1940

A Card S, like the one shown below, is punched for each sheet of the Population Schedule. In the first of the **four sections** of the card are punched the items relating to the first individual enumerated on a line marked "Suppl. Quest."; **in the second of the four sections** are punched the items relating to the second individual enumerated on a line marked **"Suppl. Quest."**; etc. for the third and fourth sections. Thus, each card represents the four individuals enumerated on the **sample lines**. The information is punched from the Preliminary Sample Transcription Sheet prepared from the Population Schedule.

The items presented in the various columns of Card S and the categories included for each item are indicated below. (For columns 13-36, the columns in each of the four sections are listed in order.)

Columns 1 and 2. State.

Column 3. Area. Rural, urban 2,500-99,999, each city of 100,000 or more separately.

Columns 4-6. City-County.

Columns 7-10. Enumeration district number.

Columns 11 and 12. Sheet number.

Columns 13, 19, 25, and 31. Live on a farm? Yes or No.

Columns 14, 20, 26, and 32. Sex.

Columns 15, 21, 27, and 33. Color. White, colored.

Columns 16-17, 22-23, 28-29, 34-35. Age.

Columns 18, 24, 30, 36. Work status.

    In the labor force:
      Seeking work, new worker
      At work
      Emergency work
      Seeking work, experienced
      With a job
    Not in the labor force
      Home housework
      Student
      Unable to work
      Not in the labor force for other reasons
    Inmate of specified institution.

December 18, 1940

**APPENDIX VI
PROGRESS REPORT AND COSTS
OF THE 1940 CENSUS**

Figure 1. General Progress Report of the 1940 Population and Housing Census by Major Process (Cumulative Percentage Completion)

Month	Receipt of Schedules	Matching of Housing and Population Schedules	Hand Count and Sample Transcription	Separation of Population and Housing Schedules	General Population Coding	Occupation and Industry Coding	Housing Coding	Individual Population (A) Cards Punched	Housing (E) Cards Punched	General Sample (S) Cards Punched
1940										
May	3.2									
June	48.7	6.2	3.9	0.3						
July	89.6	20.8	18.8	3.9	1.3	0.6	0.6	0.1	0.1	
August	99.3	57.1	53.2	18.8	9.7	3.2	6.5	0.5	0.6	0.1
September	100.0	81.8	77.9	35.1	18.8	7.8	18.2	3.4	4.6	0.1
October		99.4	98.7	72.7	27.9	18.8	27.2	8.7	11.5	0.3
November		100.0	100.0	100.0	41.6	28.6	38.9	13.7	19.0	32.4
December					59.1	40.9	62.9	19.6	28.5	100.0
1941										
January					75.3	54.6	76.6	27.5	39.9	
February					80.7	72.7	85.7	35.9	49.4	
March					85.1	81.2	90.9	47.4	59.7	
April					89.6	89.6	94.8	61.8	67.8	
May					98.7	96.1	97.4	75.0	74.9	
June					100.0	99.3	100.0	87.4	82.3	
July						100.0		97.0	95.2	
August								100.0	100.0	

11/28/47

Figure 2. Sixteenth Decennial Census Costs 1940 through 1943

Project	Total	Administration[a]	Division Cost[b]	Field	Geography	Machine Tabulation
16th Decennial Census total	$48,671,533	3,627,209	14,541,270	20,448,620	1,427,441	8,626,993
Population	17,798,022	1,052,314	4,873,517	6,905,718	991,865	3,974,606
Housing	7,206,310	248,612	1,983,509	3,339,891	52,234	1,582,062
Vital Statistics (Other)	284,788	69,202	213,525	10	—	2,052
Marriage and Divorce	165,307	19,144	70,523	48,205	—	27,432
Agriculture	10,164,544	712,571	2,672,750	4,395,322	272,030	2,111,872
Irrigation	260,054	40,392	180,669	—	17,824	21,168
Drainage	202,042	31,238	140,003	2,510	12,697	15,548
Manufactures	2,721,444	449,435	1,249,703	829,779	21,434	171,092
Mineral Industries	470,798	149,807	275,508	12,362	—	33,119
Business	8,047,406	732,661	1,725,452	4,904,945	51,322	633,026
Territories and Possessions	591,883	36,565	484,338	9,828	8,000	53,152
Publicity	173,177	85,223	86,064	50	35	1,805
National Defense	585,768	—	585,709	—	—	59

Source: Administrative Records, U.S. Bureau of the Census

[a] Administration, general research, and housekeeping functions including printing.

[b] Includes planning, editing, coding, analysis, and the writing of the report.

REFERENCES

BC. *See* U.S. Bureau of the Census.

Batschelet, C. E. 1942. "General Principles of Tract Delimitation." *Journal of the American Statistical Association* 37 (June): 245–46.

Brunsman, Howard G. 1941. "The Housing Census of 1940." *Journal of the American Statistical Association* 36 (September): 393–400.

Brunsman, Howard G., and Dave Lowery. 1943. "Facts from the 1940 Census of Housing." *Journal of Land and Public Utility Economics* 19 (February): 89–93.

Committee on Government Statistics and Information Services. (COGSIS) 1937. *Government Statistics*. New York: Social Science Research Council.

Conk, Margo. 1978. "Occupational Classification in the United States Census: 1890–1940." *Journal of Interdisciplinary History* 9 (Summer): 111–30.

Conk, Margo. 1981. "Accuracy, Efficiency, and Bias: The Interpretation of Women's Work in the U.S. Census Statistics of Occupations, 1890–1940." *Historical Methods* 14 (May): 65–72.

DOC. *See* U.S. Department of Commerce.

Deming, W. Edwards. 1940. "Sampling Problems of the 1940 Census." In Cowles Commission for Research in Economics, *Report of the Sixth Annual Research Conference on Economics and Statistics*. Chicago: University of Chicago Press.

Deming, W. Edwards, and Leon Geoffrey. 1941. "On Sample Inspection in the Processing of Census Returns." *Journal of the American Statistical Association* 36 (September): 351–60.

Deming, W. Edwards, and Frederick F. Stephan. 1941. "On the Interpretation of Censuses as Samples." *Journal of the American Statistical Association* 36 (September): 45–50.

Deming, W. Edwards, Benjamin J. Tepping, and Leon Geoffrey. 1942. "Errors in Card Punching." *Journal of the American Statistical Association* 37 (December): 525–36.

Eckler, A. Ross. 1941. "Employment and Income Statistics." *Journal of the American Statistical Association* 36 (September): 381–86.

Eckler, A. Ross. 1972. *The Bureau of the Census*. New York: Praeger Publishers.

Edwards, Alba M. 1941. "Occupation and Industry Statistics." *Journal of the American Statistical Association* 36 (September): 387–92.

Givens, Meredith B. 1934. "An Experiment in Advisory Service: The Committee on Government Statistics and Information Services:" *Journal of the American Statistical Association* 29 (December): 396.

Goldfield, Edwin D. 1958. "Decennial Census and Current Population Survey Data on Income." In Conference on Research in Income and Wealth of the National Bureau of Economic Research, *Studies in Income and Wealth*, Volume 23, *An Appraisal of the 1950 Census Income Data*. Princeton: Princeton University Press.

Hansen, Morris H., and W. Edwards Deming. 1943. "On Some Census Aids to Sampling." *Journal of the American Statistical Association* 38 (September): 353–57.

Hauser, Philip M. 1941a. "Research Possibilities in the 1940 Census." *American Sociological Review* 6 (August): 463–70.

Hauser, Philip M. 1941b. "The Use of Sampling in the Census." *Journal of the American Statistical Association* 36 (September): 369–75.

Hauser, Philip M. 1942. "Proposed Annual Sample Census of Population." *Journal of the American Statistical Association* 37 (February): 81–88.

Hauser, Philip M. 1945. "Wartime Developments in Census Statistics." *American Sociological Review* 10 (April): 160–69.

Hauser, Philip M. 1947. "The Statistical Program of the Census Bureau." *Journal of the American Statistical Association* 42 (March): 24–30.

Hauser, Philip M. 1949. "The Labor Force and Gainful Workers—Concept, Measurement, and Comparability. *American Journal of Sociology* 54 (January): 338–55.

Price, Daniel O. 1947. "A Check on Underenumeration in the 1940 Census." *American Sociological Review* 12 (February): 44–49.

Proudfoot, Malcolm J. 1940a. "New Inquiries for the Census of 1940." *Journal of Land and Public Utility Economics* 16 (February): 102–4.

Proudfoot, Malcolm J. 1940b. "The United States Census of 1940." *Geographical Review* 30 (April): 301–3.

Reed, Vergil D. 1942. "Business Uses of Data by Census

Tracts." *Journal of the American Statistical Association* 37 (June): 238–44.

Scott, Ann Herbert. 1968. *Census, U.S.A.: Fact Finding for the American People, 1790–1970.* New York: Seabury Press.

Shryock, Henry S., Jr. 1941. "General Population Statistics." *Journal of the American Statistical Association* 36 (September): 376–80.

Shryock, Henry S., Jr. 1957. "The Quality of the 1940 Census Data on Migration." In Daniel J. Bogue, Henry S. Shryock, Jr., and Siegfried A. Hoermann, eds., *Scripps Foundation Studies in Population Distribution, No. 5, Subregional Migration in the United States, 1935–1940, Vol. I, Streams of Migration,* pp. 30–36. Oxford, Ohio: Scripps Foundation.

Stephan, Frederick F., W. Edwards Deming, and Morris H. Hansen. 1940. "The Sampling Procedure of the 1940 Population Census." *Journal of the American Statistical Association* 35 (December): 615–630.

Truesdell, Leon E. 1935. "The Mechanics of Tabulation of the Population Census." *Journal of the American Statistical Association* 30 (March): 89–94.

Truesdell, Leon E. 1941. "New Features of the 1940 Population Census." *Journal of the American Statistical Association* 36 (September): 361–68.

Truesdell, Leon E. 1965. *The Development of PunchCard Tabulation in the Bureau of the Census, 1890–1940.* Washington, D.C.: U.S. Government Printing Office.

U.S. Bureau of the Census. 1939. "General Memorandum on Changes under Consideration for the 1940 Census of Population," prepared by Leon E. Truesdell. Washington, D.C.: Bureau of the Census.

U.S. Bureau of the Census. 1940a. "Alphabetic Index of Occupations and Industries," prepared by Alba M. Edwards. Washington, D.C.: U.S. Government Printing Office.

U.S. Bureau of the Census. 1940b. "The Origin of the Wage Income Question on the 1940 Population Schedule," prepared by Leon E. Truesdell. Washington, D.C.: Bureau of the Census.

U.S. Bureau of the Census. 1941. "On the Sampling Methods in the 1940 Population Census," prepared by Frederick F. Stephan and W. Edwards Deming. Washington, D.C.: Bureau of the Census.

U.S. Bureau of the Census. 1942. "The Elimination of Unknown Ages in the 1940 Population Census," prepared by W. Edwards Deming. Washington, D.C.: Bureau of the Census.

U.S. Bureau of the Census, *16th Census of the United States. Population. Estimates of Labor Force, Employment, and Unemployment, in the United States, 1940 and 1930.* Washington, D.C.: Government Printing Office, 1944.

U.S. Bureau of the Census. 1974. *Bureau of the Census Catalog of Publications, 1790–1972.* Washington, D.C.: U.S. Government Printing Office.

U.S. Department of Commerce. 1936. *24th Annual Report of the Secretary of Commerce: June 30, 1936.* Washington, D.C.: U.S. Government Printing Office.

U.S. Department of Commerce. 1938. *26th Annual Report of the Secretary of Commerce: June 30, 1938.* Washington, D.C.: U.S. Government Printing Office.

U.S. Department of Commerce. 1939. *27th Annual Report of the Secretary of Commerce: June 30, 1939.* Washington, D.C.: U.S. Government Printing Office.

U.S. Department of Commerce. 1940. *28th Annual Report of the Secretary of Commerce: June 30, 1940.* Washington, D.C.: U.S. Government Printing Office.

U.S. Department of Commerce. 1941. *29th Annual Report of the Secretary of Commerce: June 30, 1941.* Washington, D.C.: U.S. Government Printing Office.

U.S. Department of Commerce. 1942. *30th Annual Report of the Secretary of Commerce: June 30, 1942.* Washington, D.C.: U.S. Government Printing Office.

U.S. Department of Commerce, Office of Federal Statistical Policy and Standards. 1978. *Revolution in Government Statistics, 1926–1976,* prepared by Joseph W. Duncan and William C. Shelton. Washington, D.C.: U.S. Government Printing Office.

von Struve, A. W. 1940. "Geography in the Census Bureau." *Economic Geography* 16 (July): 275–80.

Sources of Materials at the National Archives

Record Group 29. (Bureau of the Census) Acquisition Numbers and File Descriptions:
NN364–101; Series A-Boxes 1–2, Series C-Boxes 1–4.
    Miscellaneous forms.
NN367-1; 7 Boxes with numbered files.
    Includes files of Alba M. Edwards.
NN36958; Looseleaf volumes.
    1939 Trial Census (2 volumes).
    1940 Census of Population (7 volumes).
    Includes forms used in enumeration and processing.
NN370–128; Box 21–File Series 2500.
    Files of the Chief Clerk, Bureau of the Census.

INDEX

Advisory Committee: ASA census, 8, 11, 12, 13; housing census, 16; on metropolitan districts, 11; technical, on population, 11, 13; to the Secretary of Labor, 4

Age: allocation of missing entries, 41, 42, 45–48; coding, 38, 42, 45–48; evaluation of item, 66; in publications, 57, 58, 59, 60; schedule item, 3, 16, 24; tabulations, 55

—at first marriage of women: schedule item, 26; tabulations, 55

Agriculture: Census of, 18, 27, 29; Department of, Secretary of, 4, 5

American Statistical Society (ASA), 4, 8, 14. *See also* Advisory committee, ASA census

Area manager, 10, 17–19, 20, 21, 23, 29, 30

Austin, William Lane, 6, 8, 13

Baker, O. E., 11

Benedict, Murray R., 8

Biggers, John D., 8

Bureau of the Census: Director, 1, 2, 5, 6, 8, 11, 12, 13, 17, 18, 19, 20, 21, 26, 30; division of geography, 6, 7, 9–11, 19, 32; division of machine tabulation, 6–7; division of public relations, 21; division of statistical research, 6, 8, 14; division of vital statistics, 39, 48; field division, 6, 7, 9, 10, 17–19, 28, 29, 31, 32; machine shop, 4; mechanical laboratory, 4, 6, 9; personnel division, 6; population division, 6, 7, 11*n*, 13, 14, 31, 32

Canvass of population and housing, 9, 15, 17, 18, 21–28

Capt, James C., 6

Census Act, 3, 11, 20, 21, 23

Census tract, 5, 9, 10, 11; in publications, 57, 58–59; tabulations, 55

Central Statistical Board (CSB), 5, 6, 11, 12

Chaddock, Robert E., 8

Cherington, Paul T., 8, 11

Children ever born: in publications, 60; schedule item, 5, 26; tabulations, 55

Citizenship status: coding, 43, 44; in publications, 57, 58, 59, 60; schedule item, 5, 16, 24; tabulations, 53, 54, 55

Class of worker: coding, 50–52; evaluation of item, 63; in publications, 57, 59; schedule item, 25

Commerce, Department of: Coast and Geodetic Survey, 10; Secretary of, 3, 4, 5, 6, 11, 12, 13

Commerce and Labor, Department of, 4

Committee on Government Statistics and Information Services (COGSIS), 4–6

Compensation, rates of, 18, 20, 29–30, 45

Constitution, 3

Dedrick, Calvert L., 5, 6, 8, 13, 14, 16

Deming, W. Edwards, 14, 45, 53

Dennis, Samuel J., 16

Dewhurst, Frederick J., 8

District supervisor, 9, 10, 17, 18–19, 20, 21, 23, 27, 28, 29, 30, 52

Dublin, Louis I., 11

Education, 13; in publications, 60. *See also* school attendance

Edwards, Alba M., 12, 50

Emergency work: coding, 51; evaluation of item, 62, 65; schedule item, 25

Employment status. *See* Labor Force

Enumeration district (E.D.), 7, 9–10, 14, 15, 17, 18, 19, 20, 21, 22, 23, 24, 26, 27, 28, 29, 30, 63, 64; identified in processing, 32, 33, 36, 39, 40, 41, 43, 45, 49; plan of division by, 9–10, 18; tabulations, 55

Enumeration procedures, 3, 17, 21–28; evaluation of, 5–6, 62–67; records, 28–29; supervision, 18, 27–28

Enumerators, 17; evaluation of, 27–28; selection and training, 15, 20–21

Farm residence: coding, 38, 41–42, 43, 50; in publications, 57, 58, 60; schedule item, 16, 24, 26, 27, 52; tabulations, 29, 53, 54, 55

Fergus, Corwin A., 16

Fertility, 13; schedule item, 14, 16. *See also* Children ever born

Field inspector, 15

149

Index

Flophouse, enumeration of, 21, 22

General Land Office, 10
Geoffrey, Leon, 45
Geography. *See* Bureau of the Census, division of geography; enumeration district; farm residence; metropolitan district; place of residence; place of residence in 1935; rural areas; urban areas
Givens, Meredith, 4
Grades completed, 13; coding, 42; in publications, 57, 58; schedule item, 16, 24; tabulations, 55; use in allocation of missing ages, 46, 47, 48

Hand count, 29, 31, 36; official population count, 52; verification of, 37–38, 39
Hansen, Morris H., 6, 14
Hart, Shirley K., 16
Hauser, Philip M., 14
Hollerith, Herman, 4
Home tenure: coding, 44; in publications, 58, 60; schedule item, 16, 24, 27, 52
Hoover, Herbert, 4
Hopkins, Harry, 13
Hotels: coding, 42; enumeration of, 21, 22, 24
Hours worked: coding, 43, 44; evaluation of item, 65; in publications, 57; schedule item, 12, 25
Household: census definition of, 24; confused with institutions, 63; enumeration of, 15, 22, 23, 24, 27, 30; enumeration schedules, 8, 15–16; in housing census, 26–27, 34, 52; in processing of population schedules, 32, 33, 34–35, 36; tabulations, 55, 59
—head: age of, 60; information on used in processing schedules, 35, 36, 38, 44, 48; race of, 52, 58, 59; tabulations, 55
—relation-to-head of: coding, 42; in publications, 58; schedule item, 16, 24, 26, 27; tabulations, 55, 59; use in allocation of missing ages, 46, 47, 48
Housing, Census of, 3, 16, 56; enumeration process, 22, 23, 26–27; enumeration schedules, 26–27; processing of schedule information, 31, 32–35, 36, 37, 38, 39, 52, 55, 56; publications, 57, 58, 59, 60
Howard, T. W., 11

Income: coding, 41, 43–44, 45; confidential reporting form, 13, 26, 39, 41, 49; controversy over questions, 12–13; evaluation of item, 64–65; in publications, 57, 60; schedule item, 12–13, 16, 25–26; tabulations, 53, 55, 56
Individual census form, 22, 32, 33, 39
Industry: coding, 50–52; evaluation of item, 63–64; in publications, 57, 59, 60; schedule item, 14, 16, 25, 26, 28; tabulations, 55
Infant card, 24, 27, 29, 31, 32, 34, 35, 39, 48
Institution: coding, 42, 43, 44; enumeration of, 10, 22, 24, 25, 34; evaluation of item, 63, 64; in publications, 60; tabulations, 55
Interior, Department of, 3, 4; Geological Survey, 10; Secretary of, 3, 4, 5
Irrigation, census of, 18

Jay, Aryness, 16

Labor, Department of: Secretary of, 4, 5
Labor force: coding, 38–39, 43, 50–52, comparability with gainful worker concept, 12; evaluation of items, 62–63; in publications, 57, 58, 59, 60; schedule items, 8, 12, 16, 24–25; tabulations, 55, 56; use in allocation of missing ages, 47. *See also* hours worked; industry; occupation; unemployment; weeks worked
Language during childhood. *See* Mother tongue
Legislation. *See* Census Act

McCormick, Ernest J., 50
McLaughlin, Glenn E., 11
Maps: preparation, 9, 10, 18; used in enumeration, 15, 19, 21, 28, 32, 35
Marital status: coding, 41, 42, 44; in publications, 58, 60; schedule item, 5, 14, 16, 24, 26; tabulations, 53, 55
—multiple marriages of women: schedule item, 26
Metropolitan district, 9, 14; in publications, 57, 58, 60; tabulations by, 55, 56; *See also* Advisory committee, on metropolitan districts
Migration. *See* Place of residence in 1935
Mother tongue: coding, 44; evaluation of item, 66; schedule item, 14, 16, 26; tabulations, 60
Myers, Howard B., 11

National Bureau of Economic Research, 11, 12
Nativity. *See* Place of birth
North, Simon N. D., 4
Nuptiality. *See* Marital status

Occupation: coding, 50–52; evaluation of item, 63–64; industrial home workers, 51; in publications, 57, 59, 60; peculiar for women and youth, 50–51, 64; schedule item, 3, 12, 14, 16, 25, 26, 27; tabulations, 5, 55
Occupational designation, 50
Ogburn, William F., 8

Perkins, Frances, 4
Place of birth (nativity): coding, 42–43; evaluation of item, 65; in publications, 57, 59, 60; schedule item, 14, 16, 24, 26; tabulations, 55
—of parents: coding, 44
Place of residence, 30; coding, 9, 11, 43, 51; in publications, 57, 58, 59, 60, 61; schedule item, 3, 13, 16, 21–22, 23, 24, 26, 27,

Index

See also Enumeration district; farm residence; metropolitan district; rural areas; urban areas

Place of residence in 1935 (migration), 13; coding, 43; evaluation of item, 66; in publications, 60; schedule item, 13, 14, 16; tabulations, 55; use in allocation of missing ages, 47

Portfolio of enumeration materials: receipt in Washington, D.C., 31–32; records of processing performed, 40–41; use in field operations, 19–20, 28; use in processing, 34, 35, 36, 37, 38, 39, 42, 45, 49, 51

Preliminary population announcement, 21, 29

Production records, 40–41, 49, 53

Publications, 57–61, 62; relation to tabulations, 55. *See also* Bureau of the Census, division of geography

Public relations, 13, 21, 64

Public roads administration, 10

Punch cards, 6, 7, 16, 52, 53; procedures, 9, 52–54; types, 54–56; verification, 48–49, 53, 54

Race: coding, 38, 42, 44; evaluation of item, 65, 66, 67; in publications, 57, 58, 59, 60; schedule item, 16, 24, 27, 52; tabulations, 53, 54, 55

Reed, Vergil D., 13

Rent: as income, 25; coding, 44; evaluation of item, 64; in publications, 58, 59, 60; schedule item, 12, 16, 24, 26, 27, 52

Residence. *See* Enumeration district; farm residence; metropolitan district; place of residence; place of residence in 1935; rural areas; urban areas

Rice, Stuart A., 4, 5, 6

Roosevelt, Franklin Delano, 4, 5, 8

Rural areas: coding, 43; enumeration, 9, 10, 19, 27, 62, 67; in publications, 57, 58, 59, 60; tabulations, 55

Sample: tabulations, 14, 54–55, 86; transcription, 36, 37–39; verification, 48–49, 51, 52. *See also* Age, at first marriage of women; children ever born; marital status, multiple marriages of women; mother tongue; place of birth, of parents; social security; veterans status

—supplementary schedule lines: coding, 36, 44, 50, 52; enumeration, 22, 23; inclusion on population schedule, 13, 14, 15; tabulation, 54, 55; transcription, 36, 37

Sampling: bias, 8, 15; design, 13, 14–15, 26, 36; introduction of, 3, 8, 11, 13–14

Schedules, absent household, 11, 32, 33, 39

Schedules, agriculture, 3, 19, 26, 30

Schedules, housing, 16, 22, 32, 33, 40, 56; occupied dwelling, 26–27, 31, 34, 35, 36, 37, 39, 52; vacant dwelling, 26–27, 31, 34, 35, 36, 37, 39, 52

Schedules, nonresident, 11, 23, 29, 32, 33, 39

Schedules, population, 3, 5, 16, 21, 22, 27, 29; coding of, 41–48, 50, 51; design of, 6, 11–12, 13, 14, 15; evaluation of, 5, 65; examination of completed, 27–28; filling out of, 23–26; processing of completed, 31, 32, 33, 34, 35, 36, 37, 38, 39, 40; shipment and receipt of, 7, 18, 19–20, 30, 31; styles of, 15; verification of coded, 49, 50, 51, 52

School attendance: coding, 42; in publications, 57, 58; schedule item, 3, 5, 16, 24; tabulations, 55; use in allocation of missing ages, 45, 46, 47, 48

Sex: coding 38, 42, 44; evaluation of item, 66; in publications, 57, 59, 60, 62; schedule item, 16, 24; tabulations, 54, 55; use in allocation of missing ages, 46

Social Science Research Council (SSRC), 4, 5

Social Security: coding, 44; evaluation of item, 66; schedule item, 14, 16, 26, 28

Special Census (Indiana), 12, 13, 15–16

Spiegelman, Mortimer, 46

Squad leader, 5–6, 10, 17, 20, 21, 23, 37, 38; selection and training, 21

State, Department of, Secretary of, 3

Stephan, Frederick F., 11, 14

Supplementary lines. *See* Sample, supplementary schedule lines

Tabulation, 52–56; equipment, 4, 9, 54; evaluation of 5, 6, 62, 64–65, 66; program, 6, 7, 11, 14

Thorp, Willard C., 8

Thorp, Willard L., 14

Tobey, Charles W., 13

Transients, enumeration of, 21, 22

Truesdell, Leon E., 13, 16

Underenumeration, 66–67

Unemployment, 12; coding, 44; evaluation of item, 62, 63, 65; in publications, 57, 60; schedule item, 25; tabulations, 55

Unemployment Census of 1937, 8

Urban areas: coding, 43; enumeration of, 9, 10, 15, 19, 23, 27, 28, 66, 67; in publications, 57, 58, 59

Vacancies: instructions for, 22, 23, 27; in publications, 59. *See also* Schedules, housing, vacant dwelling

Value of home: coding, 44; evaluation of item, 64; in publications, 58, 59, 60; schedule item, 12, 16, 24, 52

Veteran status: coding, 44; evaluation of item, 5; schedule item, 14, 16, 26

Vinton, Warren J., 16

Weeks worked: coding, 43, 44; evaluation of item, 65; in publications, 57; schedule item, 12, 16, 25

Whelpton, P. K., 11

Woofter, Thomas J., 16

COMPOSED BY A-R EDITIONS, INC., MADISON, WISCONSIN
MANUFACTURED BY CUSHING MALLOY, INC., ANN ARBOR, MICHIGAN
TEXT AND DISPLAY LINES ARE SET IN PALATINO

Library of Congress Cataloging-in-Publication Data
Jenkins, Robert M., 1955–
Procedural history of the 1940 census
of population and housing.
Bibliography: pp. 147–148.
Includes index.
1. United States—Census, 16th, 1940. 2. United
States—Statistical services—History. 3. United
States—Census—History. I. Title.
HA201 1940   304.6'0723   85-40368
ISBN 0-299-10120-7